ON
MY
WATCH

ON MY WATCH

A MEMOIR

Virginia Buckingham

CAVAN
BRIDGE
PRESS

Published by Cavan Bridge Press, New York, NY
https://cavanbridgepress.com
http://www.virginiabuckingham.com

Edited and designed by Girl Friday Productions
www.girlfridayproductions.com
Cover design: Emily Mahon

ISBN (paperback): 978-0-9987493-2-7
ISBN (ebook): 978-0-9987493-5-8

Library of Congress Control Number: 2019917943

To my loves, David, Jack, and Maddy Lowy

AUTHOR'S NOTE

The events related in this book are true and are reconstructed to the best of my memory. If I made mistakes in time or depiction, it is unintentional.

The names of some 9/11 victims and family members, whom I never personally interacted with, have been changed to protect their privacy.

CONTENTS

PROLOGUE

LETTER TO READERS

Dear Readers,

There have been many stories told about the September 11 terrorist attacks, and I know you have your own. You know where you were when you first heard. You remember who you called after seeing the TV image of the plane striking the second tower. Our stories of 9/11 are the things that unite us still, like the sense of unity we felt in those first days and months after the attacks.

Except I never felt that way. I was the head of Boston's Logan Airport on September 11, 2001. On my watch, American Flight 11 and United Flight 175 were hijacked after leaving Logan and then flown into the World Trade Center. The first news story suggesting I might be fired in response to the hijackings appeared on September 13. A media frenzy followed. Six weeks after 9/11, Massachusetts's governor forced me to resign. I was later notified that a 9/11 family had sued me, holding me personally responsible for the wrongful death of their loved one. For many years, I feared that the blame directed at me was deserved.

I was broken by being blamed for the hijackings. Not instantly, not shattered like handblown glass, but over time. Like a bottle tossed into the sea, tumbled apart bit by bit by the movement of the waves.

Some have scoffed at the notion that I was really blamed. "It's just politics," they'd say. Others would shrug and note, "Everyone needs a scapegoat."

Do we? What purpose does a scapegoat serve? And, beyond the obvious personal toll, is there a societal toll to assigning blame?

I have asked myself many times whether this story is worth telling. No one I knew personally died that day. I wasn't part of the New York recovery effort, the federal response. I do recount the events of that day and the rebuilding of a broken confidence in aviation from my perspective at Logan. More so, though, I recount the rebuilding of a broken life.

As the years passed, I came to understand how being blamed and blaming myself come from the same human impulse—life is fragile, yet we unconsciously deny its fragility. Our culture, political and societal, turns to blame to help appease our fear and anger, allowing us to avoid wrestling with the harder questions.

Nothing I write in the following pages can adequately capture the devastation of the families whose loved ones died on 9/11. Their stories are their own, and I wouldn't presume to tell them here. In some cases, I changed the names of victims or their families to maintain their privacy. In the passing years, though, I have had the privilege of contact, even friendship, with some 9/11 families. That they let me share in their grieving and allowed me to share my own grief is one of the greatest gifts I will ever receive. Their embrace helped me to move forward.

In its final report, the 9/11 Commission decreed we were a nation "unprepared" for the attacks and ascribed our nation's inability to detect the 9/11 plot as a "failure of imagination." As for Logan Airport's role, the Commission found no evidence that the terrorists specifically targeted Logan or that there was any difference in checkpoint screening there versus at any other US airport. Finally, in 2011, a federal judge dismissed Logan from the one remaining wrongful death case slated to go to trial.

In this book, I do not revisit the investigation, nor tread the well-worn path of what might have been different had political leaders, the CIA, FBI, FAA, airlines, airport operators, or any number of individuals, me included, put together the pieces of the 9/11 plot before that day. The following pages are an investigation of my heart, my mind, my soul. It is not about who knew what but about the acceptance of simply not knowing what I did not know.

I hope that my story will have some resonance with others trying to navigate deeply painful experiences, who, like me, do not meet society's expectations of how to "move on" by resolutely putting their trauma and loss behind them, who are admired for their strength, while knowing inside they are utterly broken. My story does not end neatly wrapped in a bow. I've not slammed some metaphorical door shut on the past. Instead, I have found a different sense of what resilience in the face of trauma and loss can look like and discovered that there is an important difference between moving forward and moving on.

Thank you for reading,
Ginny

PART I

CHAPTER ONE

WITNESS

December 15, 2006—101 Federal Street, Boston, Massachusetts
Deposition of Virginia Buckingham in Bavis v. UAL Corp. et al.

I looked down the long polished conference table. Dozens of lawyers leaned forward expectantly. They were all staring at me. I sat alone at the head of the table.

Except for the rustling of papers, the room was silent, tense. A video camera was set up at the far end, its lens trained on my face. There was a time when I would have turned a scarlet shade of pink if I became the center of attention, in class or at a social gathering. I never grew out of this painful shyness exactly; it just became subsumed into an intense focus on doing an increasingly public job well.

I felt the familiar anxiety creeping up the back of my neck as my lawyer leaned over and whispered that my testimony was being taped so it could be shown in court if there was a trial. The word "trial" jolted me even though I knew it was a possibility. I'd been dreading this deposition, but the idea that the wrongful death cases could end up before a judge and jury was too much to bear. Even though the personal case against me had been dropped, I knew that didn't make a difference. If Logan Airport was found liable, then so was I.

The attorney who was to be my chief questioner represented about twenty-five of the passengers who went through Logan checkpoints on September 11 and their families. He sat directly to my right and introduced himself. After a few formalities, he wasted no time in going for the jugular.

Before 9/11 did you know who al Qaeda was?

Did you know who Osama bin Laden was?

Did you know terrorists had issued fatwas against the US?

I answered each question quietly. "No."

I knew that most Americans before 9/11 would have answered the same way I did. Yet inside, the despair that had been my closest companion in the years since 9/11 immediately enveloped me in response to the lawyer's insinuation: I should have known.

I clutched my hands tightly together and resisted the desire to stand and flee. The stares from the dozens of lawyers now seemed to reflect the questioner's accusations.

The lawyer went on to ask me about my upbringing and education and professional career up until the time I was appointed to head Logan Airport. His point was to try to show I was unqualified for the position, to paint a picture of a woman ill equipped to lead the nation's eighteenth-busiest airport in its most fundamental duty—to keep the people who traveled through it safe from harm.

I answered in the affirmative when he asked if I was born in Connecticut and first came to Boston to attend Boston College. I told him how I worked my way up in state government. But there was no opportunity to really share the story, however unremarkable, that ended with me in this seat answering for the wrongful deaths of thousands of people.

***

"BUCKINGHAM—Seventh child, fourth daughter, Virginia Beth, Sept. 14 in St. Mary's Hospital to Mr. and Mrs. Thomas Buckingham (Florence Andes), Beach Avenue."

The faded square of newsprint from 1965 was tucked among a few other mementos my mother had given me after one clutter-shedding spree long after I'd moved to Boston. It was taped to what appeared to be a page ripped out of a sibling's baby book.

"It must have been fun to grow up in such a large family," friends and acquaintances have commented when they learned I was one of eight siblings. "What was it like?"

"It was quiet," I wanted to answer. "So quiet."

"But how can that be?" I knew they would ask incredulously. So I always simply answered, "It was fun."

And it often was—sledding down our long, steep hill, Wiffle ball and home run derby in the backyard, games of H-O-R-S-E at the hoop on the street in front of our house, bicycle riding, excursions for ice-cream cones and penny candy. Still, an understandable and palpable exhaustion, emotional and financial, covered our family like so much dust on an end table. A voracious reader, I remember reacting in wonder at the recounting in the book *Cheaper by the Dozen* of the cacophony of a family of twelve children, their dinner table conversations a rotating clamor for attention. Our dinner table was mostly silent, my dad often taking his meal on a tray in the living room. To earn extra money, he rose immediately after finishing to go to his second job as an umpire or a referee depending on the season. He left most mornings by five o'clock to load first his milk truck and later his Hostess delivery truck with the products he "peddled," as he liked to say. He'd take me with him sometimes on Saturdays to check the mom-and-pop stores he'd been to that week. Even though he wasn't being paid, he wanted to make sure the displays of goods were still neat and attractive. As we entered each store, he greeted the clerk and paused to straighten the racks. Some lessons, I intuited, could be taught even when delivered in the most quiet of ways. "Work hard and take pride in your work, Virginia Beth," my dad seemed to be teaching me.

In 1982, I pored over college catalogs. At that time, only three of my seven siblings had gone to college and none to so expensive or well known a school as Boston College. The soaring stone tower of BC on the cover of its catalog seemed like something out of a fairy tale. I was enamored with the idea of attending school in Boston simply based on one visit there as a child. My mom had taken me to famed Faneuil Hall

and Quincy Market on a town-sponsored bus trip when I was about
ten. I stared in delight at the street performers, flower carts, and cob-
blestones. The smells and sounds and jostle of people vying for attention at the food stalls in the center aisle were both frightening and
thrilling.

As we wandered through the crowds in the outer covered aisles, I
remember being drawn to a slanted wooden stand. It was packed with
ice, and perfectly laid out on it, as if painted with an artist's brush,
were row after row of clear plastic cups. Each was filled to the rim with
cantaloupe as deep orange as the setting sun and watermelon dripping
with sugary pink juice and shiny black seeds, finished like a master-
piece with glistening strawberries and blueberries. In that moment, I
think I understood, subconsciously, that Boston was the most beautiful, magical, almost mystical place in the world, and someday it would
be my home.

With the flimsy reasoning of a sixteen-year-old, I vowed I would
apply to Boston College, and with a stubbornness I didn't know I pos-
sessed, I declared that if I didn't get in, I wasn't going to college at all.

The early acceptance letter I received in December 1982 made me
want to skate across the linoleum-tiled floor of my upstairs bedroom
like I used to do as a young girl in my stocking feet, pretending to be
Dorothy Hamill. I could hardly contain my joy.

My mother navigated the financial assistance forms, and in the fall
of 1983 I moved to Boston. I quickly found my place at Boston College,
despite its size, making a couple of close friends and securing a job
on campus paid for with a federal work-study grant. I immediately
felt comfortable working among other students who came from more
modest backgrounds. I still had plenty of time to study and have fun—
nights at the library, sunny afternoons cheering BC Eagles football.
But throughout college, I also spent nights and weekends behind the
register at a nearby convenience store, waitressing at a local restaurant,
and delivering audiovisual equipment to classrooms across campus. I
worked hard, as if the lessons my dad taught me were hardwired.

In my junior year, I was required to find an internship related to
my communications major, so I went to the college career center and
flipped through a three-ring binder for opportunities that accepted

work-study grant students. I read an entry for the Governor's Press Office requiring strong writing skills.

Well, I can write, I thought. So I climbed on the T, as the Boston subway was called, and rode the Green Line into Park Street station on the corner of the Boston Common. I walked up the path to the steep stairs ascending into the grand marble halls of the State House and slowly opened the wooden door to room 259. I was accepted for the internship even after the office manager gently pointed out a typo in my résumé, a lesson of thoroughness I have never forgotten, and at nineteen I had my first job in politics. I was hooked.

If I was lucky, I got to be the intern who taped the remarks of the governor, then Michael Dukakis, at an event and cut them into tiny sound bites to feed into an ancient audio machine that radio stations could access for their local broadcasts. Or I would watch the governor hold a press availability outside his office and later that night see it on the news. It was exciting, but I also learned that politics matters. Government matters in people's lives. And I wanted to be part of it.

After graduation I interviewed by phone for a role in Dukakis's presidential campaign with his Iowa state director but decided to stay in the Boston area. I answered a blind help-wanted ad in the *Boston Globe* and was hired by a trade association to work on public affairs for small building contractors. I wore a "Dukakis for President" pin on my off-the-rack suits and dived into what turned out to be a wholly different job than advertised. The organization was sponsoring a ballot question that fall asking voters to repeal a decades-old law requiring union-level wages be paid on any public construction project. I was to be a field organizer, helping to gather the necessary signatures to get the question on the ballot, and then work with the advertising and media team to execute the campaign. I was skeptical about the so-called prevailing wage issue at first and an offhand comment by my father, a loyal member of the Teamsters Union, passed on by my mother gave me pause, too. "Just remind her that the only reason she went to college was because of the union," he said.

Yet, the more I got to know the small contractors who made up our membership, the more I came to agree that being forced to pay union-scale wages, especially in small towns, was unfair and that their workforce deserved a chance to compete for publicly funded jobs, too. Some months into the campaign, I was sent up to the Merrimack Valley, a northern area of the state bordering New Hampshire, to represent our side in a League of Women Voters debate. It was to be aired on a local cable station, and it was my first debate. I was still innately shy, and I battled my nerves as I fiddled with the edge of my cardigan while seated onstage waiting for the event to begin. I noticed the organizers nervously checking the door. There was a moderator but the opponent's chair was empty. "We may have to do it with just one side," I heard an organizer say. Just then, the door flung open and a number of burly-looking construction workers came in, some accompanied by their girlfriends, and filled the front row. The moderator asked me a few questions but then asked if I minded taking questions from the audience.

"Okay," I answered, hesitating for just a second.

The first union construction worker approached the standing microphone. I don't remember his question, but I nervously answered as best I could. And then as soon as he sat down, the next construction worker stood at the microphone and fired another accusation. That's how it felt, not like I was being questioned, but that I was being accused. I could feel my cheeks burning and my voice shaking, but oddly, as person after person stood at the microphone, I began to shake less and my nerves were replaced by a rising anger at the misrepresentations being thrown my way.

This is how I remember one exchange: "I build elevators, and if this law passes, elevators are going to be unsafe," the newest questioner said.

I straightened my shoulders and looked the man at the microphone right in the eye. "Do you have a license to build elevators?" I asked.

"Well, uh, yeah."

"And do you have to be trained and pass a series of requirements to get that license?"

"Yes," he answered.

"And will the fact that you have to be licensed and pass a series of requirements to build elevators in this state change in any way if this new law passes?" My questions came rapid fire, the injustice of his purposeful inaccuracies fueling my newfound courage of conviction.

"Well, no, I guess not."

I don't remember how the exchange ended or how the next several went except to say that afterward I felt, well, different. It's not that my shyness and soft-spoken manner disappeared after that, but it was more that, inside, part of who I was moved over a little to make room for a growing confidence.

As it turned out, we lost that referendum campaign, with a simple slogan "Question 2—Bad for You" on every union worker's bumper overcoming a more complex policy argument, another political lesson learned. But as the 1990 gubernatorial election approached, the trade association remained politically active and it endorsed an unusual pairing of Republicans, then state senator Paul Cellucci and a relative political newcomer named Bill Weld.

I volunteered on their campaign and joined it full time in the last few months when Cellucci received a recommendation from my then boss Steve Tocco, who was advising the campaign, that the candidate should expand his core staff. "Can I have Ginny?" Cellucci asked. So I spent the remainder of the campaign at a small desk in the corner of his chief adviser's office stuffing press kits and planning media stops around the state.

Unexpectedly, the two won, the first Republicans to hold Massachusetts's top offices in twenty years. I went with them into the State House, serving first as an assistant press secretary. With my father's unspoken mantra—work hard—in my head, I arrived at the office at about five o'clock every morning to cut out and copy the relevant newspaper stories that the interns would deliver to the governor, lieutenant governor, and their senior staff, a full-circle movement back to when I had first caught the political bug.

Slowly, my duties expanded. I traveled to press events, primarily with Cellucci, fielded media questions for the administration, wrote press releases and op-eds, booked editorial-board visits and radio interviews. Each morning I'd stand with a small group of junior staff members in Weld's impressive, ornate corner office, him at one end of the table and Cellucci at the other, the senior staff sitting in between, making the decisions of governing.

I was young, twenty-four, yet I began to sense I had strong strategic instincts, advising Cellucci and increasingly Weld about how to answer media questions and position their policies about the pressing topics facing them daily. I also grew close to the governor's deputy legal counsel David Lowy, whom I worked with on many projects. We fell in love, got engaged in 1993, and married a year later.

At twenty-nine, I was promoted to press secretary, joining the governor's senior staff and sitting at the conference table during the morning meeting. Then, after winning a landslide reelection victory, Weld turned his sights to the US Senate and took me aside and asked me to manage his campaign.

Polls showed the race against incumbent senator John Kerry close until the end, but we lost, and while licking my wounds at home, I was called by Weld and asked to come see him at the State House.

"Will you come back as my chief of staff?" he asked. At thirty-one, I took my place at the table to his immediate left. I loved the broader management role. No day was the same, as I juggled meetings with cabinet secretaries and agency heads seeking guidance on policy development, oversaw the work of the governor's executive staff, and continued to serve as the governor's chief adviser on a myriad of complex issues. David and I had by this time moved out of the city and commuted in together each morning and back home in the evenings. He had left the governor's office for a role as a prosecutor in the Boston district attorney's office. We both were exhilarated by our jobs, feeling alive and engaged and certain the future held limitless opportunities.

Weld resigned in mid-1997, automatically rendering Cellucci governor under the state constitution. Cellucci asked me to stay on as his chief of staff. I happily accepted, managing the transition between the two leaders and tackling Cellucci's priorities. When I became pregnant with our son Jack, I worked up until his birth, and there was no question that I would come back to the State House after maternity leave.

While at home caring for the baby, I indifferently followed the front-page stories about a scandal embroiling Massport, the agency that operated Logan Airport. When the scandal led to the agency's leader getting fired, though, it was not long before the first call came from the governor's chief personnel secretary asking if I would be interested in the job. I flatly said no. I loved being chief of staff and didn't want to change jobs while juggling being a first-time mother.

But after being asked twice more, including personally by Cellucci, I finally acquiesced. I wanted to help the governor, a person I respected deeply, achieve his goals. I knew I had the public administration background for the job and could help the agency's aviation and shipping professionals achieve their own operational goals by navigating the politically charged interactions with neighboring communities and political leaders. I could help the governor change the much-criticized culture at the agency and help him win approval for a new runway to aid the economy.

Once it was announced, my appointment was criticized in some quarters given my role at the State House, a critique I felt was fair game, but for the most part I was hailed in the media as just the kind of reformer the agency needed.

***

A little more than seven years later, I found myself defending my role again, with far more at stake than a career change. After taking a short break, the deposition resumed. A technician ensured the camera was still tightly focused on me at the head of the table.

Did you know the FBI thought it was only a matter of time before there was a terrorist attack?

No, I didn't.

I didn't know.

CHAPTER TWO

BEFORE

(Some of the details in chapters two and three are paraphrased from The 9/11 Commission Report.*)*

Summer 2000—*Newark International Airport, Newark, New Jersey*

Three of the 9/11 pilots arrive in the United States between May 29 and June 27. All three begin flight training in Florida.

Summer 2000—*Logan International Airport, Boston*

"Bitch," I said under my breath as I slammed the phone down. I looked over at Jose Juves, Massport's media director, waiting expectantly in my office doorway.

"How'd it go?" he asked, casually leaning against the doorframe.

"How do you think it went?" I answered. "She threatened me."

A shadow passed across Jose's eyes. We were about to issue public report cards on airline customer service. My brief conversation about the plan with Carol Hallett, the head of the Air Transit Association (ATA), the trade association representing commercial airlines in the

US, was tense. Poor customer service by airlines was such a hot issue that Congress was considering passing a passenger bill of rights. But no airport operator had taken it upon itself to publicly rate an airline's performance as a means to prompt improvement as we were about to do.

"So what's the bottom line?" Jose asked.

"She said if we went forward she'd announce the ATA is against the new runway," I answered.

"No way, really?" Jose looked genuinely surprised. He moved farther into the office and sat on the arm of one of the two leather couches facing each other in front of my desk. He understood, as I did, that if the airlines announced that a new runway at Logan was unnecessary, the project was dead.

Adding a fifth runway (some say a sixth, counting a little-used smaller runway) had been the subject of a political impasse for nearly thirty years. The airport's neighbors and their elected leaders vehemently opposed it. The business community and the governor were strongly in support because of the effect of Logan's notorious delays on the regional economy. Back in the late 1960s, the fight became a part of the local political lore, in a city rich with it, when a group of mothers—later dubbed the "Maverick Street Moms" after their East Boston neighborhood—blocked the Boston Harbor tunnels connecting East Boston to downtown in protest while pushing baby strollers.

I looked past Jose, through my floor-to-ceiling window at Boston's inner harbor. A trawler was making its way along the water's edge, scooping up floating trash, a project we had helped fund. Just beyond the trawler, I could see the East Boston neighborhood of Jeffries Point. I wrote myself a note to check on the plan to move the massive green dry dock that was half floating, half sinking into the water off the Jeffries Point waterfront.

The dry dock looked like a carnival funhouse version of Fenway Park's left-field wall, so we'd nicknamed it the "Green Monster." It had broken away when it was being towed from a nearby Boston Harbor marine repair facility. Massport didn't own the dry dock or the marine repair facility, but if something impacted the neighborhoods around Logan, it usually became our problem to solve.

I placed the note in my in-box, on top of a copy of a newspaper editorial I kept in it.

The *Boston Globe* had published the editorial a few weeks after my appointment to the agency in 1999. Headlined "Buckingham's Tasks," New England's most influential media outlet laid out what it thought ought to be my priorities:

- Better manage airport traffic
- Improve taxi service
- Build a new runway
- Replace a parking lot with a park
- Modernize two Logan terminals

I kept the editorial on my desk as both a reminder and a point of pride. Just a year into the job, I was well on the way to completing all my "tasks."

"So what are you going to do?" Jose asked.

Oh, right, back to today's problem, I thought, *or at least this morning's problem.*

"Get to my next meeting or I am going to be late," I answered.

Early fall 2000—Afghanistan

Senior al Qaeda leaders in Afghanistan started selecting the muscle hijackers—the operatives who will storm the cockpits and control the passengers.

Early fall 2000—South Boston

I hurried to the front door of Jimmy's Harborside Restaurant on the South Boston waterfront. I glanced to my left and saw the large black Town Car parked in its usual spot. *Yup, he's already here,* I thought to myself, walking faster. *He's going to be annoyed I'm late.*

I greeted the maître d' at the hostess stand. He grimaced in seemingly silent agreement that tardiness with this particular lunch partner was a bad idea.

"He's waiting for you," he said.

Congressman Joe Moakley was seated alone. A couple of waiters were busily moving around him. One poured more water into his glass. The other checked to see whether he wanted to order without me.

Moakley was the longest-serving member of the Massachusetts congressional delegation and former chairman and ranking member of the powerful House Rules Committee. No legislation moved through Congress without his okay. He was also a frequent Massport critic, admonishing the agency about noise made by low-flying aircraft over his South Boston neighborhood. Moakley's latest fight with us was about the proposed new runway. It would send additional air traffic over the heads of his neighbors, as well as his beloved neighborhood church.

I settled into my seat across from Moakley, grinning at his gruff hello.

"Hi, Mr. Chairman," I said warmly. Moakley had been ill recently, but I thought he looked great. He had on a charcoal-gray turtleneck and he'd grown a beard. It was gray-black like his distinctive bushy eyebrows. I'd heard some wise guys around the office crack that he was doing a poor imitation of an aging Sean Connery, but I found his effort endearing.

"Whaddya want to eat?" he asked, relenting, just a little, on maintaining his irritable posture. "You like swordfish?"

"Yes," I answered.

"Then have the Harborside cut. Nothin' like it."

I ordered as he instructed and settled back in my chair as Moakley launched into some of his favorite stories. He started, as always, with how he'd come down to the Southie railroad tracks as a boy. "We'd eat the watermelons that fell off the freight cars," he said.

I've heard this story so often I can tell it myself, I thought, smiling at how he told it each time with the same obvious relish. As he talked, my mind wandered to the first time I'd met with him. How unlikely it was then that I'd ever be sitting across from him as his lunch companion.

When I accepted Governor Cellucci's offer to be put before the agency's board as his choice for the new CEO of Massport, I couldn't stop myself from weighing in.

"You're going to get killed for this," I said, instinctively continuing to play the role of his closest adviser.

"Why?" he asked.

"Because I'm thirty-four, I'm your chief of staff, and I'm a woman," I answered.

Sure enough, after I was appointed, the media sought out Moakley to get his comment. The governor gave the job to "some girl sitting in the next office," Moakley growled.

The comment was red meat for members of the media, who immediately sought a response from the governor's administration. Lieutenant Governor Jane Swift, who herself had made news by running for office while pregnant, jumped to my defense. Cellucci chimed in a few days later. Critics of both me and a woman recently appointed to lead the state's highest court were uncomfortable with women in power, he said. They "should get a life."

As soon as I started at Massport, I knew I had to try to make peace with Moakley. The runway and all federal grants the airport relied on needed his blessing to go through Congress. I asked for an appointment, and as I entered his office, I took a deep breath to ease my nervousness. I could feel my cheeks burning as I sat down across the massive desk from him. "Mr. Chairman, I learned my politics at the knee of Bill Weld," I began. I knew Moakley, despite being an irascible Boston Irishman, adored the Yankee, Long Island–bred former Massachusetts governor. Weld had first suggested the new Boston federal courthouse we now sat in should be named in Moakley's honor.

Moakley's demeanor softened, slightly. "You know, I didn't mean anything by—" he started to say. I interrupted him before he could finish, even though I wasn't sure what I was going to say in response.

"I know, Mr. Chairman. Actually, my dad, who's exactly the same age as you, told me that the media should lay off because, in his eyes, I am just a girl!" My dad had, in fact, said just that during the media dustup. I murmured a silent thank-you to him for the last-minute inspiration.

**

Oh, how Moakley loves that story, I thought, smiling, as I refocused my attention on my lunch companion. He repeated it in my presence almost as often as the watermelon story. "You know what her father said," he'd begin, speaking to anyone within hearing distance. "That I was right; she is just a girl!"

The thick pieces of swordfish were placed in front of us. As we dug in, the waiters came back to fill our water glasses. The clinking ice was no competition for the rumble of jets flying directly overhead.

Fall 2000—Saudi Arabia

The majority of the Saudi muscle hijackers obtain US visas in Jeddah or Riyadh between September and November of 2000.

Fall 2000—Mayor's office, City Hall, Boston

"Talk to the neighbors. Go into their livin' rooms. Just talk to 'em about what you're doin'," Boston's mayor Tom Menino said.

Menino had built a political reputation as a "neighborhood" mayor. I'd come to his City Hall office to ask his advice about resolving a long-simmering issue involving neighborhoods abutting Logan.

At the end of one of Logan's most active runways was a wooden and concrete blast fence. It had been built years earlier to protect nearby private homes from jet-engine noise and pollution. Over the years, as aircraft were built larger, the jet engines came to sit higher than the top of the fence and its utility dwindled. At the same time both pilots and Logan's aviation team grew concerned that the fence was a danger. If a jet overran the runway upon landing, it could crash into the fence, causing a catastrophe. The *Boston Globe* had published a prominent exposé on the runway hazard in 1996. Shortly after, Massport officials vowed to remove it. Their decision, made without neighbors' input, incited a political backlash. Menino denounced the airport's man-agement for failing to include the community in the decision. Some community leaders, distrusting Logan officials' motives, contended removing the fence would allow even larger jets to use the runway, disrupting their neighborhood even more. The two sides were at an impasse. Four years later, the fence remained in place.

The mayor leaned back in his chair as I leaned forward in mine explaining the dilemma, the floor-to-ceiling window next to him framing a view of historic Faneuil Hall. "The neighbors will listen," Menino continued. "Just explain to 'em. You'll have no problem."

Over the next couple of months, Massport held dozens of small forums with community groups. At each, Logan's deputy fire chief recounted aircraft incidents involving similar runway obstructions around the country. At neighbors' urging, we explored alternatives to removing the fence. We set up an official neighborhood committee. We kept the mayor and other local public officials informed as we worked on a mitigation agreement—projects that Logan funding would support to help the community once the fence was removed.

In March of 2001, with neighborhood support, a Logan construction crew dismantled the fence piece by piece.

Fall 2000—Sarasota, Florida

Mohamed Atta and Marwan al Shehhi enroll at Jones Aviation, a flight training school in Sarasota, Florida. They are "aggressive," "rude," even fight with the instructor to take over the controls during training flights. They fail the Stage I exam for instruments rating. Soon after, they return to a different flight training school they had attended earlier in the year.

October 2000—Boston

I took a sip of hot coffee. The traffic was heavy. The slow crawl allowed me to glance away from the on-again-off-again brake lights in front of me to the ocean stretching out to my left. The water was steel gray, reflecting the sky. The surface of the water at low tide was as placid as a lake.

Thank you, God, for giving me this new day, I prayed silently, as I did every morning. *Help me to remember that nothing is going to happen to me today that you and I together can't handle.*

As the traffic speed picked up, I turned down a grittier stretch of road. The ocean was now mostly hidden by warehouses, car dealerships, and fast-food restaurants. Stopped at a red light, I glanced at the clock on the dashboard. *I'm going to be late,* I thought, growing anxious. That day was the start of Logan's two-day emergency response drill. The FAA required airport operators to conduct emergency drills every three years. We'd dubbed that year's drill "Operation Excellence." Logan rescue personnel would practice the response to a large passenger jet crashing into Boston Harbor shortly after takeoff.

Statistically, most aircraft crashes occur on the airfield within reach of airport fire and rescue crews. The FAA also required fire and rescue equipment and personnel to be able to reach the crash scene within three minutes.

"We can get there in two," a Logan firefighter told me during one of my first meetings at Logan's Massport Fire Rescue headquarters. Logan personnel had also assembled a "go team" of key first responders, he'd said. The team traveled to crash sites around the country and then applied whatever lessons they learned to their training back at Logan. With pride in his voice, the firefighter said the initiative was meant "to make Logan the safest airport in the country."

8:45 a.m.—Black Falcon Cruise Terminal, South Boston

The enormous passenger processing area of the cruise terminal had been temporarily transformed into an emergency response center. Federal, state, and local first responders were arrayed in metal folding chairs around the room. Logan security director Joe Lawless began the mock emergency exercise as I took notes from my seat at the edge of the room.

9:07 a.m.—Logan Airport, air traffic control tower, sixteenth floor

The radio crackled. "Emergency Code 3," the Massport communications specialist said over the radio. She gave the coordinates of the crash and the number of "souls on board," the total number of passengers and crew on the downed flight.

9:22 a.m.—Boston Harbor, one and a half miles from Logan

State Police divers were in the water, looking for survivors. A Massachusetts State Police helicopter hovered overhead, a video camera trained on the scene below. A live transmission of the rescue scene was being sent to National Transportation Safety Board (NTSB) investigators in Washington, DC. "We're the first to do that," Lawless pointed out.

The water was covered with vast swaths of red dye, a biodegradable substance representing oil and other biochemical hazards that would hinder rescuers in a real crash. Debris donated by the airlines was scattered across the water. Suitcases. Dislodged aircraft seats. Cushions. A sneaker. A black box containing crucial aircraft data was pulled on board the rescue boat. Dummies, representing the dead, were gently recovered. This part of the drill trained responders in how to handle human remains.

Twelve members of the Massport Fire Rescue crew were treading water in red survival suits. They were the passengers who had survived.

8:00 a.m. the next morning—Logan Airport Hilton hotel

The Massport Care Team had transformed an entire second floor of the Logan Hilton hotel into a family assistance center for day two of the drill. More than fifty employees had volunteered to help families of passengers who might come to Logan after yesterday's simulated crash. Logan wasn't a hub airport, meaning it didn't serve as the base of operations for one or more major airlines, like Chicago's O'Hare or Hartsfield in Atlanta. Most major airlines have their own care teams, but we were concerned these airline teams would be delayed in arriving at Logan since they were not based here. An agencywide email solicited volunteers for our own care team. Massport engineers, administrative assistants, airfield development planners, and others volunteered to be trained for a challenge far different from their normal tasks of assigning terminal gates or haggling with contractors.

A group of Emerson College drama students arrived in the Hilton meeting room. They would play the parts of anxious family members.

8:15 a.m. Betty Desrosiers, Massport's Care Team leader, who normally headed the airport's planning department, approached the podium. She told the assembled "families" she had little news to report.

"What we know is that Flight 157 is down one and a half miles off of Runway 15-Right," Betty said. "We don't know how many, but we do know that there are some survivors."

There were sobs and shouts from those gathered in the room. "I want to know whether my husband is dead or alive," a young woman cried out, burying her face in her hands. A volunteer patted her back.

As I watched from the back of the room, their acting was so convincing that I wiped tears from my eyes. When a young family member fainted, the Massport emergency medical staff paused in their role-play. "Are you okay?" they asked.

The tension in the room grew as the families pressed Betty for more information. I noticed Jim Hurd standing nearby. His son Jamie had been killed in the TWA 800 crash off Long Island in 1996. We'd invited Jim to observe the drill so he could share what he'd learned firsthand from dealing with the airlines in the aftermath.

"Thanks for coming," I said, touching his arm. He smiled gently, his eyes betraying a depth of grief that no role-play, however convincing, could match.

After the briefing, the families dispersed to other smaller rooms off the hotel hallway. There, American Red Cross volunteers would take them through the difficult process to come. In one room, a forensics team was set up. Their job was to ask family members to gather dental records and report any of their missing loved ones' identifying physical marks. Clergy of various faiths waited nearby to offer whatever comfort they could.

A few hours later, I returned to my office and tried to shake off a sense of foreboding as I sifted through my in-box. It was piled with decision memos on development deals for Massport property, environmental analyses of the new runway, and customer service recommendations.

Some weeks later, we held a briefing on the next steps for our emergency preparedness plan. I had a particularly sharp exchange with the head of Troop F, the State Police unit assigned to the airport. In the event of a real emergency, he said, they would shut off access to the airport, closing down entranceways from the highway. "Then how will families get here?" I asked him. He dismissed me, with a little wave that was not unfamiliar from my years of dealing with politics' sometimes "old boy" culture. He said something like, "We'll figure it out."

"That's not good enough," I said, looking him straight in the eye. "Come back to me with a better plan."

"It's eerie," I said to Tom Kinton, Logan's director of aviation, as we left the conference room. "The drill makes it feel like something is really going to happen." Tom grimaced and nodded in agreement.

Spring 2001

The level of reporting [among counterterrorism officials and Washington leaders] on terrorist threats and planned attacks increases dramatically, to its highest level since the millennium.

May 29, 2001—Boston

I stood discreetly on Logan's tarmac behind dozens of former and current congressional staffers as the honor guard approached the military jet. The flag-laden casket carrying the body of Congressman Joe Moakley was brought down the steps and placed on a wheeled platform on the tarmac.

June 1, 2001—St. Brigid Church, South Boston

The funeral service was packed. President George W. Bush, former president Bill Clinton, former vice president Al Gore, and many other dignitaries took their places in the front row. Like Moakley himself, the service was a blend of South Boston tradition and modest pageantry.

Near the end of the service, a security guard approached my pew. "Come with me," he whispered. I wasn't sure where we were going until I saw the presidential limousine parked near a waiting area. Inside a small white tent were a few local residents, including military service members or their families selected to greet the president. White House chief of staff Andy Card—a close friend of my old boss, Governor Cellucci—and his wife, Kathleene, were there, too.

President Bush entered the tent. He shook hands with the small gathering. As I said hello, reintroducing myself, he asked me, "How's Jack?" I was amazed he remembered my son's name.

I had first met the president when he was governor of Texas. I was serving as Weld's press secretary and had become friendly with Bush's communications director, Karen Hughes. I was pregnant with Jack when I chatted with Governor Bush at a Republican Governors Association meeting. He was kind and congratulatory about my son's impending birth. "What a real blessing," he said. "That's great." His warmth reminded me a lot of Cellucci, and I felt an instant connection to him.

When he was running for president, I took seven-week-old Jack to a fundraising event at the Park Plaza Hotel in Boston. It was being hosted by Weld and Cellucci for Bush's first presidential campaign. The four of us posed for a picture. I was holding Jack, Governor Bush on one side, Weld and Cellucci on the other. The Bush campaign later sent me a signed copy. "To Ginny," Bush wrote. "A rose between three thorns." Cellucci later told me that when Andy Card visited him at the ambassador's residence in Canada and the two reminisced about Massachusetts politics, Card remarked, "The president really loves Ginny Buckingham."

Now I stood quietly and listened as President Bush and Andy Card conferred about their schedules over the next few days.

"I'm staying here because I have to give a speech," Card said. "I'll see you at Camp David."

"Okay, I'm heading to the airport," the president replied. "Anyone need a ride?" He turned and looked at me. "Would you like a ride to your place of business?"

I shook my head, too dumbfounded to speak. I was as surprised that the president of the United States was offering me a ride as I was that he remembered I now ran Logan Airport.

In just a few short months, and in the years ahead, I would wonder if he made the same connection when attacks launched from my airport became indelibly imprinted on his presidency.

Summer 2001

Mohamed Atta (American Flight 11), Marwan al Shehhi (United Flight 175), and Ziad Jarrah (United Flight 93) take the first of several cross-country surveillance flights on the same type of aircraft each will pilot on 9/11. At various times and in various cities, the other pilots do the same. They and the muscle hijackers also build their strength at local gyms and purchase small knives. Atta travels to Spain to meet with an al Qaeda liaison to Osama bin Laden. He confirms the muscle hijackers have arrived in the US; the pilots have been assigned to their attack targets (the Twin Towers, the US Capitol, and the Pentagon). "If I can't reach the World Trade Center," Atta tells the al Qaeda liaison, "I'll crash the plane into the streets of New York."

Summer 2001—Marblehead, Massachusetts

"Mama!"

I hurried up the stairs to answer Jack's cry. He'd lately developed a fear of monsters. In his two-year-old mind, his room had become a potential den of dangerous creatures.

"D'ere," he said, pointing to the closet as I entered the room. "D'ere." He pointed and followed it with "Door," his broadening vocabulary serving as a road map to his fears.

Normally impatient, I checked each place he pointed to, trying to rebut his certainty that I would surely find the monster if only I looked in the right place.

"No monsters here, little love," I said to reassure him.

But each spot deemed monster-free only brought forth another request to check or recheck a corner. Suddenly, I got an idea. I turned to Jack with a broad grin.

"I have a can of special monster spray, Jack, right here," I said. I held up my right hand, three fingers and my thumb encircling an imaginary can, my pointer finger poised on the unseen button.

Jack looked at me with a quizzical expression. My change in tactic had clearly gotten his attention.

"This gets rid of monsters," I said. "Watch this, buddy." I arced my arm back and forth across Jack's room, making what I thought constituted a decent spraying sound by putting my tongue behind my teeth and hissing. *"Sssssss. Ssssssss."* I aimed the "can" at the closet and cried, "Take that, monsters! And that!"

Jack was giggling as he started directing my aim. "D'ere, Mama, d'ere!"

"That will show those monsters," I said. "They won't come near this room now."

After several minutes of this new game, I could see Jack rubbing his eyes and reached to shut off his light. I covered him with his blanket and sang "Edelweiss" from *The Sound of Music*, as I had done every night since I first learned I was pregnant. In minutes he was asleep.

I crossed the hall to our bedroom. The nightstand light was on. David was reading the rest of the newspaper he hadn't gotten to that morning.

"Jack was a little tough to get to sleep tonight," I said as I clicked on my light and reached for the mystery novel I was halfway through.

"Hug?" David asked, grinning warmly as he reached for me. I put my book down and moved closer to lay my head on his shoulder.

"Seven years and I love you more today than I did the day we were married," David said, squeezing my shoulder and bringing me closer as if for emphasis.

When we met at the State House in 1992 we had quickly gone from being close friends to falling in love. David liked to say we are each other's *bashert*, a Yiddish word for soul mate. I felt the same way, like our relationship was predestined and therefore indestructible.

"Do you want me to read to you?" he asked.

"If you must," I answered, teasing him, pretending to groan. I took off my glasses, placing them next to the water glass on the nightstand. I knew I would be awakened later when David turned the sheets upside down and groped under my pillow in search of his own glasses. Unless I removed them for him after he fell asleep, they'd slip off in the night. I smiled at the comfortable familiarity of our routine and closed my eyes.

"This is one my dad always read to my mother," David said, beginning the poem "When You Are Old" by Yeats.

> When you are old and gray and full of sleep
> And nodding by the fire, take down this book,
> And slowly read and dream of the soft look
> Your eyes had once and of their shadows deep . . .

David's voice was the last thing I heard before falling into a deep, undisturbed sleep.

No monsters here.

Between August 25 and September 5, 2001

The hijackers purchase nineteen plane tickets for cross-country flights departing from Logan, Dulles, and Newark airports on the morning of September 11, 2001.

CHAPTER THREE

THE DAY

September 11, 2001, 5:43 a.m.—Portland International Jetport, Portland, Maine

"Looking for US Airways?" Michael Tuohey asked the two Arab businessmen who appeared confused. Tuohey had transferred to Portland from Logan Airport in 1986. A native Bostonian and self-described "tough guy" who grew up in the projects, he enjoyed a quieter life in Maine. When he wasn't working the early shift at the airport, he happily puttered around his garden. He was one of a few ticket agents on duty at the counter.

Mohamed Atta and Abdulaziz al Omari approached and showed Tuohey their identification. He saw they were booked on the 6:00 a.m. Colgan Air flight to Boston. Atta was checking two bags, al Omari none. Tuohey asked Atta routine security questions about his luggage. When Atta confirmed he'd packed his own bags and kept them in view, Tuohey handed the men their boarding passes.

Atta looked angry. "They told me 'one-step check-in,'" he said, clenching his jaw. Tuohey hadn't issued boarding passes for Atta and al Omari's connecting flight in Boston even though, under airline rules, he could have. Something about the men was making him uncomfortable. Requiring the two to check in again in Boston meant they would have to deal with another ticket agent before going again through security.

Tuohey didn't like the look in Atta's eyes. *The deadest eyes I've ever seen,* he thought. *Like the devil himself.*

There is nothing in airline protocol or regulation that gave Tuohey any standing to detain the men. He'd be in big trouble with the airline if he needlessly hassled two legitimate businessmen. Instead, Tuohey looked straight into Atta's eyes. "Mr. Atta, if you don't go now, you will miss your plane."

6:00 a.m. Colgan Air Flight 5930 departs for Logan.

6:15 a.m.—Marblehead

I pulled on the shade next to Jack's crib, once, twice, until it stubbornly inched up to let the sunlight in. I hated waking him up, but if I didn't, David would be late for work and I would be late for my flight.

"C'mon, my sweet boy, time to get up," I said softly, pulling Jack's blanket back and gently taking Special Doggie, a favorite stuffed animal, from his arms. He reached up for me and snuggled his head into my shoulder. For a moment, I breathed into his hair and pressed his sleep-warmed body into mine. I sighed as I carried him to the changing table, wishing for more time.

6:20 a.m.—Logan Airport, Terminal C

Ahmed al Ghamdi and Hamza al Ghamdi walk up to the United Airlines ticket counter. The customer service agent they first approach is unsure about a document one of the men presents, so she sends them to a more seasoned representative to check their paperwork.

"I need a ticket," one of the men says to the second representative.

"No, you have a ticket," she answers after looking at his documents. "You can check in."

With two bags to check, the representative asks the routine security questions. "Did you pack your bag yourself? Has it been in your possession the whole time?"

Each man seems to have trouble understanding the questions. She very slowly repeats them. Once the men finally answer to her satisfaction, she hands them their boarding passes. The two men walk quickly to the nearby security checkpoint.

6:30 a.m.—Marblehead

Jack settled back on our bed, and I tucked a blanket around his legs as David handed him a sippy cup of juice. I reached for the remote, then turned on the TV and flipped the channel to the PBS station, hoping *Sesame Street*, Jack's favorite, was on.

"Hey, I already called first shower!" I teased David, as I raced him to the bathroom door. He grabbed me in a bear hug and answered, "Only if you kiss me first."

I happily obliged, and as I stepped under the hot stream of water, I counted the seconds in my head until the next step in our morning routine. There was a loud knock on the bathroom door. *Here it comes,* I thought, already smiling.

"Hey, hon!" David called. "Doug's on the phone."

I played along. "Doug, who?"

"Doug MacDonald from the water department. He says he's getting complaints that someone in Marblehead is using up all the hot water."

If David took his shower first, it was me at the other side of the door making the "Doug" joke. There was simple intimacy to our goofy joking, and we grinned at each other as David headed into the bathroom for his turn. I reached to pick up Jack and settled him on my hip to carry him downstairs for breakfast.

6:45 a.m.—Logan Airport, Central Parking Garage

Three men, Wail al Shehri, Waleed al Shehri, and Satam al Suqami, pull their rental car, a white Mitsubishi, into a space in the Logan garage reserved for long-term parking. Another Logan passenger has just parked in the next spot and is still sitting in his car. One of the three men opens the passenger side of the rental car door. He stands there with the door open, fiddling with something in the front seat. He either doesn't know or doesn't care that he's blocking the man in the next car from being able to open his own door.

After a few minutes, the Logan passenger gets tired of waiting for the man to move and carefully opens his door, pushing the door of the Mitsubishi. The Logan passenger expects a reaction—a glare, or even an apology for blocking his way—but the man does not react at all. Neither do the two still sitting in the car. They just stare straight ahead. The passenger thinks their behavior is strange but has no reason to be concerned beyond that. He heads to his terminal to catch an early-morning flight.

6:45 a.m. Marwan al Shehhi checks a single bag onto Flight 175.

Approximately 6:46 a.m.—Logan Airport, Terminal B

Atta and al Omari walk off the Colgan Air flight from Portland into the US Airways concourse of Terminal B. A baggage handler immediately begins unloading the checked bags from the belly of the plane. He sees Atta's bags are tagged for transfer to American Flight 11.

Shouldering their carry-on luggage, the two men cross a parking lot to the other Terminal B concourse. The signs are unclear and they stop and ask someone for directions. They then walk quickly to the sliding glass doors leading to American Airlines.

6:52 a.m.—Terminal B

Atta's cell phone rings. It's al Shehhi calling from a Terminal C pay phone. The two men knew each other well, having spent much of the year before together at the same flight training school in Florida. They confer for three minutes.

6:53 a.m.—Terminal C

Fayez Banihammad and Mohand al Shehri check in at the United ticket counter. Banihammad checks two bags, al Shehri, none.

7:15 a.m.—Marblehead

"Bye, little buddy," I said to Jack, kissing him on the head. "I love you."

"Love you, hon," David called, carrying Jack's backpack in one arm and Jack in the other as he walked down the front steps. "Have a great day."

7:20 a.m.—Terminal C, United Airlines gate 19

Passengers couldn't help but smile back at the redheaded gate agent with the twinkle in her eye. "Good mornin'," she said. "Have a great flight!" Marianne MacFarlane had been at work since before dawn. Her mom had dropped her off, as usual, at the lower level of Logan's Terminal C. She planned to board United 175 last, after she'd helped board all the passengers, to head to the West Coast for a short vacation.

Marianne loved everything about working at an airport and had since the moment she started selling flowers out of a cart in Terminal D as a teenager. But she especially loved the benefit of flying for free. She and her mom, Anne, regularly flew to Disney in Florida—her favorite place on the planet!—just to get haircuts at the Contemporary

Resort She had four cross-country flights to choose from that morning and settled on Flight 175.

7:23 a.m.—Terminal C, gate 19

Fayez Banihammad hands his boarding pass to the gate agent. He's followed by Mohand al Shehri. The two men walk down the jet bridge and take seats in first class, 2A and 2B.

7:27 a.m. Marwan al Shehhi boards with Ahmed al Ghamdi. They sit three rows apart in business class.

7:28 a.m. Hamza al Ghamdi boards the United flight. He sits in business class, 9C, in the same row as Ahmed al Ghamdi, who's in 9D. All five hijackers are now on board United Flight 175.

7:31 a.m.—Terminal B, gate 32

Wail al Shehri and Waleed al Shehri hand their boarding cards to the gate agent. They walk down the jet bridge and settle into seats 2A and 2B. Just minutes before the boarding door is closed, Atta and al Omari walk onto the plane. Their seats are in business class, 8D and 8G. Satam al Suqami walks right past them and sits in 10B. All five hijackers are now on board American Flight 11.

7:32 a.m.—Marblehead

Taking advantage of a few rare minutes of quiet at home, I reached into my briefcase and pulled out the background memo for my meeting in Washington later that afternoon.

It was entitled "Meeting with Jane Garvey" and dated "September 11, 2001." Garvey was the administrator of the Federal Aviation Administration, the agency that regulated civil aviation in the United States.

The memo was from Kristen Lepore, a well-regarded Massport colleague and state public-policy expert whom I'd worked with at the State House. I read her succinct summary: "It is my understanding that you will be meeting alone with Jane Garvey. Assistant Secretary Michael Jackson is planning to stop by during the meeting. Items you should raise include: 1) Filing of the Final Environmental Impact Statement (FEIS); 2) The MITER Study; 3) Timing for the Record of Decision."

Kristen's briefing memo made clear what I already knew. Today's meeting with Garvey was a critical step to receiving federal approval for Logan's new runway. I'd been working on this regional economic priority nonstop for the two years I'd been at Massport. But since it had taken nearly thirty years to get the controversial project to the edge of approval, I knew I needed to navigate these last steps perfectly.

As I continued reading, though, I shook my head in frustration. The technical points I'd make in the meeting about the length of the runway, its projected use, and its environmental impact weren't going to make a difference. *She knows all this!* I thought to myself. I had been getting nowhere with Garvey, once a Democratic political operative from Massachusetts who was intimately familiar with Logan's operating constraints. At one point, she was aviation director there, essentially the person who ran the airport, before moving to federal posts in Washington. I'd often thought about our somewhat parallel career tracks and wondered if I, too, would eventually move to a federal position.

I figured Garvey was caught between a rock and a hard place on the runway decision. The state's all-Democrat congressional delegation and Boston's Democratic mayor still fiercely opposed the project because of neighbors' fears it would lead to increased air and ground traffic. So I'd requested that Assistant Secretary Jackson, from the US Department of Transportation, attend today's meeting to make the point to her, without subtlety, that the Bush Administration supported building new runways at the nation's airports. I hoped the counterpressure would prompt Garvey to agree to a compromise.

Today's meeting is my checkmate move. I hope so anyway, I thought, closing the briefing and putting it back in my bag.

7:40 a.m. American Flight 11 pushes back from gate 32 and begins taxiing to the runway.

7:58 a.m. United Flight 175 pushes back from gate 19 and begins taxiing to the runway.

7:59 a.m. American Flight 11 takes off from Logan.

Shortly before 8:14 a.m. Flight 11 reaches an altitude of 26,000 feet, just shy of its cruising altitude of 29,000 feet. The flight attendants begin preparations for cabin service. An FAA air traffic controller radios directional instructions: "American 11 turn twenty degrees right." Flight 11's crew replies: "Twenty right American 11." Seconds later, air traffic control radios Flight 11 again, this time instructing the aircraft to climb to 35,000 feet.

There is no response.

8:14 a.m. United Flight 175 takes off from Logan.

8:19 a.m.—On board American Flight 11

Flight attendant Betty Ong contacts the American Airlines Southeastern Reservations Office in Cary, North Carolina, via AT&T airphone to report an emergency aboard the flight. "The cockpit is not answering. Somebody's stabbed in business class," she says. "I think there's Mace. We can't breathe. I don't know, I think we're getting hijacked."

8:21 a.m. Someone in the cockpit switches off the transponder, which relays the aircraft's location to air traffic control.

Shortly before 8:25 a.m.—FAA Boston Center, Nashua, New Hampshire

An air traffic controller monitoring Northeast air traffic hears two clicks over the frequency assigned to Flight 11. "Is that American eleven trying to call?" the controller asks. Five seconds later, a man with a foreign accent tries to address the passengers but mistakenly transmits a message to air traffic control: "We have some planes. Just stay quiet and you'll be okay. We're returning to the airport."

Approximately 8:45 a.m.—Swampscott, Massachusetts, en route to Logan

"Do you mind pulling over so I can get a cup of coffee?" I asked my colleague James Roy, who was dropping me off at Terminal B for my flight. "Want one?"

I have plenty of time, I thought to myself. *I don't take off until ten.* Getting through security should only take a few minutes.

Back in the car, coffee in hand, I reached over to flip on the radio. I turned the dial to the local news station, WBZ Newsradio 1030. Once I found the right station, I rummaged through my briefcase—a last-minute check to make sure I remembered the plane ticket. The paper ticket was still stapled into its travel agency–issued envelope, and I glanced at the details: "US Air Flight 6517. 10:00 a.m. lv. Boston, arr. Washington Reagan 11:31 a.m. Date: 11 Sept. Status: OK."

Status: OK

As James pulled to a stop at a light, I went through a mental checklist. *Ticket. Briefing. Did I pack a change of clothes for Jack? Backgrounder and directions for meeting tonight.* When I returned to Boston later, I would be observing a focus group of Logan passengers. They'd be questioned about their attitudes toward renaming Logan's terminals. The terminals were named A, B, C, and E, skipping D. The missed letter is a quirk from years past when a wing of an existing terminal was used by one particular airline. Someone at the time thought it would be easier for travelers to find their gate if the airline had its own terminal designation. When the airline moved, D was dropped, leaving Logan with its alphanumeric dilemma. That night, I'd get to gauge the reaction of regular and occasional Logan travelers to the proposed solution of numbering the terminals like they did at New York's JFK airport, or whether simply changing the name of E to D would help or be even more confusing.

8:49 a.m.—En route to Logan

"Listen to this," James interrupted my thoughts. There was a breaking news report. A plane had hit the World Trade Center, the announcer said.

I assumed the crash was an accident, caused by a small private plane. "Wow, that's terrible," I said, turning up the radio. "I'm glad we're not going to New York. It's going to be a mess down there."

My cell phone rang. "Ginny, it's Julie. Did you hear?" Julie Wasson was my assistant. "Do you want to cancel the trip?"

Canceling hadn't crossed my mind. "No, I'm not letting Garvey get out of this," I answered.

8:52 a.m. An air traffic controller asks Flight 175 to recycle its transponder to the proper code. There is no response.

8:53 a.m.—Logan Airport

The radio crackled in Rudy Chiarello's Massport truck. Rudy, a Logan veteran, typically spent his shift on the airfield, monitoring activity. His radio call signal was "Port 25." Logan's air traffic control tower supervisor advised Port 25 that "American Flight 11 from Boston to Los Angeles had lost radio contact."

Rudy immediately radioed John Duval, "Port 20," the airport's deputy operations director. John was sitting at his desk on the fifth floor of the air traffic control tower. He had just hung up from a call with his son. "Dad, a plane just hit the World Trade Center," his son had told him, having seen the breaking news report on TV. John also thought it was probably a small single-engine plane. Until the radioed alert from Rudy: "John, something big is happening and it can't be good."

John immediately called Ed Freni, his counterpart on the aviation staff who dealt with Logan's airline issues. Ed was in a management training seminar at Logan Office Center and stepped into the hall to take John's call. After hearing the news, he walked quickly back into the training session, ironically named "How to Deliver Bad News," to tell the leader he had to leave. "I've just been told the worst news possible," he said.

My radio call signal was "Port 1." Believing I was already in Terminal B waiting for my flight, Logan officials began paging my name over the public address system with an urgency I was later told caused some passengers to wonder if something was wrong.

8:57 a.m. Flight 175 turns to the northeast and levels off at 28,500 feet. One minute later, it heads toward New York City.

Approximately 8:58 a.m.—Revere, Massachusetts

The phone rang in the Revere "double-decker," the two-family home where Anne MacFarlane lived with her daughter Marianne. Anne had been up since before dawn after waking Marianne and dropping her off at the airport for her morning shift. "Otherwise she'd never get there," Anne recounted later. She reached for the phone. It was her son George, a firefighter in Chelsea, Massachusetts, calling from the station. "Ma, turn on the TV, a plane has hit the World Trade Center in New York."

Approximately 9:00 a.m. The FAA's New York Center informs the United Airlines air traffic control coordinator that Flight 175 is missing from radar.

9:03 a.m.—Revere, Massachusetts

Anne, still watching television at home, gasped as she watched a jet-liner fly into the World Trade Center during the live broadcast.

The second plane striking the tower. The explosion. The ball of fire. The black smoke. When I thought later about the image of 9/11 many of us carried most closely, I always thought about the families of passengers on United 175 like Anne who saw it live. Not knowing at the time that they were watching their children or spouses being murdered. But knowing later. Then knowing always.

9:03 a.m.—En route to Logan

James and I listened as a reporter described the chaotic scene from street level in New York.

"Another plane has just crashed into the South Tower!" he exclaimed.

"Oh my God, it's terrorism," I gasped.

My phone rang again minutes later. It was Joey Cuzzi, Massport's director of communication, who was coming with me to Washington.

"They're saying that one, maybe both planes are from Boston." Joey's tone was even but insistent. "Two planes are off the radar."

I closed my eyes, just for a second, and whispered a quick prayer. *God. Please, no. Not our planes. Not our people.*

"Okay, we're headed in," I told Joey and disconnected the call.

"Jack." My first thought was of my son. I wanted to tell James to turn around. I wanted to drive straight to Jack's day care center. I wanted to take him in my arms and keep him safe from whatever this was.

"I'm taking the back way in," James said. "It's faster."

"Good," was all I said in response.

9:07 a.m.—North Tower

Fire companies begin to ascend stairwell B.

9:07 a.m.—En route to Logan

"The kind of plane they're describing is not in our fleet mix," James said. WBZ had switched to airing live New York City radio coverage. One caller into the station who had witnessed the crash described the aircraft as a DC-3, an old prop-driven cargo aircraft.

I wanted to hang on to this trace of doubt, but Joey's words echoed in my head: "Two planes are off the radar."

9:09 a.m. to 9:10 a.m. All air traffic controllers in Boston Center use their radio frequencies to advise aircraft in their airspace to heighten cockpit security.

Approximately 9:11 a.m. As I listened to the radio reports describing the chaos in Lower Manhattan, James and I raced through back streets of Lynn, Revere, and East Boston. The buildings and streetscape were deeply familiar. Double- and triple-decker houses next to Italian delis, statues of the Virgin Mary next to convenience stores with signs in Spanish, Dunkin' Donuts outlets, fast-food Chinese and burger joints. The aboveground tracks of the Blue Line subway, its trains rumbling past, heading in and out of Boston.

How was it possible that it still looked just as it did yesterday and the day before? Exactly the same as it did just a few hours before, when surely some of the passengers on the two planes—*"Two planes are off the radar"*—drove by here to park at Logan, or be dropped off at the terminals' curb?

James pulled to a stop at a busy intersection. We were in the Beachmont section of Revere, an old neighborhood of working-class families, directly under the approach to Runway 22-Left, one of Logan's busiest. Local leaders here had been pushing me hard to fund sound-insulation windows to shield residents from the noise of low-flying aircraft overhead.

The incongruity of what was, just yesterday, just hours before, a pressing priority with what was happening in New York jarred me as I stared out the window.

"Two planes are off the radar."

Joey's refrain echoed among the other questions reverberating in my mind:

Were there more out there?

"Two planes are off the radar."

Were the planes that crashed in New York from Logan?

"Two planes are off the radar."

How did this happen?

"Two planes are off the radar."

Again and again, I asked myself variations of the question that would take investigators years to answer: *How?*

Approximately 9:12 a.m. As James turned onto the road leading to the back entrance to Logan, I could see the one remaining house on East Boston's Neptune Road. The rest of the homes were taken by eminent domain decades earlier by Massport officials in their relentless march toward expansion. Whenever I spoke to Logan neighborhood activists, I was still asked questions about Massport compensating the community adequately for the loss of the Neptune Road homes and the destruction of nearby Wood Island Park. No matter how many years later, as Massport's leader, I understood I bore the responsibility of answering for the agency's past decisions.

But I didn't know yet, just several minutes after the world was changed forever by the hijackings of two planes from Logan, that I would soon be asked to take responsibility for something that would prove nearly impossible to bear, the deaths of thousands of innocent people.

Approximately 9:15 a.m. After confirming that two airliners had struck the World Trade Center, American Airlines orders all its airborne flights to land.

Approximately 9:15 a.m.—Logan Airport, Air Traffic Control Tower, eighteenth floor

Logan security director Joe Lawless activates the Emergency Operations Center at Logan's Massport Fire Rescue headquarters. Airline, airport, federal, state, and local public-safety agencies are notified to report immediately.

9:15 a.m.—Logan Airport, Logan Office Center

James screeched to a stop in front of Logan Office Center. It had been twelve minutes since I'd heard the live report of the second plane flying into the tower. Before getting out of the car, I took a deep breath. I steeled myself. I knew I couldn't freeze in the face of the horror that was taking place. I couldn't, as I wanted to, weep as I heard the reports coming out of New York.

I could not scream. I could not cry. I don't think I actually thought these words but I felt them. Felt them more deeply than I had ever felt anything.

I had to do my job. I had to do my job better than I had ever done anything in my life. I was the leader of more than one thousand Massport employees at Logan. There were sixteen thousand more who worked for the airlines and other contractors. Millions of Logan passengers relied on all of us for their safety. I had to lead Logan through this. Whatever "this" turned out to be.

9:17 a.m. All New York airports are shut down by the FAA.

9:18 a.m.—Logan Office Center

The lobby was eerily empty as I walked quickly across it. I impatiently jabbed my finger on the elevator call button. Once. Twice. A third time. My office was on the second floor. As I quickly walked toward it, I saw several people gathered around the TV in the office next to mine.

I wanted to see this alone. I had to see this alone. I stepped into the doorway, and stopped in front of my desk. The TV, some fifteen feet away, was already on. I wrapped my arms protectively around my chest. As if I were cold. As if I were freezing. I stood perfectly still, squeezing my arms so hard to stop myself from shaking that I left red finger marks. The images I had been able to conjure in my mind from the radio reports were no match for the reality.

It came out of nowhere.

Impossibly low. Unbelievably fast.

The explosion.

The ball of fire.

The black smoke.

Against the backdrop of a perfect blue sky.

"Two planes are off the radar."

Joey's words. I swallowed the vomit that rose up in my throat and reached for the phone to call Acting Governor Jane Swift.

9:28 a.m. Russ Aims came into my office. He'd been my deputy since I was chief of staff for Governor Weld. "Can you give the official okay to open the family assistance center?" he asked. His exceedingly thin face looked thinner and paler than usual. We briefly locked eyes. The Logan Hilton hotel was the headquarters of the Care Team. The families who gathered there would be looking for answers. For comfort. Just like we'd practiced in the drill the year before. Except this was nothing like we'd practiced the year before. My saliva burned as I swallowed. I took a deep breath to ease the sensation.

"Yes, get it open right away," I answered.

9:25 a.m. The FAA institutes a national ground stop.

9:36 a.m. Fearing that the Logan air traffic control tower itself might be a target, employees evacuate.

9:37 a.m. American Airlines Flight 77 flies into the Pentagon.

Approximately 9:39 a.m. Oh my God, did they get the people out? I thought as I looked at the image on the television of the smoking hole in the side of the Pentagon. *How many more planes are out there?*

9:42 a.m. The FAA halts all flight operations at US airports.

9:43 a.m. Ed Freni and John Duval tried to confirm with the FAA that the planes that hit the towers were from Boston. No one seemed to know for sure. Freni was able to get some information from the airlines, but even that was inconsistent. He called to tell me it was American Flight 77 that crashed into the World Trade Center and United 175 was safely on the ground.

The TV in my office was still on, and as I placed the phone back in its cradle, a question posed by an anchor to a reporter on the ground in New York drew my attention. "Do you think the towers will fall?" the anchor asked.

I looked up and glanced over at James, who was standing nearby. "What do you think?" I asked. "Is that even possible?"

9:59 a.m. The South Tower of the World Trade Center collapses.

10:02 a.m. My direct line rang. It was John Duval. "We can't reach Delta Flight 1989. They have no radio contact," he said. The Delta flight was another one from Boston to Los Angeles. John's voice trembled with emotion. He and Ed, he said, were working with air traffic control to account for all Boston originating flights. "I'll keep you updated."

"Okay, thanks." I took another deep breath as I absorbed the possibility that another plane might be missing from Logan.

10:03 a.m. United Airlines Flight 93 crashes near Shanksville, Pennsylvania.

10:18 a.m.—Logan Airport

John Duval called again from the tower. "Delta 1989 has landed safely in Cleveland," he reported.

"Thank God," I answered, exhaling, as if I had been holding my breath for all of the fifteen minutes since he told me the flight was missing.

10:28 a.m. I noticed Russ standing, open mouthed, at his office door. His hand gripped the right doorframe as if for support. "What is it?" I asked him.

"They're gone," he said. I followed his gaze to the television. The North Tower had collapsed, too.

Approximately 10:34 a.m. My assistant Julie said my mother was on the phone. "Are you okay?" she asked.

"I'm okay," I answered. I wished I could have said in response, *The towers, Mom, the towers are gone. Thousands, maybe tens of thousands, of people are dead. Oh my God, Mom, the planes came from Logan.*

But I couldn't, even then, change the dynamic of a family relationship in which I was always the "good one," the "successful one." The okay one.

A devout Catholic, my mother in turn tried to comfort me with our shared faith. "God always has a reason," she said.

"God would never stand by and let this happen," I snapped back, my voice rising. I paused a second to try to speak more calmly. "I refuse to believe in that kind of God."

The all-powerful God she raised me to believe in "opens a window when a door closes." He answered prayers, worked miracles. How could He stand by and let hijackers murder thousands of innocent people? Barely concealing my rising fury—at her, at God, maybe at both—I said shortly, "I can't talk about this now. I have to go. I'll call you later."

Neither she nor I knew then that a major foundation of my life—my belief in God—had shifted. A faith that had been as tangible and present as the ground I stood on—solid and unmoving—was gone. Destroyed in a matter of hours as completely and as unimaginably as the Twin Towers.

Approximately 11:00 a.m. My private line rang again. It was David. "The courthouse is being closed for security reasons," he said.

I don't remember what else either of us said, beyond my urgent plea: "Just please go get Jack and bring him home." I tried to steady my voice. "Please keep him safe."

"I will," David answered. "I love you."

11:05 a.m. Massachusetts State Police searched the air traffic control tower and Logan's communications tower for any signs of a follow-on attack.

Ed and John came to my office. They sat on the edges of the two opposing leather couches, poised as if they might have to get up and race back to the tower for another emergency.

John updated me that the remaining aircraft on the airfield were being secured so each could be searched for potential evidence. Passengers were continuing to be cleared from the terminals. He noted that the Care Team was preparing for the first arrival of families at the Hilton hotel, his voice catching as he related details of the operation.

As he spoke, I envisioned the drill the year before in which the students' convincing performance as family members brought me to tears. John looked over at me. With a thick shock of white hair, he had always looked older than he was. Now he looked older still. We held each other's eyes for a long moment and nodded, a silent acknowledgment of the shared grief we could not yet allow ourselves to express.

Ed, too, had pages of notes, jotted as he continually called contacts he had at American, where he used to work, and United Airlines. A father of eight, Ed still looked like the college hockey player he once was. He confirmed that it was American Flight 11 that had been the first plane hijacked.

"I know these people. I used to work with them," he said, the shock evident even through his professional recital of what he had learned. A flight attendant, Madeline Amy Sweeney, he said, had called the American control center from the back of the plane. The manager on duty told Ed what Sweeney had told him: "They're in the cockpit. Two flight attendants have been stabbed." I leaned forward. I folded my hands in front of my mouth, not conscious that I may have wanted to shield my reaction.

"She said a passenger had his throat slashed." A sharp gasp escaped through my now-clenched fists blocking my mouth.

This was the first time I would hear about the murder of Daren Abelman, though not by name, the only passenger thought to be killed on Flight 11 before the plane crashed. Abelman had once served in the Israeli military, and it's likely he leaped to the defense of the flight attendant being attacked, unaware another hijacker sat directly behind him. Some two years later, I would hear of him again in a call from my lawyer, telling me I had been personally sued for wrongful death. For Daren Abelman's wrongful, horrifying death.

I could see the harbor and the Boston skyline silhouetted beyond the floor-to-ceiling glass windows, the same view I had every day. Again, this struck me as odd, just as the familiar street scenes had this morning on the ride in. I kept expecting everything to look different in the wake of a world completely changed in a few short hours.

"They used a box cutter," Ed continued, relating what Sweeney had reported. I crossed my arms in front of my chest then and dug my fingers deeper into the skin of my forearms.

"What's a box cutter?" I asked, unfamiliar with the term.

Ed described the flat metal sheath holding a razor blade. It was most commonly used in supermarkets to open boxes, he said. Sweeney was likely right about the kind of knife it was, he added, because airline employees more typically used a utility knife to open boxes, with a thick handle and small blade that could be extended with a click of a button. Either could be bought in any hardware store.

Approximately 11:30 a.m.—Terminal C

Anne MacFarlane, still waiting at home in Revere for her daughter Marianne to call, decided to drive back to Logan. Maybe some of Marianne's United Airlines colleagues had heard from her. She parked and hurried to the departures level of Terminal C.

As she approached the ticket counter, she couldn't help but notice the abnormal quiet. On any other Tuesday, the terminal would be abuzz with activity. Passengers rushing to get to their gates, others peering at the arrival and departure listings. Children crying. Baggage being wheeled across the tiled floor. Just ahead, she saw a group of United Airlines employees gathered by the ticket counter. They were talking quietly. When they saw Anne coming toward them, several began to cry. It was then that she knew for sure: her daughter was on one of the hijacked planes.

Approximately 11:45 a.m. Julie handed me a stack of pink message slips. I sorted through them. I couldn't return any of them now, but I appreciated the calls from friends and acquaintances who were simply showing their support. I was startled, though, by the name on the message slip at the bottom of the pile: "Fred Salvucci," the state transportation leader under former governor Michael Dukakis who was no fan of Massport. The message he left was equally unexpected: even if Israel were in charge of Logan, this still would have happened.

11:59 a.m. United Airlines confirms there were fifty-six passengers and nine crew on Flight 175.

12:10 p.m. Logan Airport officials are notified that four international flights bound for Boston from Europe have been rerouted to Canadian airspace, joining some 250 flights and more than thirty-three thousand passengers that will be diverted to airports across Canada by the end of the day.

Approximately 1:00 p.m.—Logan Airport, Massport Fire Rescue headquarters

Ed placed a faxed sheet of paper on the table in the upstairs conference room. We'd moved to Massport Fire Rescue headquarters, next to the airfield where the Emergency Operations Center had been set up. Dozens of federal, state, and local first responders were in the auditorium downstairs. Had a plane gone down on the airfield or in the harbor, we'd have coordinated rescue efforts from there just like we'd practiced in the response and rescue part of the drill last October. Instead, there was a restless energy in the room as the emergency response unfolded hundreds of miles away.

I stood behind Ed and leaned over his shoulder to read the passenger manifest for Flight 11. "It's generated from scanning the boarding passes," Freni explained, "so these are the people actually on the plane."

I noticed someone had written "AA #11" in thick black permanent marker along the margin of the list of names. The manifest listed the seat assignments, too. As I scanned the names, I pictured the organized chaos of a typical plane boarding—passengers waiting patiently while the person in the aisle in front of them pushed and tugged a too-big carry-on into the overhead bin, others fastened their seat belts, tucking a water bottle into the seat-back pocket, alongside the folded morning newspapers.

"But look at these," I said to Ed and the other Massport senior staff gathered around him. I pointed to the abbreviated Arabic names of passengers who were seated toward the front of the plane.

American Airlines officials had actually tried, Ed said, to locate the two al Shehris in the gate area before the flight. The manifest noted they were "club" members, entitled to relax in a special area reserved for first-class and business travelers.

The room went quiet. The realization that every single person on this list was dead seemed to hit each of us at the same time.

"Two planes are off the radar."

The reality of that haunting phrase was right in front of me. On American 11, seventy-six innocent passengers, two pilots, and nine flight attendants. Ninety-two people in all dead. On United 175, fifty-one innocent passengers, two pilots, and seven flight attendants. Sixty-five people in all dead. Each of those passengers and crew had gotten up that morning. *As I did.* Followed their normal routine. *As I did.* Kissed their spouse and their children goodbye. *As I did.* Traveled to Logan to catch a flight. *As I did.* Did they die instantly? Did they suffer?

I needed to be alone for a few minutes. I nodded to the firefighter seated at the desk by the entrance as I stepped out the door to the parking lot. For the first time, I noticed the details of the special access badge he was wearing, the same one I put on as I arrived at Fire Rescue headquarters. It was yellow with an illustration of an airliner on it. The airliner was cracked in half. But large pieces remained intact, making survival, rescue, a possibility. I imagined for a second what the badge would look like if the illustration tried to capture what had happened that morning.

The plane striking the second tower.
The explosion.
The ball of fire.
The black smoke.

Fingering my own badge, I walked slowly toward the chain-link fence separating the Fire Rescue headquarters from the airfield. I stopped and listened. Something didn't feel right. It took me a minute more to figure out what it was. Silence.

I looked up and saw nothing but sky. On the tarmac ahead of me, planes were lined up against empty jet bridges. Unmoving. No fuel trucks, no maintenance vehicles driving on the perimeter road. No workers directing or refueling planes on the ramp. No baggage handlers. The runways at Logan Airport, the eighteenth-busiest airport in the country, were completely and unnaturally empty.

The sky above? Emptier still.

1:30 p.m. to 1:30 a.m.—Logan Airport

For the next twelve hours, we focused on the massive operational task of closing down and securing 1.2 million square feet of terminal space. The more than fifty Massport volunteers who made up the Care Team took on the emotional task of providing support to the growing stream of families coming to the Logan Hilton.

I sat at the head of the conference table and looked across at the people I'd worked with day in and day out for the past two years. Chris, Massport's head of the multibillion-dollar modernization project underway at Logan; Joe, the chief of security; Ed and John, the leaders of aviation operations; Mike, the head of Massport's cargo and cruise facilities in the Port of Boston; Joey and Jose, the communications and media leaders. Leslie, Tommy, and Dave, the agency's finance, government relations, and legal teams. Given the runway fight and other difficult negotiations with the community over airport-impact issues—the intense forums, the public hearings, the media scrutiny—I felt I knew each of these people better, more personally, than I would in an ordinary work situation. Now on each face I saw the same recognition I knew was on mine. What we had seen so far that day and what was yet to come would be beyond any experience we'd ever shared.

I asked each operational head to provide a status update on their area of responsibility:

"The American Red Cross is on-site with the families at the Hilton. Father Richard is on his way."

"We're bringing cots and supplies to the Exchange Conference Center for passengers who have no place to stay."

"We're already getting calls from families in East Boston offering their homes for people to stay in."

"Canine units are being deployed."

"No word from the FAA on the airspace reopening."

"An employee's daughter was on United 175."

"Wait, what?" I stopped John and asked him to repeat what he'd said. A Massport customer service agent's daughter, who worked for United, was on Flight 175. "Marianne MacFarlane," he said.

The operational reports continued:

"All construction sites have been shut down."

"The governor is going to need another update before her next press availability."

"The tower says everything was normal leaving Boston airspace."

"We've opened a media center at the Hyatt. We need someone to make a statement."

Ed came into the room. "American Airlines," he said, "has found luggage in the bag room that mistakenly hadn't been loaded onto Flight 11. State Police are on the way over to open and search it."

In the first major break in the investigation, the luggage turned out to be Mohamed Atta's. In it were an instructional flight video and a fuel consumption calculator.

Shortly before 4:00 p.m.—Logan Hyatt ballroom

Logan security director Joe Lawless ascended the makeshift platform in the media center set up in the Logan Hyatt ballroom. I stood on the side of the room. We'd asked the FAA and representatives from the airlines to join him, but they'd refused. Still, we felt we had an obligation to attempt to satisfy the intensifying restlessness of the gathered media.

In a short prepared statement, Joe said that Logan's priority was dealing with the needs of the passengers' families. He provided phone numbers the airlines had made available for them to call. He then confirmed it was American Flight 11 and United Flight 175 that had been hijacked.

As we expected, there were some questions about Logan security procedures. Joe, a highly respected state homicide investigator and head of the governor's security detail before running Logan Airport security for the past eight years, said, "We have a very high security standard here. We are as secure, if not more secure, than any other airport in the US."

Since the hijackers had successfully boarded and taken over four planes at three different large East Coast airports at almost exactly the same time, I expected the media and political leaders would see the security issues as national rather than Logan-specific. And that the immensity of this world-changing event would trump any tendency to turn the terrorist attacks into some kind of political football. I believed the target of understandable collective anger and fear would be the terrorist sponsors who launched this horrific attack.

On all three counts, I had never been more wrong in my life.

Approximately 5:00 p.m.—Massport Fire Rescue headquarters

As we reconvened in the conference room, Ed related the story of a passenger who had called police to describe an encounter with three Arab men in the parking garage that morning. "When he heard about the hijackings, he immediately contacted authorities," he said. Because of the passenger's report about the odd behavior of the men who sat in their car staring straight ahead as he tried to open his car door, investigators recovered the hijackers' rented white Mitsubishi, the second big break in the investigation. In the car they found Arabic-language flight manuals.

A check of Logan's parking garage records, which tracks the license plates of cars entering and exiting Logan garages, indicated the hijackers' car had been in and out of Logan several times in the preceding days, a further indication that the attacks were carefully orchestrated.

8:00 p.m.—Logan Hyatt ballroom

Some twelve hours from when American 11 and United 175 had pulled back from Logan's gates, I approached the podium set up in the make-shift media center. Tom Kinton, Logan's director of aviation, had arrived at the airport under police escort after traveling for hours from a meeting he was attending in Canada.

Reporters packed the room, many more than were there that afternoon. Cameras, mounted on tripods, lined the back wall. Working with Joey, I had quickly jotted an opening statement on the way to the media center.

"Good evening," I said, looking straight ahead into the cameras, the notes I had made on three sheets of yellow paper in front of me.

"On behalf of Massport, I want to express our deepest sympathy to families of loved ones on the aircraft involved in these incidents. Even as our response has focused on the safety and security of our passengers and employees, the pain of these families has been foremost in our minds. These incidents triggered our emergency response plan. Throughout the day Massport has worked with public-safety agencies at the federal, state, and local levels. We've trained extensively for disasters, though certainly today's events are beyond our worst imaginings."

Reporters scribbled furiously in their notebooks.

"I also want to thank the Hilton hotel and the numerous volunteers who have responded to the family assistance center to support those families who came to Logan in search of information.

"We appreciate the patience of the press throughout this long day. We've attempted to provide you with whatever information was made available to us, and we will continue to do so throughout the hours and days ahead. This media center at the Hyatt will stay open as long as this crisis continues. Finally, from the onset this morning, we pledged our wholehearted support for ongoing law-enforcement efforts and will continue to do so. Nothing is more important to those of us in the aviation industry than finding out how this could have happened. Thank you."

I turned the microphone over to Tom Kinton, who made a similar statement and then, in turn, introduced Joe Lawless. Lawless barely finished before the questions started coming rapid fire.

Row after row of reporters poised, pens or microphones in hand, on the edge of their seats jostled for their turn:

How did the hijackers access the planes?

What weapons did they have?

Is it true other Logan flights were targeted?

Were the weapons snuck onto the planes from the ramp?

Is it true five Arab men were seen running from another plane?

Tom, Joe, and I fielded each question, but we had few answers. I could see the frustration on the reporters' faces. It mirrored our own.

After the press conference was over, I received a call on my cell phone from Frank Phillips, the head of the *Boston Globe*'s State House Bureau. "You look awful," he said.

I hadn't realized until then that the press conference had been carried live on some local television stations. I'd known Frank for years, from the days when I was a young assistant press secretary in the governor's office and he, even then, was a crotchety senior reporter on the state political beat. We typically had fun repartee, teasing each other about politics and media coverage from the vantage points of our disparate ages.

"You okay?" he asked, his voice serious.

"I am horrified," I answered quietly.

10:00 p.m.—Massport Fire Rescue headquarters

I spent the rest of the evening with Tom Kinton and Joe Lawless in the Emergency Operations Center, overseeing incoming reports and operational updates.

"Med flights are being allowed now."

"The American Airlines Care Team has touched down and is headed to the Hilton."

"There are twenty families there. We're going to keep it open overnight."

"One hundred passengers are sleeping in the Exchange Center."

"Did you hear about the flags?"

"No, what flags?"

American and United employees, without direction or permission, had gone out on the tarmac at some point during the day to the jet bridges connected to gates C19 and B32, the departure gates of the two flights. On the top of each one, they mounted an American flag, the first Logan memorial to the passengers and crew.

Approximately 1:30 a.m.—Marblehead

James drove me back to Marblehead, neither of us saying anything on the short, solemn ride. Candles were still burning along the side of the road, illuminating homemade signs, remnants of earlier spontaneous vigils. As we drove through Swampscott, near the spot where we first heard the radio reports that morning, there was still one man, standing alone, waving an American flag.

James dropped me off in my driveway. "Good night," I said. "Thank you."

"I'll pick you up in the morning," he said. "Six o'clock?"

"Right," I answered. I'd scheduled a staff meeting for 6:30 a.m., five hours later.

David opened the front door and immediately took me in his arms. I tried to accept his embrace for a few seconds but I needed to see Jack. I pulled away and ran up the stairs. David joined me by Jack's crib, and I leaned back into his chest. He wrapped his arms around me from behind. For several moments we just stood there watching Jack sleep. He was so peaceful. His little breaths going in and out. Special Doggie in his arms as always. Just as it was when I woke him that morning.

Just that morning.

Suddenly, there was a roar overhead. David and I literally jumped. My heart pounded as I quickly followed him downstairs to the front door. We stepped outside and peered into the darkness in the direction of Boston. The city was far beyond our line of sight, but we both wondered, *Is this another attack?*

"It's a military plane," I suddenly realized. "It must be patrolling Boston's airspace."

I read many years later in President George W. Bush's book *Decision Points* that the White House had experienced a similar scare that night, pulling the president and Mrs. Bush from their bed as an unknown aircraft approached. It was a reminder that, at times, my 9/11 experience was similar to that of many others, including the president himself, but I had no way of knowing that at the time. Nor did I know that within a few short days my 9/11 experience would take a painfully isolating turn.

As the sound of the plane's engine died away, David and I stood in the darkness. "Let's go upstairs," David whispered.

For the rest of what remained of the night, we lay in bed, holding hands, waiting for dawn.

CHAPTER FOUR

SHUT DOWN

September 12, 2001, 6:00 a.m.—En route to Logan

I couldn't let myself feel anything. I had to be intensely focused on the job in front of me. When the horror of the attacks, the fear of what was still unknown, coursed through me, I pushed those feelings away, to be dealt with at some later time. At first I did this consciously, then increasingly, automatically.

I could not let myself feel anything else.

Focus. The airport. I needed to make it safe.

Was it over?

Were there more?

Stop.

The twisted metal. Smoking pile.

Stop.

The plane striking the second tower. The ball of fire.

Stop.

How many were dead? Six thousand? Seven thousand?

Stop.

My hand went to my stomach.

The baby. Was it okay?

Stop.

The airport was shut down. I would keep it closed. I would make it safe. I had to make it safe.

But it was too la—

Stop.

September 12, 2001, 6:30 a.m.—Logan Airport, Emergency Operations Center

The airport's senior staff and I gathered around the conference table. "The FAA has put out several new security directives. They came in all night," John Duval said. He and Joe Lawless noted that airports and airlines had to comply with each one before reopening.

"Let's go through them," I answered. My pen was poised over the yellow legal-sized notepad on the table in front of me.

"Curbside check-in must be discontinued."

"Only plastic knives in the food service areas beyond the security checkpoints."

"Cars can't be parked within three hundred feet of the terminals."

I put my pen down.

"Access beyond the checkpoints is limited to passengers with tickets."

"All the terminals have to be swept with K-9 teams."

I could feel my cheeks burning with frustration.

"Suspicious items or activities have to be reported immediately."

"No cargo or mail is allowed on commercial flights."

John and Joe stopped their recitation.

"And?" I said. "Is that it?"

"So far," John answered evenly. "More are coming in. Some are for the airlines. Some for us. We have a checklist that we're going through. The expectation is airports will reopen tomorrow."

"We're preparing to reopen," he said, "like we would after a major winter storm."

I felt my cheeks burn redder.

I understood what was driving him and the aviation team. It was a point of pride in "snowbelt" airports to reopen quickly if storms forced runway closures. Every fall we even held a "snow parade" of gleaming, peak-condition snow equipment—I'd once driven a plow at the head of it—to demonstrate to our airline tenants our readiness for winter.

But this is no snowstorm, I thought. *It's a terrorist attack.*

It might be acceptable to every other airport to reopen after banning curbside check-in and removing metal knives in concession areas. It was not acceptable for us. I tried, unsuccessfully, to push away the intrusive image.

The second plane strikes the tower.

The explosion.

The ball of fire.

The black smoke.

Stop.

I took Tom Kinton aside in the hallway outside the conference room. "Tom, this isn't a fucking snowstorm," I said, the still-simmering frustration detectable in my voice. "That's not what this is about."

Tom looked me in the eye for a long second and then nodded in agreement. "You're right," he said.

We reconvened around the conference table. "Reopening quickly is not the priority," I said. "Reopening safely is."

Joe and John immediately suggested developing our own checklist of security measures beyond what the FAA had required.

"We should station uniformed state troopers at every security checkpoint," Joe said.

"What else?" I picked my pen back up and started writing.

"Random checks of passenger identification beyond the checkpoints."

Everyone around the table started contributing ideas.

"Security sweeps of all ramp areas, crawl spaces, construction sites, air vents on the roofs of the terminals."

"Inspection of vehicles."

"Increased patrols of perimeter roadways."

The list grew. I excused myself and stepped out of the room to make a private call to Acting Governor Jane Swift. I wanted to fill her in on our strategy. I wanted to make sure she agreed keeping Logan closed was the right thing to do.

Jane was elected lieutenant governor on a ticket with Governor Paul Cellucci in 1998. She had made national news because she was pregnant during the campaign. We were the same age, and though not necessarily close, we at least became friendly colleagues. She had lent me maternity clothes when I was pregnant with Jack. I had a picture of her holding him in the hospital. Then, shortly before I took the job at Massport, an agency where she briefly worked herself between elected roles, she took me aside. She suggested I reregister to vote under my maiden name—Buckingham—which I used professionally, instead of being registered under my married name. "You could run for office someday," she said. "You're in a different category now."

When Cellucci was named US ambassador to Canada in 2001 and resigned, Jane became the state's first female governor.

My call was put right through to her office. "Jane, most airports will reopen tomorrow, but I don't think we should," I said. I shared our plan to go beyond federal security requirements. I told her Joe's suggestion to position uniformed state troopers at the security checkpoints.

"I'll tell the media you directed us to do it," I offered.

Swift agreed while imposing this caveat: "I don't think I should be involved in the actual decision to reopen the airport."

I instantly understood her unstated message. Insulating political leaders from the fallout of damaging events was Politics 101. Yet this wasn't politics as usual. Or, for her, was it? I was uneasy as I replaced the receiver.

A day after our call, she told the media, "When a tragedy of this enormity happens, it is obvious to all of us—two terrorists got on a plane at Logan—there was a problem. Once we have the facts at our disposal, there's no doubt in my mind that changes will be warranted."

Sources at the State House told reporters these "changes" might include my firing.

September 13, 2001—Emergency Operations Center

When I read the comment about my potential firing, I swallowed my surprise and resolved to dismiss it out of hand if anyone on the staff brought it up. There was too much to do, and I wasn't going to let the political swirl take any of our energy or attention.

Commercial airports were allowed to reopen at eleven o'clock. Logan remained closed. I entered a large meeting room in the Emergency Operations Center. The top federal, state, and local public-safety experts in the region filled every seat. We'd invited them here to review and, we hoped, add to the extra security measures we were implementing.

Joe went through the more than thirty items on our Logan-specific checklist.

"We've asked the FBI to conduct terrorist background checks on all contractors working at the airport."

"Ongoing security sweeps of all ramp areas."

"Random inspections of all vehicles."

As Joe talked, I looked around the room. Oddly, to a person, the attendees looked uncomfortable. Like they'd rather be anywhere but here.

As the meeting ended, I went through the room and tried to thank everyone personally for participating. One State Police detective took me aside.

"I want you to see this," Detective Marty Robichaud said. He was holding a ballpoint pen. When he took the cap off, I took an involuntary step backward. Where the nib of the pen should have been was a tiny, sharp blade. The pen had been converted into a weapon.

"How are you going to stop this from getting through security?" he asked.

I thought about that moment often. In retrospect, maybe that's why all those experts looked so uncomfortable. We were asking them to help us develop a foolproof plan to reopen Logan safely. Perhaps they understood, better than most, that there was no foolproof plan. Not against suicidal terrorists.

September 13, 2001—Emergency Operations Center

"Thanks for joining, everyone," I said into the speakerphone. On the conference call were the members of the Massachusetts congressional delegation and FAA administrator Jane Garvey.

I outlined the additional security steps we were taking before reopening and invited the legislators to ask questions.

"What are the hiring standards for security checkpoint employees?" one said.

"Was this an inside job?" asked another.

"What triggers additional screening of passengers?"

"How soon after takeoff did the planes go off course?"

The questions continued. After Garvey and I answered all we could, I sensed the leaders seemed comfortable with our approach to reopening. I ended the call, promising to continue providing them and their staff as much information as we could.

"I'm satisfied that in the circumstances we're in, the measures are good and that they are erring on the side of caution," senior congressman Michael Capuano told the media afterward.

But one of his colleagues admitted anonymously, "We are embarrassed the planes came from Logan."

September 14, 2001—Marblehead

"Happy Birthday," David whispered when he woke me before dawn with a kiss. His birthday wish jarred me. I'd forgotten that I was turning thirty-six.

"*Shh*, let's talk about it next year," I answered, putting my finger to his lips. Celebrating anything seemed obscene.

As I got ready to go back to work, I glanced at the headline in the *Boston Globe*. "Political Ties Strong at Airport."

The story was about my background as an adviser to Massachusetts's governors. It also described Joe Lawless's experience as the head of Governor Weld's security detail as akin to being the governor's driver. I read that Jane was asked whether political appointees at Massport would be reconsidered.

"In the days and months ahead as the investigation gets us more information, there will be no question that isn't explored as to how we can avoid these tragedies in the future," the acting governor said.

After reading the paper and before leaving for the airport, I sat on the family room floor and played with Jack. We lined up his Batman characters, "bad guys" on one side and "good guys" on the other. "Bam!" "Bang!" Jack hit his figures into mine. One by one my "bad guys" fell to the ground.

"Batman win!" Jack said with glee.

It was time to go to work. After getting changed, I came back into the family room, with my briefcase in one hand. Jack got visibly upset.

"Don't go, Mama. No go to airport," he said. "You no save people anymore."

His words brought me up short. Someone, probably David, must have explained my recent absence by saying I was at the airport "saving people."

"No, Jack," I said softly, stroking his blond hair. "I'm not saving people. It's too late for that."

Four years would pass before Jack would ask me what happened on 9/11 and why I left my job at Logan. "Some bad guys took some planes," I began, trying to figure out, even as I spoke, how to explain to him how these "bad guys" had any connection to me, to us.

US senators Edward Kennedy and John Kerry asked to receive a personal briefing at the Emergency Operations Center later that day. I had invited Acting Governor Swift, too, but she had declined. I was grateful the two senators were willing to come.

Tom Kinton, Joe Lawless, John Duval, and I sat across from the state's two senators in a conference room.

"Just tell us what you need," Kennedy said without hesitation.

We, again, detailed the added security measures. "We may need additional federal funding," I said. We also discussed our support for turning the checkpoints over to federal security agents, a controversial initiative Kerry, in particular, was pursuing.

They'd been at the State House before coming to Logan. "Take a look at what I said to the media," Kennedy said. "It's just not productive to try to assign blame."

"I appreciate that, Senator," I answered. I suggested the two go downstairs to the auditorium to address the first responders still working there.

As we started to leave the room, Kerry paused in the doorway. Despite the fact that I ran former governor Bill Weld's tough campaign against him in 1996, there was nothing but kindness in his eyes. He squeezed my shoulder. "I know it's hard," he said gently, "but at some point you have to make the call on reopening the airport."

He was right. It was my call to make and it was time to make it.

Through the rest of the afternoon and evening, the Massport team and I scrubbed the security checklist to ensure we and the airlines had complied with every item. One airline had not yet provided us certification it was in compliance with the new FAA directives, arguing it didn't have to under federal law.

"Fine," Tom Kinton said bluntly. "Tell them we'll reopen but they're not operating." Soon after, we got its certification.

Joe had one final idea to add to our expanded security list. "I want to deploy State Police troopers armed with submachine guns in the public areas of the terminals," he said. "But, it will be controversial."

Joe didn't have to remind me that we used to get regular complaints from state tourism officials about the traditional uniform of the Logan police. "It's too militaristic," they'd say. "It's off-putting to foreign tourists."

Referring to the submachine guns, Lawless noted, "It's never been done in an American airport."

"Do it," I told him.

I placed two more calls before giving the final okay to reopen the next day at 5:00 a.m. My question was the same to both the FAA's Jane Garvey and Charles Prouty, the FBI's special agent in charge of the Boston office. "Do you know of any specific threat to Logan or any reason at all that should keep us from reopening tomorrow?"

Each answered, "No, there's nothing."

The Logan team completed the security checklist in the wee hours of the morning. The terminals were evacuated and searched one last time. Tom held a final briefing with the aviation staff at the Emergency Operations Center. "In the past," he said, "when we got the airport reopened we would feel relieved."

"Now," Tom said before he paused and looked every person in the eye and perhaps in his own mind's eye at this:

The second plane.
The explosion.
The ball of fire.
The black smoke.

"Now, it should just make us feel sick."

September 15, 2001, 6:50 a.m.—Logan Airport

United Airlines Flight 168 was the first plane to land. As the pilot taxied from the runway to Terminal C, he saw the familiar ramp workers. They waved him into the aircraft's assigned gate. But there, on the tarmac, just beyond the jet bridge were more than a dozen United Airlines and American Airlines employees. They stood in a horseshoe shape, as if to give the giant aircraft and its passengers and crew a simultaneous embrace. Many were crying. All were waving tiny American flags.

"Welcome home," they mouthed. "Welcome home."

As plane after plane touched down through the morning, passengers on board burst into spontaneous applause. Some joined together singing the national anthem. One pilot opened his cockpit window and, with a grin as wide as a Boeing 757, set an American flag flapping in the breeze.

In all there were more than three hundred arrivals and departures that day, some one thousand less than normal. That evening, I briefed the press on the opening day's operations. "Given the circumstances and significant changes we've made to Logan operations, I think the first day went very smoothly," I said.

In a nearby terminal, a state trooper patrolled. He was dressed all in black. His expression inscrutable, his eyes intense. In his hands was a submachine gun.

***

Four days after 9/11, I had reopened Logan.

For many, many more years, I stayed shut down.

To get through those first days, I had closed myself off emotion-ally. Probably as soon as I got the call reporting "two planes are off the radar." At first, it was intentional, necessary. Intellectually, I had to remain intensely focused. I couldn't let in the horror of what had happened to the people on the planes and the people in the towers. And then being shut down became something less deliberate and more reflexive.

The ability to dissociate—to erect a wall between your heart and your head—I've since learned is common. Common, that is, among people exposed to intense stress and trauma, be they soldiers in a war, victims of a violent crime, or, as it turned out, me.

It is also common to stay shut down for a very long time, if not forever.

CHAPTER FIVE

BLAMED

The search for a scapegoat is the easiest of all hunting expeditions.

— Dwight D. Eisenhower

Massport Chief Pledges Accountability

"If there are specific flaws that are unique to Logan, people here, including myself, will accept responsibility and whatever consequences there are," Buckingham said. She said she has not focused on whether her "personal future" is at stake. . . . Asked whether she believes Massport is a victim of a search for scapegoats, she said, "No. It is simply that everyone is trying to deal with and understand a tragedy of extraordinary proportions."

— *Boston Globe,* September 16, 2001

September 16, 2001, mid-morning—Logan Airport, Delta Airlines hangar

The song "God Bless the USA" by Lee Greenwood echoed through the vast concrete expanse of the aircraft hangar.

Tom, Joe, and I stood in the back of the cavernous space. It was large enough to shelter a Boeing 767. Now it was filled to overflowing with airport and airline workers. Massachusetts State Police trooper Dan Clark, in full dress uniform, stood alone at the microphone, summoning the depth of the feeling in the space with his soaring voice.

Many of the gathered employees clutched one another's arms, as if standing erect alone wasn't possible. Others tightly held small American flags, as if the red, white, and blue cloth, too, was transmitting some kind of temporary strength. I fingered the tiny red, white, and blue ribbon pin on my lapel. "I made it in honor of the New York firefighters," I was told by the Massport employee who handed it to me in the Emergency Operations Center a day or so earlier.

My tone in that morning's *Boston Globe* story had "pleased" the governor, my deputy Russ told me before we headed to the service in the hangar. I understood immediately why. The public's anger and fear in the aftermath of the attacks, combined with three days of mounting criticism of my qualifications to run Logan and its past security record, amounted to a demand I step up and accept responsibility. I'd meant what I'd said. I would take responsibility if Logan was found to be at fault. I would accept the consequences.

The second plane.

The black smoke.

Bodies falling.

How many dead?

Six thousand? Seven thousand?

Joe put his arm around me. My shoulders began to shake with the effort of trying not to weep.

Trooper Clark's voice built to a crescendo.

Joe squeezed harder. I saw Tom wiping away tears under his dark sunglasses. I closed my eyes tightly.

Stop.

I couldn't.

Tom stepped to my other side and took my arm.

I couldn't stop.

My entire body was wracked with sobs.

Oh my God, what possible consequences could be harsh enough if I was responsible for this?

**Management at Reopened Logan Airport
Under Scrutiny**
—*Washington Post*, September 16, 2001

Massport Records Detail Security Breaches
—*Boston Globe*, September 16, 2001

September 16, 2001, late afternoon—Emergency Operations Center

US Transportation Secretary Norm Mineta's press conference was being carried live on TV. I watched as he announced the formation of two rapid-response task forces to make security recommendations, one on airports and one on aircraft. My neck stiffened as he read the roster of appointees. All were veteran Washington or industry figures long involved in aviation debates. "What about counterterrorism experts?" I asked out loud, my voice rising. "Jesus, these are the same people he would have appointed if September 11th hadn't happened!"

Jose Juves, Massport's media director, looked around the room at the rest of the gathered senior staff. "We're on our own, guys," he said.

He voiced what I was thinking. We weren't going to get the guidance we needed from Washington on further security improvements.

"I want to call Crandall and Barclay," I turned to Tom and Ed.

Bob Crandall, the former chief executive of American Airlines, was one of the most respected aviation leaders in the country. He was known as a maverick, willing to buck conventional wisdom. I'd seen him on TV over the past few days supporting a growing call in Congress to turn the airport checkpoints over to a new federal security force. Chip Barclay, the head of an influential airport trade association, was serving on one of Mineta's task forces. Ed got me their numbers.

I called Crandall first from the Logan fire chief's private office. After I expressed my frustration to him about the Mineta announcement, he gave me this advice: "Keep pressing them in the media. That's what I am doing every chance I get."

I knew he was right. The intense media scrutiny of me and Logan had one upside. I might be able to influence the debate over federalization of security.

The following days were sixteen-hour tsunamis of decision-making and crisis management. Despite the new security procedures, media reports around the country indicated passengers continued to successfully, if accidentally, bring pocketknives and other banned materials through checkpoints at several airports. Some checkpoint doors were left unlocked or unguarded. Terminals were repeatedly emptied of passengers and searched with K-9 teams. At Logan, a false report that a terrorist had taken a tour of the control tower days before 9/11 got wide coverage in the press. Other media reports falsely claimed that several Logan ramp passes were found in the terrorists' rental car. The passes would have allowed full access to the airfield.

Those false reports escalated the media frenzy. Talk radio. The top of the six o'clock newscast. Influential columnists. All raising questions that had no good answer if what you wanted was an easy one. I stopped for coffee at a Revere Dunkin' Donuts early one morning on the way into the airport. A man in line whispered to his friend, "That's her."

In my daily staff meetings, I tried to be matter-of-fact about the media coverage. "We have a lot of work to do," I said. "Dealing with the press goes with the territory. As the facts become known, the focus on Massport will decrease." I hoped that because I was unfazed by the criticism, staff morale would stay high. I was also largely dismissive because I still found it hard to believe anyone could seriously blame one airport operator for the attacks. "If they want to fire me because terrorists attacked America, let them," I said on a brief call with my sister.

I told Jose to answer all inquiries about my future at Logan by saying, "She and everyone here are staying focused on doing their jobs."

***

Massport Needs Leadership, Not Patronage

Confiscating bagel knives or prohibiting curbside
parking is not enhanced security. It's a joke. Acting Governor Swift should declare the death of a
culture of patronage at Massport and the dawn of
a new culture of professionalism.
—*Boston Globe*, September 18, 2001

*September 18, 2001—St. Rose of Lima Church, Chelsea,
Massachusetts*

I stood in a line of mourners stretching three blocks long. As I waited
to pay my respects to the family of Marianne MacFarlane, who had
died on United 175, I became conscious of the stares of others nearby.
What if I'm not welcome here? I suddenly realized.

Maybe Anne, Marianne's mom and a Logan employee, would be
offended, given the questions that had been raised in the media. I looked
around. There were a few whispers. Discreet glances in my direction.
There was no way to make a quiet escape. My heart started beating
faster. I was trying to decide whether to walk away when Kathi-Anne
Reinstein, the state legislator from the area, approached and asked if I
wanted to go inside with her. I walked up the stone stairs with a group
of other officials. My heart pounded in my chest as I followed Reinstein
into the rear of the church where the family was gathered.

The vestibule was dark and cool. Familiar. The smell of incense in
the air evoked an instant sense of connection. I had attended paro-
chial school from first through eighth grade. The nuns made us attend
funerals regularly, sometimes weekly, a group of uniform-wearing children filing by the caskets of total strangers during Holy Communion.
A gesture to comfort the grieving.

What if my being here brings them more pain, not comfort? I worried. It was too late to turn back. I tried to breathe slowly. To slow my
heart rate. There was no casket in the church. No trace of Marianne
had been found. I shook hands and murmured condolences. Anne was
the last person in the line. Redheaded and shorter than the people

standing next to her—her sons I later found out—she exuded a presence that made her seem taller. I approached slowly. As I reached to
take her hand, I was momentarily startled by the pin sparkling on her
jacket. It was in the shape of an airplane.

"I'm sorry for your loss," I said softly, not meeting her eyes. Anne
gripped both of my hands in hers. The strength of her grasp caused me
to look straight at her.

"Don't let them tear our airport apart," she said. "Promise me."

I didn't know how to answer this surprising request. Anne held my
hands tighter. Her gaze was steady. I finally said, "I won't. I promise I
won't." I had no idea how or if I could fulfill my pledge.

At the end of the service, Anne led the congregation down the
stairs of the church singing "God Bless America."

Anne's strength would save me many times in the years ahead, like
a life ring thrown to someone drowning. Then one day, after we'd been
getting together for lunch or coffee a few times a year, Anne called me.
Her request was as simple and surprising as the one made at Marianne's
service. "Can I lean on you for a while?" she asked. For a few seconds
I didn't know what to say. Can the drowning in turn save the rescuer?

> It's been over a week now, and Ginny Bucking-
> ham still isn't a stay-at-home mom. Thousands
> of Americans have been murdered . . . in jetliners
> hijacked out of this hackerama of an airport.
> —*Boston Herald*, September 19, 2001

September 19, 2001—Emergency Operations Center

> The future of Massport director Virginia Bucking-
> ham is also open to question.
> —*Boston Globe*, September 19, 2001

Pressure is building for a high level shake-up at
Massport—from director Virginia Buckingham on
down.

—*Boston Herald*, September 19, 2001

"What's that?" I asked Tom and John, who were surrounded by a few
other Logan operational staff. They were peering at a list of names. As
I got closer, I could see it was a passenger manifest for a flight.

"They're members of the Bin Laden family," Tom answered, his
tone serious. "Some of them live in the Boston area and a plane is landing here to pick them up."

I took the list from John and read it, incredulous at the almost
twenty names, several with the surname Bin Laden.

The entries were complete with addresses, passport numbers, even
telephone numbers.

Tom said he was told the Bin Laden family members feared for
their safety. "They're being airlifted from all over the country on a
Saudi-chartered jet."

"Have they been questioned?" I asked. He didn't know.

It was not yet well known, and certainly not known by us, that
there had been a public break between the family and the terrorist
leader. All we knew was that there was still a ban on international
flights from certain countries and we didn't know whether this flight
violated it and whether intelligence agencies and the FBI had cleared
the Bin Ladens' mass departure. I asked Tom to call Washington, DC,
authorities, including the State Department. "Maybe there's a way to
stop them," I said. "How can they let them go barely a week after the
attacks? There must be some mistake."

After several hours, Tom reported back that for each call he made,
he got the same answer. "Let them leave."

Craig Unger, a former editor of *Boston* magazine, wrote a book in
2004 that discussed the Bin Laden family airlift. He tried to interview
me but I declined. I didn't feel I could provide additional information.
Instead, he quoted from an article I'd later written about the frustration I'd felt that day. It would be years, after reading his book and other
accounts, before I understood that the decision to let the Bin Ladens
leave was made at the highest levels of the federal government. I was in

no position to second-guess it. It's just one illustration of a dichotomy that took me years to accept. While the local media and political leaders placed me at the center of 9/11, the reality was this: I was nowhere near it.

Swift Special Panel to Review Massport

Administration sources said the commission's findings . . . will greatly influence whether Massport executive director Virginia Buckingham and her director of security, Joseph Lawless, remain in their jobs.

—*Boston Globe*, September 20, 2001

To the Editor:

When I was governor, Logan was the responsibility of two executive directors of Massport who were competent, able, experienced public managers.
. . . The same cannot be said for their successors.
—Michael S. Dukakis, Boston
—*Boston Globe*, September 20, 2001

Change Ahead for Troubled Boston Airport Agency

—*New York Times*, September 21, 2001

As the critical media coverage began extending beyond Boston, from my sister-in-law Leah's bedroom I watched the news coverage of Jane's announcement that she was appointing a commission to review Massport. It was Rosh Hashanah and David and Jack were downstairs with his family celebrating the Jewish New Year.

"Airport operations will never be the same anywhere in America, and certainly we have a moral responsibility at Logan to take that very seriously," Swift said.

Tears flowed down my face. The direction she was heading was obvious. The acting governor was following a familiar political playbook. It was a playbook I had recommended to governors before her when a scandal in state government raged in the press.

In reports about the formation of the commission, an administration source made her intent clear: Jane had no "desire to scapegoat. . . . She cares that Ginny go out with dignity, if she has to go," the source said.

For the first time since the attacks, my belief that I couldn't rationally be blamed for the hijackings slipped, my assertion in the conversation with my sister, "if they want to fire me, let them," looking more like the hubris it was. Yet, this wasn't a scandal in state government. This was an attack on America.

Wasn't it?

September 20, 2001—Marblehead

I shifted under the sheets. Uncomfortable. Sweating.

I was in a courtroom surrounded by angry people. Every seat was filled. The aisles were packed with more people standing.

I groaned and turned again, tightly gripping the blanket covering me and David.

Why were they all glaring at me? Leaning forward. Shaking their fists. Menacing. I wanted to shout, "I didn't do it." Instead, my face reddened with shame. A tiny voice inside whispered, "But what if I did?" I said nothing. My eyes were cast downward. Tears dripped down my face.

I woke up with a start. I looked over at David. He was soundly sleeping. I didn't wake him.

My first recounting of this dream was in a *Boston Globe* Sunday magazine essay I wrote in 2002. I knew Massport was preparing for eventual litigation against the airport so I'd let the lawyers read a draft before I submitted it. I didn't want to catch them off guard. They were adamant that I take out the dream sequence with its obvious overtones of my deepening sense of responsibility. So I removed it in the final submission. The magazine's editor emailed me and asked, "What happened to the dream? I loved it!" He asked if I would reconsider its use and I eventually agreed.

"It's just a dream, Joe," I said to my lawyer when I told him the dream was back in the piece.

It was just a dream.

***

Will Heads Roll at Massport?

Are the calls for a housecleaning at Massport legitimate, or are they fueled by politics and the need to offer up a scapegoat to an anxious public?
—*MetroWest Daily News*, September 20, 2001

Too Early to Whack Massport Chief

Stop the scapegoating. . . . Will you feel a whit safer if Ginny Buckingham is fired or forced to resign tomorrow?
—*Boston Herald*, September 20, 2001

September 21, 2001—Governor's office, State House, Boston

"Ginny, can you wait a minute? I'd like to talk to you privately." Jane stood up from the head of the conference table in her office. As the others at the table—mostly cabinet and subcabinet officials from her administration with responsibility for public-safety issues—filed out of the ornate room, I looked around. The heavy, worn blue drapes, the chipped yet still regal white-painted woodwork, the massive fireplace behind the governor's desk, the large varnished wood table where we'd been sitting. Every inch of this office was deeply familiar, like I'd stepped back into my favorite room in a house I'd lived in years before.

I thought back to the first time I entered the Corner Office at the State House when I was a nineteen-year-old intern helping Governor Michael Dukakis's press secretary with a routine photo opportunity. The governor was harsh and impatient when it was only us in the room, and blandly pleasant as citizens filed in to receive a proclamation and pose for a photo. I was confused by the contrast, my first experience of commonplace political posturing. As Jane Swift sorted some papers at her desk, I jumped ahead a few years in my mind's eye and saw myself in the same room, perched on the side of a nearby leather chair as Governor Weld and his senior advisers debated firing a young commissioner who had made an innocent error in judgment, my heart sinking as the decision was made to let him go, my first lesson on the harshness of the field I had chosen. And there I was at twenty-eight, sitting in the middle seat at the same table—the governor's chief spokesperson, forcefully arguing, whether the issue was taxes, crime, or welfare reform, for a strong, clear message to support the governor's position. Now as Swift came back to the head of the conference table, I remained standing behind the chief of staff's chair that had become mine at thirty-two.

"I know Massport had nothing to do with the hijackings," she said, shifting uncomfortably on her feet when she saw I had no plans to sit down. "There's nothing you could have done to stop them."

When I didn't respond, Swift continued. "I can't promise you how this is going to turn out, but the only reason I can sleep at night is I know you understand how the media and politics work."

In a room where I had witnessed and participated in all manner of coarse political discussions, I was still taken aback by the raw cynicism of her comments. All I could bring myself to say was the same mantra Jose and I had used with the media for the past two weeks. "I'm staying focused on doing my job," I told her. I walked out of the office I had essentially grown up in without looking back, feeling less certain than I had ever been of what was ahead.

Hard Times Call for Gov, Mayor to Step Forward

The question is how to ease Buckingham out without subjecting her to national embarrassment.

—*Boston Herald*, September 24, 2001

Misguided Blame

The planes-turned-missiles in the attack on America were hijacked from airports in three cities but only in this one has the attack been followed by continuous calls to find someone to blame.
                    —*Boston Globe*, September 24, 2001

Questions About Massport Won't Stop
                    —*Boston Globe*, September 25, 2001

Breakdown: Buck Knife and Bullets Slip by Logan Checkpoints
                    —*Boston Herald*, September 26, 2001

September 26, 2001—Logan Office Center, Boston

The press conference was jam-packed. On easels behind me were poster boards containing the list of recommendations we were making to US Transportation Secretary Mineta on improving security nationwide. In my opening statement, I described some of the items contained in a letter to Chip Barclay, the member of the task force I'd called the day of Mineta's announcement.

When I finished making an opening statement, a reporter called out, "Are you going to resign?"

"I'm willing to resign or do whatever the governor wants me to do if a specific flaw at Massport related to the hijackings is found," I answered.

"Is the airport safe?" another reporter asked.

"Certainly the airport is safer than it's ever been," I answered, "but it doesn't mean it is safe enough." I pointed out the story in that morning's *Herald* about the knife and bullets getting through Logan's checkpoints as further evidence in support of federalization. "These kinds of items are going to continue to get through until we have a law-enforcement professional with the right training at all the checkpoints."

A story the next day in the *Herald* termed it an "extraordinary admission" that I would say Logan was still vulnerable. Others had a similar tone.

Massport Says It Can't Offer Fix; Buckingham Seeks Federal Monitoring of Checkpoints
    —*Boston Globe*, September 27, 2001

Passing the Buck Won't Fly at Logan
    —*Boston Herald*, September 27, 2001

September 27, 2001, 6:30 a.m.—Logan Office Center

The *Today* crew had set up in the second-floor lobby before dawn. I moved around in the chair, trying to get comfortable. I was conscious of keeping my back straight, the bottom of my blazer tucked under me, following the advice I used to pass on to governors over the years so they wouldn't look rumpled on TV.

Jose had advised me to pass up the interview request. He was worried the issue of my personal future would come up on national television.

"I can't miss this chance to talk about the need for federalization," I told him. I was still taking Bob Crandall's advice—"press them in the media"—every chance I had.

"Matt Lauer will interview a counterterrorism expert first," the producer explained now through my earpiece. "Can you count to ten for the audio check?"

"Lauer will toss it back to Katie Couric," he added, "in the studio in New York."

An American flag, flapping in the breeze outside, was just visible over my left shoulder. I was wearing the red, white, and blue ribbon pin. I could hear Couric in my earpiece but I couldn't see her. As the red light went on, I looked straight into the camera.

Couric got right to the point. "FAA data analyzed by the *Globe* shows not only did Logan Airport rank near the bottom when it comes to security violations, but it also had the highest number of serious violations, those where federal agents were able to smuggle hidden weapons through security checkpoints. What is your reaction to these findings?"

Most of the violations reported in the recent *Globe* story were the responsibility of the airlines, which oversaw the checkpoints under the scrutiny of the FAA. But I didn't point that out to Couric. I wasn't going to be drawn into blaming the airlines. I blamed no one but the terrorists.

"We're not happy with the state of security at our airport or the nation's other airports. So far evidence has pointed to the fact that these hijackers used the current system of security. They didn't breach it. And if that's the case, it's a huge wake-up call to Logan Airport and every airport. We need a dramatic overhaul in airport security, particularly at those screening checkpoints."

Couric then asked whether President Bush's recent proposals on more background checks and training for security personnel go far enough.

"Well, I think his proposals go a long way to fortifying the aircraft themselves." I shifted in the seat, uncomfortable. I didn't like criticizing the president's proposals. But he was only supporting funding for the installation of hijack-proof cockpit doors in commercial aircraft, not turning the checkpoints over to a new federal security force. "They don't go far enough to fortify the airports," I said.

Couric's questions grew more intense. "Meanwhile, you claim it's not within your purview in terms of the airlines themselves hiring or contracting out people to do the security. Should you not have been more aware of all the violations and infractions that were occurring at Logan, in your position?"

"Well, we certainly were aware of it," I answered, "and, in fact we had just begun a program of testing those screening checkpoints ourselves. We had brought in a security consultant to do a top-to-bottom review of all the security problems. But this is going to require action by Congress."

Couric was wrapping up. "I understand within Boston there has been some pressure for you and your chief of airport security to resign. Is that something you're considering?"

I paused for a fraction of a second. "I've said if evidence points to some specific flaw in Logan security that led to these incidents, then I'm willing to step up and accept responsibility for that and whatever consequences that may bring," I answered.

"Thank you for joining us."

"Thank you." The red light went out.

It was 7:14 a.m.

***

Logan Brass Should Atone by Resigning
—*Boston Herald*, September 27, 2001

I walked down the hall to my office to finish reading the morning papers.

Later that morning, I hesitated outside a holding room in Terminal A. Inside, former president George H. W. Bush was waiting for a flight out of Logan, a planned public show of confidence in the nation's aviation system. I pushed open the door and he strode over, hand outstretched. "Thank you for coming here, Mr. President," I said. I shook his hand, holding on to it for a few seconds too long. A bit too tightly.

I explained that we'd first met when I worked for Governor Cellucci but that I worked here now. "Oh, oh, you run the place," he said. When I last saw him in 1998, he had come to visit his newly elected friend Cellucci, who had been one of his first supporters in 1979 when he challenged then governor Ronald Reagan for the Republican nomination. "Where's the chief?" he'd said then, as he strode into the Corner Office reception area, reaching out to shake my hand. Now at Logan, he gave me a warm smile but didn't say anything else. An aide pulled him away to get ready for an interview with Tom Brokaw that would be taped in the lounge behind us.

Brokaw probed former president Bush's deep knowledge of world affairs for context on the 9/11 attacks. As I watched, I felt silly and small when I considered my need for him to acknowledge what was happening in the Boston media. *Why would he think to say, "Hang in there" or "This is a bunch of baloney,"* I berated myself. *He has more important things to think about. But oh God,* I thought, tears biting the corners of my eyes as I watched the former president. *That is all I want. Please just say, "It wasn't your fault."*

Of course, he didn't. And the deeply rooted desire I had for someone in a position of authority like him—or his son—to exonerate me would persist for many years.

CHAPTER SIX

TIDE

August 1975—Dunes Park Beach, Weekapaug, Rhode Island

"Here comes one!" my youngest brother, RJ, shouted. He was seven, I was ten, and I was certain I was going to win this time. The wave came toward us. We bent our knees slightly, leaning forward to take the wave head-on. The made-up game we played—Hold-Your-Ground—required a delicate balance. We couldn't lean too much. We had to figure just how to position our shoulders. The goal was to be rocked back into position without falling forward, readying ourselves immediately for the next wave. Whoever withstood the push and pull of the tide, keeping their feet firmly planted on the ocean floor—whoever held their ground longest—won.

I looked over. We were both still standing in the same place. "Here comes one!" I shouted the warning this time.

There's no way I'll get knocked over, I thought, my feet buried deep in the sand. Without warning, a powerful wave lifted me up. Forced unwillingly into a somersault, I turned and twisted under the water. I opened my eyes. The salt water burned like acid. I couldn't breathe or find my footing. My head struck bottom and I scraped against some rocks. My father, standing on the shore's edge keeping watch, ran into the water. He reached down, firmly grasping my forearms in his large hands. He lifted me back up onto my feet.

At least that's how I remember the story. But I'm not sure it's true. Not the wave knocking me over part. I remember that vividly. But did my dad really reach in and rescue me? Like most young American girls, I grew up with fairy tales of knights rescuing their princesses. My white-knight stories were mostly of the black ink on white paper variety, with occasional glorious colored illustrations, in the years before Pixar ensured every little girl went to bed with visions of being rescued in her head. I'm not sure whether my dad was actually there that day, or if that's just how I prefer to remember it. That I was rescued. It would be years, fourteen exactly, before I finally understood the truth in something I was told soon after I left Logan: no one was going to rescue me from the pain of being blamed for 9/11. I had to be my own hero.

Patronage Still Rules the Roost at Logan

It has been two-and-a-half weeks since the greatest attack on the American mainland was launched from Logan Airport, and Virginia Buckingham is still running Logan. . . .

We may never know the extent that unqualified executives played in terrorists assuming that Logan was a cinch. . . . it cannot be an accident that terrorists thought they could board not one, but two airplanes at Logan.

—*Boston Globe*, September 28, 2001

September 28 to November 9, 2001

The media spotlight grew even more intense after my *Today* appearance. It became harder and harder to ignore, to believe the misplaced blame and fury would blow over as the facts became known.

But it was a lead editorial in the *Patriot Ledger*, the state's third-largest newspaper, that hit me as powerfully as that wave did when I was a child.

New Leadership for Logan

> Swift must act immediately to remove Virginia
> Buckingham. . . . The long chapter of political
> patronage at Logan must come to an end, now
> that we've seen the devastating consequences of
> putting unqualified political appointees in strate-
> gic positions involving public safety.
> —*Patriot Ledger*, September 29–30, 2001

"Now that we've seen the devastating consequences of unqualified appointees." My lack of aviation experience led to the attacks? Is that what she's saying? I asked myself. I knew the editorial page editor of the *Ledger* from my days in the State House. I always thought her coverage was smart and fair.

The second plane.
The explosion.
The ball of fire.
The black smoke.
Thousands dead.
"Devastating consequences."
She's saying it's my fault.
Oh my God.

I had to start my daily staff meeting and welcomed the return of emotional numbness. I walked into the small meeting room. I went through the agenda item by item.

"Security update?"

"Federalization push next steps?"

"Upcoming legislative committee briefing?"

"Presentation to Boston business leaders on Logan operations?"

"Anything else?" I asked after we discussed all the items. I went around the table so each colleague could raise any issues they had. It was a management tactic I learned from Governor Weld, who had done the same at his daily staff meeting.

As I walked back to my office, I noticed copies of the local weekly paper piled on a low-standing table near the door. The *East Boston Sun Transcript* closely covered goings-on at the airport. I picked one up out of curiosity. As I opened the paper to the editorial page, I was not conscious of breathing as I was picked up and tossed by another powerful wave.

Time to Decide

> Buckingham is now carrying the weight of the world on her shoulders. It is a heavy weight that will never go away.
>
> The enormity of what began in Boston is impossible for Buckingham to mitigate. She is being swept away, literally by events almost entirely out of her control. Yet she is struggling to keep her self-respect, struggling mainly, like the salmon trying to swim upstream, fighting against a tide of rushing river water. The salmon struggle and fight and give everything they have until they run out of energy and are swept away. . . . What began at Logan on Buckingham's watch is a disaster whose outcome will follow her the rest of her life. . . . Call it bad luck, bad timing, call it a mixture of chance and fate, call it what you will, Buckingham cannot come back from this.

I stood dead still in the office foyer. I didn't move. I couldn't move. I held the paper. I stared at the words.

They seemed to swirl around me. Encircling my throat. Choking me. *"Rest of her life . . . swept away . . . cannot come back from this."*

They were right.
"Rushing water . . ."
The ocean wave. It picked me up off my feet. I struggled to hold my ground. I couldn't.
"Swept away."
"Devastating consequences."
A glass bottle. Tossed in the pounding surf.
Broken.
Stop.
Hold on.
I couldn't.

Letter to the Editor:

Certain places where atrocious events were allowed to occur are forever branded with the dark
stain of shame. To this black roster we now add
Boston's Logan International Airport, where
terrorists waltzed aboard two airliners and killed
6,000 innocents in New York. . . . It's time for
Massport Executive Director Virginia Buckingham
and company to pack up their bags and go.
—*Boston Herald*, September 30, 2001

Voters Poll: Dump Massport Director

More than half the voters polled by the Herald
said Massachusetts Port Authority Chief Virginia
Buckingham should resign or be fired in the wake
of unprecedented airport security lapses.
—*Boston Herald*, October 2, 2001

Letter to the Editor:

Now we have a former gubernatorial aide running
Massport. After an extensive national search, this
is the best our governor can do? As a Republican,

my advice to Gov. Swift is to clean house immediately, before more people die.

—Boston Globe, September 30, 2001

October 2, 2001—Logan Office Center

"Peter, she shouldn't do this." My tone was heated. Jane Swift was giving a live televised address from her office that evening. Her aides had
leaked that Logan's security director, Joe Lawless, was being fired. This
was the second heated conversation I'd had with her chief of staff in
the past week. Several days earlier he had called me to say I could no
longer speak with Jane directly. "If you need to tell her anything, call
me," he'd said. I knew then that the protection of Jane's political future
was now paramount in her and her staff's view. I was a problem to be
managed, controlled, disposed of. Like Joe.

"Joe shouldn't be fired," I told him now. "This isn't right, Peter. Joe
didn't do anything wrong." After several minutes of debate, Forman
agreed to talk to Jane again. Less than an hour later, he called back to
report she had agreed instead to transfer Joe to Massport's maritime
division.

I watched Jane's live address on my office TV. "We've all been
searching our souls these past few weeks," she said. "That two of those
planes took off from Logan Airport is particularly painful for us, and
has raised serious questions about the airport's security procedures."

Fired Up: Swift Tightens Security at Logan

Apparently joking with aides who were gushing
over her performance, [Jane Swift] proclaimed on
the live microphone, "Yeah, they work for me . . .
and they know I'm in a firing mood."

—Boston Herald, October 3, 2001

Early October 2001—Logan Office Center

"Where do they do this best?" I asked at my daily staff meeting, referring to airport security.

"Israel," was the unanimous answer.

I learned Rafi Ron, the former security director at Israel's Ben Gurion Airport, was currently in the United States. As soon as we tracked him down, I invited him to come to Logan. At our initial meeting, we talked about the American system's focus on technology to protect aviation from terrorism.

"You will never be able to stop all weapons," he said, referring to the security of checkpoints. "You have to stop the people." Ron told me a true story about a pregnant Irish-born girlfriend of a Palestinian traveling through Heathrow to visit her boyfriend's parents in the West Bank. I was riveted as he described how careful questioning by the El Al airline employee revealed the presents she'd packed for the prospective grandparents of her unborn child were not wrapped by her, but by her boyfriend. A search of her luggage found explosives, not gifts, in the packaging.

Ron then described a training program he'd designed that would teach airport and airline employees to identify certain behaviors that should raise a red flag.

We hired him on the spot.

Some ten years after 9/11, the federal government formally adopted the behavioral awareness program we started at Logan as a pilot program. I was both proud and frustrated. It was the right thing to do and it shouldn't have taken a decade to do it.

October 2001—Marblehead

"Jack, honey, someone is at the door. I'll be right back," I said, trying to put Jack down on the floor with his toys.

"No, Mama, hold me." He had a slight fever and hadn't let me put him down all evening. I shifted him to my hip and opened the door.

The camera light went on. Jack, who was wearing his favorite plastic fireman's hat, stared into it.

"Can we talk to you for a minute about your future at Massport?" the TV reporter asked. I shook my head. "I don't have any comment."

"Who's that, Mama?" Jack asked. I gently shut the door. The camera was still rolling. "It's just some people from work, sweetie."

October 2001—South Londonderry, Vermont

I didn't want to go when friends offered us their home in Vermont for a night over the weekend. I didn't want to be that far away from the airport.

"What if something happens?" I said to David.

"C'mon, honey, there's a phone there. And we can get back here in a few hours if we need to," David urged.

Reluctantly, I agreed. As we passed over the border into Vermont on Interstate 91, I could actually feel my shoulders relax, like a burden was being lifted. I reached over and squeezed David's hand in gratitude.

The leaves in the backyard of our friends' house were brilliant orange, golden yellow, and rust red. I raked a huge pile for Jack to jump in. He giggled and attacked each pile with glee. "Again, Mama, again!" he yelled. I felt a rush of joy so intense, tears rolled down my cheeks. *How is it possible to still experience happiness?* I wondered. I got on my knees and hugged Jack tightly. Then I gathered the scattered leaves back into a pile.

A community of Benedictine monks lived in nearby Weston. My mother had taken me there when I was a little girl. I remembered buying a handmade Jacob's Ladder toy at a country store on the way. Its flat wood blocks were held together by ribbons and tumbled into a different order depending on how you held the highest block. Jacob's ladder was "how you climb to heaven," my mother said, an explanation I accepted without question, as I accepted all matters of faith.

The monks wrote their own music and welcomed visitors to join their services and song. "Can we go?" I asked David. I wanted to pray. I wanted to talk to God as I always had. Maybe there, in a place preserved so perfectly in my childhood memories, I'd be able to.

David parked near the unassuming stone and wood buildings. Jack toddled down the gravel path ahead toward the chapel. I heard music, the strumming of a guitar. I had mastered a few of the monks' songs on my own guitar in high school.

I didn't recognize the song the monks were playing as we approached the post-and-beam chapel beside a small stand of white birch trees. They were seated in a semicircle, dressed in simple tunics and slacks. I stood in the sunshine, among the pots of mums and bundles of hay decorating the entrance. I closed my eyes. I tried to pray. "Dear God," I began, wiping away the sudden tears. "Please . . ."

I stopped. *"Please" what? What is the point of a God who couldn't, or worse, wouldn't, stop 9/11?*

The monks continued to sing.

I turned away.

Tough Questions About Massport

What, exactly, is a hack? Does Virginia Buckingham, the executive director of the Massachusetts Port Authority, qualify as one? The answer is relevant but not conclusive to the debate that is raging in Massachusetts in the aftermath of the Sept. 11 hijackings out of Logan Airport. In its most simplistic form, the controversy is framed like this: Do hacks run the Massachusetts Port Authority? Are they somehow responsible for the terrible events that began at Logan and ended in those deadly explosions in New York City? Would their firing produce a better, safer airport?
                    —*Boston Globe*, October 18, 2001

October 19, 2001, 6:00 p.m.—Logan Office Center

Dems Rip Gov on Massport Patronage, Logan Woes
                    —*Boston Herald*, October 19, 2001

I sat at my desk going through phone messages I hadn't had a chance to return. The TV was turned on. I could hear the anchor of the local evening news but I wasn't watching it.

"Massport Director Virginia Buckingham"—the mention of my name caused me to look up—"is three months pregnant."

The "news" that I was pregnant—barely five weeks along when the planes struck the towers—broke in the *Herald* that morning. The reporter had called Jose the night before and asked for confirmation. I hadn't told anyone about the baby except family and close friends, but as I reached the end of the first trimester, I thought it was appropriate to let the governor and her staff know through a third party. The *Herald* story cited an unnamed State House source.

Gov: Pregnancy Won't Affect Buckingham Decision
—Boston Herald, October 20, 2001

Since the hijackings, I'd tried not to think about the baby during the day. But late at night, before I went to sleep, I'd read through the pregnancy handbook I kept by the side of my bed. The pages on miscarriages were dog-eared. I didn't know if stress could cause the baby harm. "Headache. Numbness. Baby movement." I jotted notes of symptoms to tell my doctor. I didn't remember from my pregnancy with Jack what was normal.

A week or so earlier, I'd lain on the examining table as my doctor inserted the long needle required for the amniocentesis test. I'd had one with Jack also. That first time, I was consumed with anxiety over the possibility of miscarrying him, a risk of the procedure. This time, as the long needle was withdrawn, I could see the same worry in David's eyes. I knew I could never admit to him the thought I tried to push from my mind: *If I lose the baby, maybe I deserve to.*

Pregnancy Is No Excuse for Ginny's Fiascos
—Boston Herald, October 21, 2001

October 23, 2001—State House, Boston, Joint Committee on Transportation hearing

I'd been called before a legislative committee to testify about Logan security. The small hearing room was packed. Legislators were arrayed behind a horseshoe-shaped wooden table. Newspaper photographers sat in front of me on the floor, aiming their cameras at my face. TV crews lined the side of the hearing room. Still more reporters piled tape recorders on the table.

"Those were our planes up there, and our people," I began, reading my prepared statement before taking questions. I was wearing on my lapel the American flag ribbon given to me by a Massport firefighter despite the fact that I had been ridiculed in a recent newspaper column for wearing it "like a shield."

The Democratic Senate chairman of the committee, Robert Havern, was the second questioner. I didn't know him personally, only in the context of his legislative role. "When was the last time you spoke to the governor?" he asked.

I tried to be vague. "I haven't spoken to her at length for a while," I answered.

"The marks on your back and on Joe Lawless's back are clothespin marks, because you've been hung out to dry," Havern said in disgust.

As the intense questioning continued from the rest of the panel, I unconsciously slipped one hand onto the side of my stomach. It was rare to feel a baby's movement so early. But the flutter, the twitch in my left side, was unmistakable.

The baby is moving! Oh my God, she's okay. I didn't know for sure that I was carrying a girl but I thought so. I hoped so. For the first time in many weeks, I no longer felt alone.

After the hearing ended, the media crowded around me in the hallway. Videographers jostled with one another to get the best angle. "Is it true the governor hasn't spoken to you in weeks?"

"Do you agree with the chairman's comment that she is hanging you out to dry?"

I was asked the same questions over and over again. I tried not to answer directly. I also didn't say what I was really thinking: the senator's comments had provided me an opening to resign before I was fired. I walked away from the gathered press feeling relief at the return of a small sense of control, like a car finally reaching dry pavement after trying to gain traction on a patch of black ice.

Month Long Silence Echoes Between Gov, Buckingham
—*Boston Herald*, October 24, 2001

October 25, 2001, 4:00 p.m.—Logan Office Center

The large meeting room on the first floor was packed with reporters and Massport colleagues. I walked straight into the crowd of news photographers and TV videographers who parted as I moved into the room toward the podium. *No one teaches you,* I thought, randomly, *that a crowd of photographers will move aside if you walk straight toward them,* despite all instincts to stop and wait for a path to clear.

Do not cry, Ginny, do not cry, I admonished myself silently.

I looked straight ahead into the bank of TV cameras and read from my prepared statement.

"Six weeks ago, nineteen hijackers changed our lives forever," I began.

"The fact that our airport was used in an unimaginable plot that killed thousands of innocent people is something I will carry in my mind and heart forever."

Head of Agency That Runs Logan Airport Resigns
—CNN, October 27, 2001

Buckingham Resigns at Massport
—*Boston Globe*, October 26, 2001

Swift under pressure as scapegoat resigns
—*Boston Herald*, October 26, 2001

November 7, 2001—Logan Office Center

I put the *Herald* down on my desk. "Jane Knew" was the blaring head-line splashed across the front page, over Jane's picture. I had negotiated a severance package with the Massport board after asking an interme-diary to get Jane's signoff on the general financial scope. When the deal became public, igniting another media controversy, Jane denied she knew about it in advance. She called on the Massport board to rescind part of it.

"Doesn't Ginny care about her reputation?" my intermediary was asked by one of Jane's aides, as the media controversy got hotter.

"Her reputation?" the intermediary asked, amazed at the question. "She's basically been called a murderer in the media for the last six weeks."

I winced when he repeated the story to me.

Murderer?

Is that how I will be thought of? Is that what I am?

I agreed to reduce the amount of the severance.

Murderer?

November 8, 2001—Logan Office Center

As I packed up the rest of my boxes, my assistant Julie told me Jim Coull, a longtime Massport board member, was on the phone.

"Why aren't you staying until the fifteenth," he asked, "as you'd planned?"

I held the phone loosely against my ear and considered my answer to why I was leaving a week earlier than I'd announced. I could still see the huge green dry dock out my window. Despite our efforts to relocate it, it sat there, immovable.

Some obstacles were simply too big to overcome.

"I just want to go home," I finally answered.

As I pulled out of the parking garage a lone TV camera and reporter were waiting for me. David Muir, who later would serve as ABC's national news anchor, called out to me. I backed the car up and rolled down the window. I answered his first question as Jose and I had planned. I was leaving to give Jane the flexibility she needed. "What's next for you?" Muir asked. The question surprised me. I didn't have an answer. "I don't know. I'm sure good things."

As I drove out of Logan I turned into the tunnel toward the city instead of my usual route north. Jack and David were waiting at his parents' apartment, where we planned to stay for a couple of days. Even though the State Police had assigned an unmarked cruiser to sit in front of my house, we felt it was safer for us, especially Jack, not to be at home given the continuing intense media coverage. I clutched the steering wheel with both hands to keep the car under control as I wept so hard my whole body shook.

The ball of fire.
The black smoke.
Bodies falling.
"What's next for you?"

CHAPTER SEVEN

HAUNTED

January 2002—Watertown, Connecticut

I could hear Jack's even breathing as he napped in the crib nearby. The sky-blue walls in my childhood room were pocked with tiny holes, remnants of the posters I'd tacked up as a teenager.

There was one still hanging on the wall near the window. It was the poem "Desiderata." I didn't remember where I'd gotten it or why it hadn't been discarded or packed away with all my other things. "Go placidly amid the noise and haste. And remember what peace there may be in silence," I read.

"Peace." I'd brought Jack here to my parents' house for a few days with the hope of finding peace, making peace with what had happened.

Besides the one poster, there was little else still left in the room I had last lived in more than twenty years earlier. *I wonder what happened to all my collections?* I thought to myself. *The Madame Alexander dolls and favorite books must be packed away in one of these closets.*

I'd looked for them before, without success, when I'd come home on other visits. My mother insisted I took them with me after college. I insisted they were here somewhere. "What about the shells, Mom? Have you seen those anywhere?"

I'd kept my modest shell collection in four glass bottles partially filled with sand, topped with cork stoppers. I'd gathered the shells and sand each summer at the beach in Rhode Island. In the winter, I used to lie on this same bed, turning the bottles this way and that to see what shells would emerge from the sand.

Jack cried out a little in his sleep, and I could see his hand was stuck between the pad that was tied around the edge of the crib and the mattress. I gently moved it and re-covered him with a blanket as I picked up Special Doggie off the floor where it had fallen. "Sorry, doggie," I said softly as I kissed the top of the furry stuffed animal's head and placed it next to Jack.

I shook my head and smiled a little as I lay back down. I may have lost the belief but not the childhood habit of worrying stuffed animals and other inanimate objects had feelings and could be hurt.

That's the thing about the shells I collected, I now remembered. They weren't all especially beautiful. As I walked along the shore, eyes downcast, I'd see one and reach for it. From a distance, it looked unique—an unusual shape or patch of color. Yet, when I stood back up and took a closer look at the treasure in my hand, I'd discover it was broken or just not particularly pretty or different. But when I moved to toss it back down onto the sand, most of the time I found I couldn't. It was silly, I knew even then, but I didn't want to hurt the shell.

Jack was stirring. I knew he'd be a little frightened when he woke up since he was in a strange room. I stood by the crib so he saw me when he opened his eyes.

"Two planes are off the radar."

I used to fear I'd hurt a stuffed animal or a seashell. How could I possibly bear the idea that I'd hurt . . . thousands of people?

***

Later that morning, I made Jack a snack and took out a bag of wooden blocks to help him build a tower. My father watched from his recliner, laughing each time Jack knocked down the blocks and immediately demanded, "Again!"

"Do you mind if I take a walk, Dad? Can you watch him?"

"Sure," he answered. "Be careful. Do you want me to go with you?"

"No, thanks," I answered. *Careful of what?* I wondered.

My father had come up to stay with us a few weeks before I resigned. My dad's Yankee reserve made him better suited to extending kind gestures like coming up to help with Jack—or offering to go with me on a walk—than knowing the right thing to say.

"They rough on you today?" he asked one night when I got home late, referring to the media.

"Not too bad," I answered. I turned away so he couldn't read my expression. I, too, had inherited my family's habit of not expressing what I felt.

Now the snow was coming down gently, little wisps blowing across the driveway.

I reached the bottom and paused. The neighborhood of small Cape Cod–style and colonial houses built in an old apple orchard looked the same, I thought, looking around. Maybe a tree or two was missing. The rest, in my parents' yard at least, were still standing, bare except for the coating of snow clinging to gnarled branches.

My brothers' basketball hoop was gone, but there, in the neighbor's front yard, was the rock—*was it always that small?*—that had been our pirate ship one day, a deserted island the next.

I kept one gloved hand on my now-protruding belly and decided to follow the route I had taken with my best girlfriend, Kathleen, every afternoon to walk her dog.

The green wooden bus shed was gone. The woods behind it had been developed into a new neighborhood of houses. I smiled as I remembered the Saturday morning when Kathleen and I had taken buckets of water and washed the shed's walls. An elderly neighbor stopped her car and rolled down the window. "What nice girls you are!" she exclaimed. Kathleen and I looked at each other guiltily and glanced over at the bags full of chalk that we'd brought.

"Thanks," we answered.

When the sun dried the back panels of the shed, we covered every inch with every swear word we knew. One, in particular, took up a good bit of space. I have no idea where we, two parochial-school girls, had learned it: *cocksuckerfuckermothertwoballedbitch.*

One long word. We even said it with a singsong giggle as we wrote it across the shed's back wall.

As I walked by the site of the shed, I knew I was still too embarrassed to tell anyone, even David, that it was this childhood memory that popped into my head as I walked into the packed resignation press conference. *Cocksuckerfuckermothertwoballedbitch.* I repeated it to myself a few times before speaking. It's what stopped me from crying in front of the cameras. Why did it come to mind then? I didn't know. Maybe it reminded me that at one point in my life saying that word and writing it on the shed was the worst thing I had ever done.

I turned up East Street, the steep hill that connected my street, Beach Avenue, to Longview. At the top, I stopped for a few seconds to catch my breath. From there, I could see vast stretches of my hometown arrayed in the distance like a painting. The white steeple of the Congregational church, the sports fields of Taft School, the wooded hills beyond. It, too, looked the same as it always had.

It was me who had changed.

Susan Brophy, a childhood friend, used to live around the corner. Her parents still did. As I approached, I saw the same big monogrammed *B* adorning their property that had always been there.

"Susan Brophy's husband was killed in the towers."

I suddenly remembered my mother calling and telling me about Susan's terrible loss while I still worked at Logan. They'd been married just a year. They lived in Manhattan. "So sad," my mother had said.

The second plane, the explosion.

Which tower? I can't stop the question from coming into my mind now. *Which floor?*

The ball of fire.

Stop.

Before I got to her driveway, I panicked. *I can't walk by here! What if they recognize me? What if Susan is staying with her parents? What would I say? What would she say to me?*

I took quick, shallow breaths.

I could hear Susan's voice in my head. *Why? Why did you let it happen?*

And, then, strangely, it felt as if the soul of her husband was on the street with me. A shadowy, pained presence. *Why did you let me die?*

Shivering, I tightened my coat around me and pulled my hat low. I turned and walked hurriedly back the way I'd come. Despite my unsure footing on the slippery pavement, I looked back and then began to run.

I didn't stop until I was at the foot of my parents' yard. Panting with exertion, I looked up toward their backyard. I saw the old apple tree where I'd sit for hours, a shy, excessively serious girl, and write poems in my journal. Just beyond it was the spot where my mother would pose us for pictures when the trees were in bloom. I had just looked at one the day before in an old album I'd found in my room. I was wearing my white Communion dress and veil. My palms were pressed together, fingers straight. I had practiced for hours to do it just as the nuns had taught me. Perfectly.

I blinked.

Fire.

The apple tree was on fire.

The second plane.

It hit.

Not a tree. A tower.

The explosion.

The ball of fire.

The black smoke.

I didn't know how much time had passed, possibly only seconds, before the trees were simply trees again. I entered the house from the back door. I didn't stop to take off my coat. I rushed into the living room and pulled Jack into my lap. I buried my face in his hair until all I could smell, all I could feel, all I could see was him.

CHAPTER EIGHT

QUESTIONS

May 2002—Marblehead

Jack and I were in a rowboat in Boston Harbor. It was a beautiful star-filled evening. We watched the planes take off, one after another. "Look, honey, isn't that amazing?" I said, pointing to the jet soaring overhead, backlit by the moon.

Wait. Something's wrong! The plane wasn't climbing high enough, fast enough. It was going to hit that apartment building!

"Turn, turn!" I shouted, but it was too late. Fire shot out of the windows. Bodies fell to the ground. Another. And another. I covered Jack's eyes with my hands. "No, no, no!" I screamed.

What is wrong with me? I was afraid. The nightmares were coming more frequently, each more vivid than the one before. Although the details in the nightmares were slightly different—a different kind of plane, flying in a different place—the endings were always identical. I tried to get to the scene of the crash. I wanted to try to rescue people. I wanted to save them.

I never got there. Not once.

The night before, my strangled breaths had woken David. He shook my shoulder gently. "Hon, wake up, wake up," he said. "What's wrong? What happened?"

"Nothing. Just a bad dream," I mumbled, rolling over so I faced away from him.

I didn't want him to know the truth. *He's going to think I'm crazy. He's going to think I can't take care of the baby.*

I had no reason to think this. David hadn't said anything or done anything to make me doubt his support. Except. Whenever I worried out loud that there might have been something I could have done to prevent the hijackings, he quickly shut me down. "That's ridiculous," he'd say. "If you'd made people wait in long lines and take their shoes off to go through security, you'd have been hauled away by people in white coats."

I'm not making it up," I would respond heatedly. "They said it was my fault." By "they" I meant the media accounts and the public who chimed in on talk radio and in letters to the editor. But David had a ready answer for that, too.

"At the time they were saying that, they had no understanding. They were judging it with post-9/11 information." David's voice was calm and logical, like it was when he presided over a trial. "They had no interest in explaining how security worked before. They were trying to sell newspapers."

Like the newsprint itself in which I was blamed so viciously, to him it was that black and white.

Later that same morning, after the Boston Harbor dream, I lay next to Maddy, just weeks old, on our bed. David had already dropped Jack at day care and gone to work.

"You're such a good girl," I whispered. Already she was sleeping for long stretches. Her tiny fingers were wrapped tightly around my forefinger. I stroked her soft, dark hair and searched her face for any signs of distress.

I also hadn't told David that whenever I saw a plane flying overhead, I immediately pictured it exploding. Breaking apart into pieces.

And I hadn't confided in him or anyone that, sometimes, when I took a walk along the water and looked toward the Boston skyline, I saw black smoke pouring out of the top of the tallest building.

Have I hurt you somehow? I wondered silently, as I watched Maddy sleep. Was trauma or depression or whatever was wrong with me toxic to a baby in a mother's womb? Like smoking, or eating certain kinds of fish?

Am I hurting you and Jack still?

"It'll be okay," I whispered, trying to reassure us both.

The days—and nights—after Maddy's homecoming followed a similar pattern. David took Jack to day care and I stayed home to care for her. The nightmares, and my fear when I heard a plane overhead, continued. The pattern of David's and my interactions about 9/11 continued, too.

"No one even remembers, hon, what happened in the media in Boston," he said. "I know that hurts, but it's true."

He said these things out of kindness, out of love. He said them to protect me. And he said them without knowing that, each time, with each word, he left me feeling even more alone.

Late spring 2002—Brookline, Massachusetts

"You have post-traumatic stress disorder," the grief counselor said, as straightforwardly as if she were repeating my regular order for coffee at a Starbucks counter.

"What?"

No one moment, no single nightmare had brought me here. I was sitting in a therapist's office because a deepening sense of despair had begun to seep into each day.

Maddy was buckled into an infant car seat at my feet. David was sitting in the chair next to me.

"The term 'post-traumatic stress disorder' is really a misnomer," Andrea Bredbeck was explaining, as I tried to give her my full attention. "It really should be called 'post-traumatic stress *order*.'" I'd been referred to Andrea, a specialist in treating trauma survivors.

"Your brain is actually trying to give order to what has happened. To make it make sense," she said.

I had, of course, heard of PTSD as it related to Vietnam veterans. I knew the condition had something to do with soldiers reliving the horrors of battle. But how could that have anything to do with me?

Andrea's dark, thick hair was pulled back in a messy bun. Her clothes appeared to be vintage sixties. Her glasses were perched on the end of her nose.

We couldn't have been more different and yet in the years ahead there would be no one who understood me as completely. Or knew how to help me find my way back to myself. And even then, she knew what I long refused to accept, that "myself" had been irrevocably changed.

"Is it like alcoholism?" I asked. "Will I have it for the rest of my life?"

I continued to press for clarity.

"Is it like the flu, something I will just get over?"

After we talked for a while longer, I committed to meeting with Andrea regularly. "Can I bring the baby?" I asked.

"You can," she answered, "but as we get into the work you may not want to."

Andrea used the term "dissociation." It was the first time I'd heard that my sense that I was shut down inside had a name.

"It's the common response to trauma," she said, "a kind of automatic defense mechanism."

I picture myself driving into Logan. "Two planes are off the radar," Joey had said.

Did the dissociation begin then?

Or was it in my office, seeing that moment for the first time?

The second plane.

The explosion.

The ball of fire.

The black smoke.

"Dissociation allowed you to do your job excellently," Andrea was saying now. "But as we explore your feelings about what happened you could scream," she added. "You could lose control."

"No way," I said, shaking my head vigorously. "That is not going to happen."

I just wanted to know the answer.

"Am I guilty or innocent," I said, rather than asked, like a declaration or a challenge. "That's what I need to know, no matter how it turns out."

David sounded exasperated. "She's the only person who thinks she could have done something to stop the hijackers."

"You can't know what you don't know," Andrea said. I didn't understand what she meant. My frustration grew with both of them.

They didn't get it.

What if I should have known? What then?

I didn't tell Andrea or David. But I had already come to my own answer.

Several days earlier—Devereux Beach, Marblehead

The tide was out, and though it was May, there was no sign of the coming warmth in the brisk breeze. I dug my hands deep into the pockets of my ski coat and buried my chin in its collar. I continued the silent debate raging in my mind.

If there is a distinction between blame and responsibility, how much responsibility is mine to bear?

Can I bear it?

What if I contributed to the deaths of thousands of people?

I looked across to the horizon. I'd been raised to believe in doing penance. But no Act of Contrition could compensate for this.

The water and gray sky framed more questions.

Why didn't I hold daily press conferences demanding the security checkpoints be fixed?

Why hadn't I testified before Congress about that, instead of runways?

I watched a gull pecking at a mussel shell near the low-tide line, methodically breaking it open to reach the pink meat inside. Another gull flew overhead, calling out as if it were asking its own questions. In answer, the first gull picked up its food and flew away, the mussel tightly clenched in its beak. It landed farther down the beach and resumed its meal.

I resumed my self-interrogation.

I was a leader in developing customer service programs. I was a national spokesperson for the need to ease air travel delays.

But doesn't a real leader go where others cannot see?

My steps slowed. I turned to look back at my path in the sand. I used to carry a small laminated card in my wallet with the story "Footprints" printed on it. It told of a man who questioned God after looking back at his life. He didn't understand why he saw only one set of footprints in the sand during the most difficult times. "It was then that I carried you," God answered.

I could see only one set of footprints behind me now. But I was not being carried. Of that I was certain.

Murderer?

Could I have done anything to stop them?

I looked again toward the horizon. I tried not to blink or look away.

The voices of people and institutions I'd relied on as I built my career, and my sense of self, said at some level it was my fault. No other airport directors at the three other airports where the hijackers boarded planes were being blamed. But those blaming me were smart people, not nameless critics, in the media, in politics, whose opinions I had tried to sway, yes, when I worked on behalf of two governors, but whose opinions I also deeply respected. Could they all be wrong? And even if I were simply an easy answer to point to, to assuage fear, could I bear being forever linked to the deaths of thousands?

If I could not hold on to what I knew deep down was true, that I was not to blame, if the volume of external voices drowned out my inner voice, there was only one answer.

I couldn't bear to live.

***

"It's still possible to make meaning. To find joy," Andrea was saying, as we set our next appointment.

Make meaning? Find joy?

How?

CHAPTER NINE

MARIANNE AND ANNE

June 2002—Revere

The phone rang twice, three times. I was about to hang up when I heard the click of the answering machine. "You've reached Marianne and Anne. We're not home right now, so please leave a message."

"Uh, uh," I stuttered as I tried to speak. It was Marianne's voice. Though she had been dead for nearly nine months, Anne had left her daughter's message on the machine.

"Uh, this is Ginny Buckingham. I don't know if you remember me, from Logan, but I wonder if you'll meet me for coffee?" I left my number. When I hung up, my hands were shaking.

Anne called back within a few hours. "Of course I remember you," she said. She suggested we meet at the International House of Pancakes in Revere, near her house.

As I walked in the restaurant door, I recognized her right away.

"Hello," she said simply as I slid into the booth seat across from her. I nodded yes to the waitress's offer of coffee.

"Thanks for coming," I said. I noticed she had a large heart-shaped pendant around her neck with a picture on it. "That's Marianne," Anne said when she saw me looking at the pendant. "Joe and George, my two sons, gave it to me."

I didn't know what to say, but Anne filled the silence.

"Hey, I brought you something," she said as she handed me a small teddy bear. The stuffed animal was wearing a T-shirt with "Always In Our Hearts—Flight 175" printed on it. I squeezed the bear hard.

"And for your kids," Anne said. She passed me a laminated certificate and letter from Sean O'Keefe, the NASA administrator. In the letter, O'Keefe noted that the space shuttle *Endeavour* had carried six thousand American flags to the International Space Station in December to honor the victims and heroes of September 11.

"This one's for you," Anne said. She handed me a small laminated memorial card with Marianne's picture on it. I cradled it in my palm.

I'd wanted to ask Anne to bring a picture, but felt uncomfortable. I was already invading her privacy enough by asking to meet with her. Somehow, though, she knew to bring one anyway. Maybe she instinctively understood I would want to look in Marianne's eyes. That I would want to know her. To grieve specifically for someone who had died on 9/11. To put a name and a life to my feelings of loss and guilt.

Anne and I talked easily. She, who herself had started working at Logan as a stewardess for Northeast Airlines in 1957, told me Marianne had a deep love of aviation. "Her first job was selling flowers out of a cart in Terminal D," Anne said. "Once you work at an airport, you just can't work anywhere else."

Marianne's guidance counselor at college had tried to dissuade her from pursuing an airport career. "Not for women," he'd told her. But Marianne wasn't dissuaded. "She became the manager at US Airways in Bangor, Maine." Anne's pride was evident in her twinkling blue eyes.

"Then one day, she called me and said, 'I'm coming home.' I asked, 'For the weekend?' And she said, 'Nope, for good.'"

Marianne moved into the upstairs of Anne's double-decker Revere home. Anne's two sons, Joe and George, lived in another two-family house right next door. There was a shared pool in the backyard. "The MacFarlane compound," Anne liked to joke.

Her voice grew quiet as she talked about the last time she saw her daughter. Marianne worked the early shift as a gate agent for United Airlines in Logan's Terminal C. "I usually got up by four o'clock to take her," Anne recalled. "Otherwise, she'd never have gotten there."

On September 11, Marianne was working for a few hours before taking a flight out west to meet some friends for a short vacation in Las Vegas. "Marianne usually never said goodbye when I dropped her off," Anne said. "She'd just throw an 'I'll see ya' over her shoulder as she walked toward the terminal door."

"But that day, she said, 'Goodbye, Mom.' I almost stopped the car to roll down my window to ask, 'Why goodbye?'"

I pictured the scene as Anne talked. The curb, typically filled with cabs, buses, and limos jockeying for position, must have been empty at that time of day, Marianne's "goodbye" echoing in the stillness.

"I was home when the first plane hit. George called me from down at the fire station." Anne wasn't looking at me now as she talked. She was staring past me, at her own memories. "He said, 'Turn on the TV, Ma.'"

"I saw the second plane," she said. "I didn't know Marianne was on it."

Anne's voice was hypnotic. I saw what she was seeing.

The second plane.

The explosion.

The ball of fire.

The black smoke.

"I waited by the phone. Marianne would've called, if she could have," Anne said. "After a while, I couldn't sit around and wait anymore so I went to the airport."

"As soon as I approached the ticket counter," Anne said, "I knew."

Anne would learn that Marianne was seated in the first row of the plane. She had helped board the other passengers first. She sat next to a coworker, J. R. Sanchez.

"I'm glad she wasn't alone."

Inside the plane.

Oh God.

I couldn't think about what it was like inside the plane.

Stop.

I refocused on Anne. She was telling me about a conversation Marianne had had with a family friend, Phyllis, just weeks before 9/11. "Marianne told Phyllis that if her plane was ever hijacked, she would just close her eyes, go to sleep, and wake up in Cuba."

That was the protocol then—before—to cooperate with, not confront, hijackers. As unlikely as it was, I could tell Anne was trying to hold on to the possibility that her daughter had done just that in the moments before she died. Closed her eyes and gone to sleep.

"I'm so sorry," I said, tears flowing freely now down my cheeks. I mustered the courage to pose the question that haunted my dreams.

"Do you blame me for what happened?" I tried to meet Anne's eyes as my hands squeezed the edge of the table.

Anne didn't look away. She didn't pause to consider her words, not even for a second.

"You're no more to blame than Marianne is."

You're no more to blame than Marianne is.

"I had no idea you felt that way," Anne added.

I tried to steady my voice.

"I know I didn't lose anyone on September 11," I explained. "I have my husband and two children and my health. I know it's not comparable to what you and others lost, but on September 11, I lost myself."

Anne didn't look surprised. She didn't even ask what I meant. She just said, directly, "So what are you going to do now?"

"Get through the one-year anniversary, write my story, try to reclaim who I am," I answered.

"Then do it," Anne said. "Do it in Marianne's name."

***

Anne's words were not a magic elixir. They didn't erase my pain, just as my words of condolence didn't erase hers. But for each of us, the connection we made that day became a touchstone. A place to go to be strengthened. Comforted. Reached and understood on a journey through loss that largely was made alone.

I also came to understand, in retrospect, that I knew I was likely safe asking Anne whether she blamed me, given her response to me at Marianne's memorial service. Was choosing her to answer my hardest question some kind of survival instinct? Did I know I needed a family member to tell me I wasn't to blame? To hold on to that, even if it was just one family, even if others felt differently? Maybe. What I didn't know at the time was that Anne's certainty would help me hang on—in the most literal sense—in the hardest times yet to come.

CHAPTER TEN

WORDS

September 3, 2002—Marblehead

"Jack, get down and stay on the sidewalk, will you please?" I said, immediately wishing I hadn't spoken so sharply. I couldn't get Maddy's infant car seat to unhook from the metal bars of the shopping cart. Jack kept climbing on the front of the cart, pushing it slightly backward.

"Dammit," I said, as I finally caught the hook under the seat, moving it enough so that I could lift it before it snapped back on my finger. With Maddy's car seat in one hand and a bag of groceries in the other, I said, "C'mon, honey," to Jack, suddenly wearier than a trip to the grocery store was responsible for.

"Can I help?" a voice said softly over my shoulder as I put the bag down on the hood of the car. I looked up. A dark-haired, middle-aged woman who looked vaguely familiar stood there. She was already reaching for the grocery bag.

I nodded, grateful. "Yes, thanks a lot." As I snapped Maddy's car seat into its frame and buckled Jack into his, she started loading the rest of the bags into the back of the car.

"I'm Katie Reilly," she said.

"Oh, right, hello," I answered, realizing why she looked so familiar.

Katie was a bit of a character in town, standing out for driving an old white SUV that was completely covered on the outside, doors, hood, and all, with bumper stickers of all sorts. I'd long admired her quirkiness for another reason, too. A few years earlier, the navy warship USS *Constitution* had sailed to Marblehead Harbor from Boston to celebrate its two-hundredth anniversary. Thousands of people had come to see it. The best vantage point was from a park out on Marblehead Neck, a wealthy neighborhood of beautiful waterfront homes. Visitors to town walking to the park were greeted with signs and yellow tape on neighbors' lawns. Keep Off the Grass, Private Property, and the like. But not at Katie Reilly's house. The sign at the end of the driveway leading to her white oceanfront mansion read Welcome. Katie had invited hundreds of complete strangers to take advantage of her view.

Now she was standing less than a foot or so from my car, a similar inviting expression on her face.

"I'm Ginny," I said. "Ginny Buckingham. Thanks again."

"I know who you are, Ginny," Katie responded. "I see you walking in the morning by the beach. I've wanted to say hello, ever since 9/11, but I didn't want to interrupt you." As she spoke, I pictured seeing a group of people each morning sitting at a picnic table at the beachfront hamburger shack, sipping coffee. I remembered catching her eye a few times.

"I read your book," I said. Katie looked pleased. She had self-published a book after both her parents died called *Nobody's Daughter* that was carried in the local bookstore.

"You know," she said, "when I'd see you, I always felt a soft connection between us. I can't explain it."

I couldn't either but I knew what she meant. I'd felt it, too.

"So, what are you doing now?" she asked.

"I'm trying to start a career as a writer," I answered. I told her that a piece I'd written about 9/11 was going to be published that coming weekend in the *Boston Globe* Sunday magazine.

"It's a chance to talk about the 9/11 experience from my perspective at Logan Airport," I explained.

I didn't tell her that it had taken some convincing to get the *Globe* to agree to run the piece. Frank Phillips, the paper's State House Bureau chief, had broached the possibility with the magazine's editor after I called to ask for his advice.

"I hope you're not going to try to rewrite history," the editor, Nick King, said when I first talked directly to him. After I submitted the first draft of the essay, King called me, clearly surprised. "I picked it up to take a glance at it and I couldn't put it down. I read it all the way through," he said. We then talked about the courtroom dream I'd opened the piece with. King asked, "Do you remember anything else about the dream? Were you in the dock?"

"No, no, that's it," I said, feeling bad about the lie. Even as I said it, I felt them. Handcuffs. In the dream I was in handcuffs, their cold metal tight on my wrists. Only the guilty were handcuffed. Only the condemned. I couldn't bring myself to write that because I couldn't admit to anyone, not King, not David, a horrifying reality: when I felt the most despair over 9/11, I would feel the handcuffs digging into my skin. Or sometimes, what it might feel like if I cut into my wrists myself.

"I'll look for the article," Katie said as I closed the trunk. We smiled at each other as she started toward the door of the store.

September 8, 2002—Marblehead

David and I fell into each other's arms and onto the couch, laughing and crying at the same time. "Words!" he exclaimed. "Your words!"

I was thrilled and humbled when King told me he'd decided to make my essay the issue's cover story, substituting it for a cover essay he had solicited from the famed writer Christopher Hitchens. But I had no inkling that instead of a picture or illustration, the cover would be simply words that I had written. White print on a black background. A few words in red. My long-held aspiration had been to be a professional writer. That a seasoned *Globe* editor thought my words, alone, were worthy of the front cover seemed an extraordinary validation, reducing David and me to tears of joy.

My words!

Then theirs.

Approximately ten days later

I held the large white envelope, hesitating before I opened it. The *Globe*'s masthead and return address were in the upper left corner. I knew the envelope contained copies of the letters the paper had received after the magazine's publication. In an email, Nick King had written he would forward them to me. "Some are pretty tough," he'd warned.

I carried the envelope into the sitting room. I tore it open and unfolded the first letter.

"Having read her words, I have come to the conclusion that while Ms. Buckingham was following all of the guidelines and rules set down by the FAA on Sept. 11, she is still ultimately responsible for the flights that left Logan on that fateful day. She has failed to come to grips with this or fully grasp the most baseline principle of leadership, being responsible for what occurs on your watch."

The next was no better: "Ms. Buckingham should have been screaming for improved security measures prior to 9-11" at "sieve Logan."

I opened another. "Never have I witnessed a more self-absorbed person displaying such a lack of sensitivity. Does she expect us to pray for her as well as the 3,000 souls who lost a little more than their reputations on September 11, 2001?"

My wrists.

I rubbed them and read the next letter.

"The one person who had the power but not the knowledge, training or experience to somehow influence the events of 9-11 and uses it to ask for sympathy. What about the victims and their survivors?"

Murderer.

"Mama, I need help," Jack called from the family room, where he was playing with his Batman characters and watching TV.

"Okay, I'll be right there," I answered, trying to keep my voice steady. I opened one more.

"She should stop whining and admit that her blind ambition contributed to the deaths of nearly 3,000 people."

The handcuffs were cutting into me. Cutting my skin. Cutting open my wrists. *Stop.*

"Mama! Mama!" Jack called again. "I have a boo-boo."

"*Shh*, you'll wake the baby," I said, hurrying into the family room while wiping my cheeks with the backs of my hands.

"Want a Band-Aid, Mama," Jack said, as I checked and kissed the tiny, barely visible scratch on his finger.

I started to tell Jack he didn't need a Band-Aid. But I stopped myself and got one from the cabinet. Gently, I wrapped it around his small forefinger, kissing it to seal it. I couldn't explain to a three-year-old that sometimes a wound has to be exposed to heal. How could I? I didn't yet understand that myself.

Over the next several days, I got more letters. Some were supportive, many were not. I smiled as I read the old-fashioned cursive written on yellow lined paper from one of the toughest neighborhood activists, who fought Massport at every turn. Alice Christopher bitterly opposed the dismantling of the blast fence at the end of Runway 22-Left, her advanced age no obstacle to her activism. "Because of the removal of the blast fence I was no fan of Virginia Buckingham," she wrote, "but the fact of the matter is—fan or not—you are not the least bit responsible for the horrific events of 9/11. . . . History will record that you just happened to have the wrong job at the wrong time. You're young! Be strong! Step up to the plate."

"This quote was given to me, many years ago from a friend, when my husband was diagnosed with Parkinson's," I read in another letter. "'Courage isn't having the strength to go on—it's going on when you don't have the strength.' You are a very courageous woman. We are proud of you."

And this from someone who realized I would turn thirty-seven just a few days after the first 9/11 anniversary. "Happy Birthday. It wasn't your fault."

I picked up a sheaf of mustard-yellow paper and reread a final letter. I'd found it in my foyer on the day the *Globe* article was published. It was from Katie Reilly.

She wrote that my article "is from the deepest, most sensitive part of you that feels that somehow, that if you 'confess' . . . then perhaps you will be forgiven. I can only surmise that you will forgive yourself for the horror that two planes left your 'house' that morning and changed the world as we know it."

Katie continued, "I have had friends who have had teens leave their homes late in the evening only to receive a call saying there had been a car accident, one teen injured fatally, two others critical. I had a friend who had a toddler drown in her pool at her son's birthday party. To this day, the parents of the surviving children feel guilt because they did not lose their own child, though they are desperately grateful they did not.

"May I say to you, we forgive you. . . . Please forgive yourself." Her letter was coming to an end, and I hugged it to my chest as I picked up the framed poem she'd also left in the foyer. It was a poem she'd written about traveling the world as seen through the eyes of her children.

I turned it over and reread the note she'd put on the back of the matting.

"Virginia, forgive yourself first, take your time—then move forward. The world will be waiting for your wisdom. Till then, bring your wisdom home . . . welcome home Virginia Buckingham, Welcome Home."

Home.

Before the magazine article ran, the *Globe* had sent a photographer to my house.

"I should get a picture of that," he'd joked when I clenched the plastic handle of Maddy's pacifier between my teeth as I buckled her into the infant swing in the corner of the kitchen.

He looked around for a spot to set up. "I read the piece. You came through it all whole," he said.

Whole.

I don't remember if I responded. Maybe I nodded in assent.

Whole. Home.

No.

Not yet.
Not ever?
Stop.

CHAPTER ELEVEN

LOST

September 11, 2002—Boston College campus, Chestnut Hill, Massachusetts

It was the same sky. Clear blue. Just like the year before.

"Over that way," I said to David, who turned Maddy's stroller in the direction I pointed. We fell in with the stream of students leaving class. It was quiet, despite the growing number of people. There was no tossing of a Frisbee. No idle speculation about the weekend's football game. Oddly, the solemnity seemed as natural as the backpacks flung casually on the students' shoulders.

The service started at noon. It was the same time students had gathered in front of Boston College's O'Neill Library a year earlier.

I hadn't known where to go to mark the first anniversary of 9/11.

"Do you want to go to the Logan chapel?" David had asked when we talked about it.

"No," I answered. I didn't feel right going to any of the official memorials in Boston either.

I didn't belong anywhere. I hadn't been invited to join my former colleagues at Logan, and I feared coming face-to-face with 9/11 families at a Boston event. Nothing had eased the severity of the isolation I'd felt from the moment I was first blamed. In some ways it had worsened as the 9/11 narrative turned to reflection nearing the first anniversary. I was not a first responder, not a survivor, not a suffering family, not an everyday American pausing to mark a solemn anniversary. I was nothing. No one. Lost.

When I read in the paper a few weeks before that Boston College was holding a memorial service, I felt a wave of relief.

Boston College. The place I first embraced as a new home as a seventeen-year-old freshman. *I'll be welcome there,* I thought. *Safe.*

Safe? The unbidden thought surprised me. *Safe from what? From being blamed,* I responded, answering my own question.

Now, we continued down the main driveway of middle campus. The imposing limestone walls of the old Bapst Library on our right and Gasson Hall's tower, "the tower on the heights," rose before us. I noticed the wheels of Maddy's stroller crunching the fallen leaves scattered across the driveway.

September. It had always been my favorite month. But it was lost, too. Gone, its possibility as a beginning.

I'd contacted a former college classmate whose father worked for the college president's office to ask if it would be all right to go to the BC service. After checking, he called right back. "Of course," he said. "Do you want to park on middle campus?"

I swallowed my disappointment that this was the only offer extended. I was embarrassed that I'd hoped BC would ask me to participate in some way, an unrealistic hope that somehow leaders there would intuit I wanted—needed—some acknowledgment that 9/11 was my story, too.

As we neared the edge of the open concrete plaza in front of the library, David stopped pushing the stroller. I leaned in to straighten Maddy's blanket as a shadow fell across her face. Father Neenan, the dean of the College of Arts and Sciences when I attended BC, was peering down at her. Tall and thin, rakish and scholarly at the same time, he had always reminded me of Gregory Peck.

"You have to get through Good Friday to find Easter Sunday," he said, looking at me and then David. He smiled down at Maddy, who was starting to stir. "She is the future. She is Easter Sunday."

Like the blanket covering Maddy, there was a soft security offered in his words. The hope I was raised to believe in—the hope of resurrection.

I smiled softly at him. "Thank you, Father."

David and I found a spot to sit on the ground on the edge of the plaza. I held Maddy cradled in my lap. Students all around us, wearing flip-flops and jeans, leaned on one another. Their faces were streaked with tears, illuminated in the bright sunshine.

Almost directly in front of us, a large wall had been erected. It was covered with paper. After the service, students were invited to come forward and write a message that would be preserved as a memorial somewhere on campus.

"Do you want me to write something?" David offered.

"No, I will," I answered. I passed Maddy carefully to him and stood. I approached the wall. A young man handed me the Sharpie marker he'd just finished with. I held it, staring at the white space. Others wrote and then passed on their markers to those waiting.

I took the cap off. I pressed the tip to the paper.

***

After the main service, we drove the mile or so to BC's law school campus, where I had lived as a freshman. A smaller service was being held in the chapel, the place I had spent hours in alone, thinking, praying, in the middle of the day. Maddy had fallen back asleep so David stayed in the car with her. I sat in the very last row, in a corner seat against the wall.

The names.

I shrunk into the corner, trying to make myself invisible as the service proceeded. *How could I be so oblivious?*

I was deeply ashamed that I hadn't focused on the twenty-two BC alumni who had been killed in the attacks. "Thomas M. Brennan, Class of '91," the speaker read. "John B. Cahill, Class of '66; Kevin P. Connors, Class of '68; Welles R. Crowther, Class of '99; Thomas Fitzpatrick, Class of '87." The last name was familiar, a nice guy I hadn't known well but would see at parties and football tailgates.

His name and the others swirled around me, encircling me. I pressed my body farther into the corner. I wanted to disappear.

It was late by the time we got home. We picked Jack up from day care, fed and bathed him and the baby, and got them into bed. David fell asleep while reading. I carefully extracted my hand from his and went downstairs.

I'd avoided watching any TV in the last few days. I didn't want to chance seeing the footage of that day replayed.

I always saw it.

I turned on the TV.

Oh my God.

It was not the second plane or the towers on fire. The camera was tight on the face of a woman. She was talking softly. Calmly. Only her eyes revealed the horror she was describing. They were open wide. Staring beyond the camera.

She had gotten a call from her husband, she said. He was trapped in one of the towers.

Trapped.

I sat heavily on the floor, unable to move, unable to look away, to avert my eyes. The camera seemed to get closer to her face. Her eyes. They were looking right at me.

Her lips were moving but it was her eyes that seemed to be talking to me: *This hurts this hurts this hurts so badly please make my pain go away please make my pain go away.*

"He said he was going to try for the roof," she told the interviewer. He said, "I love you," and then the phone went dead.

Her eyes seemed wider as she finished talking.

The second plane.

The explosion.

The ball of fire.

The black smoke.

Her eyes.

I curled into a fetal position on the floor in my dark house. I tried to make myself as small as I could. I squeezed my arms. Tucked my legs close under me. I rocked back and forth.

"Make meaning. Find Joy. For Jack, Maddy, and Marianne." That's what I had written on the memorial board at BC that morning. Inspired by Andrea's encouragement and Father Neenan's ray of hope.

The silent house absorbed my choking, keening sobs.

Stop.

I couldn't.

I was lost.

PART II

CHAPTER TWELVE

MISSING

November 2002—Marblehead

"You don't have to go," David said.

"Yes, I do," I insisted.

I had to see it. Ground Zero.

"There's nothing to see there," my mother said in a last phone call before my trip, trying to dissuade me. "Why do you want to go?"

No, why do I have to go, I silently corrected her.

I felt like I was following an internal checklist. Visiting Ground Zero was near the top of the items I had to complete before I could move on from 9/11.

"Move on." That's what everyone said it was time to do. David. My mother. My sisters. My friends. Even if they didn't say it out loud, I could see it in their faces. I could hear it in their voices. "Move on." "Put it behind you."

What did that even mean? How was moving on from something as horrific as 9/11 even possible?

My brother Bill, who was a frequent visitor to New York City, offered to meet me at the site. Ann, my friend and neighbor, said she'd drive down with me.

I didn't ask David to go to the site of the Twin Towers with me. Nor did he offer. At the time, this didn't strike either of us as odd. He'd stay with Jack and Maddy. Get them to day care. Bring them home at night. I had a friend and my brother coming. I didn't need him.

But, of course, I did.

Anne MacFarlane told me she'd gone to New York with a group of families just a few weeks after the attacks. "First the bus took us to 9/11," she said, referring to Ground Zero.

This appellation did strike me as strange when she first said it—"took us to 9/11"?—but in retrospect, it seemed as fitting a name as "Ground Zero." The common term for an area directly beneath a detonation began to be used in the media within hours of the attacks. But to Anne, perhaps, "ground zero" didn't quite describe the totality of the horror. United 175 and American 11 weren't "directly beneath the detonation." The two flights in which 147 innocent people were instantly killed were the detonation.

"Mayor Giuliani was speaking when I got there," Anne added. She and her family stayed at the ceremony for just a few minutes, listening to the speeches. There, for the first time since she went to the Logan Hilton to meet with the Care Team on the actual day of the attacks, she was surrounded by people who had suffered the loss of a spouse, a parent, or a child, as she had. Yet, she found no comfort in the sad company. "Let's go get a cup of coffee," she said to her son Joe.

"Then they took us to the pier," Anne said, meaning the pier where the New York City medical examiner's office had set up operations. "We sat in a big tent," she continued, filling out forms and providing DNA samples. "They gave us an urn before we left."

"What was in it?" I asked.

"Dirt," she answered. "From 9/11." She didn't have to add, "In case nothing else is found."

If Anne can go there, so can I, I told myself.

Anne, too, had been admonished to "move on," I knew. She still had Marianne's voice on her answering machine and got more than a few uncomfortable comments about it. I was even asked about it when

I saw former colleagues from Logan. "Is Anne all right? Have you called her and heard the message?"

Of course she's not all right, I wanted to snap back. *How could she be?* Instead, I demurred and said I hadn't talked to her in a while. It was as if there were some sort of grieving test we were both failing because a year later we still hadn't "moved on."

New York will help me do it, I thought. *That's why I have to go.*

I didn't think "go back," though. I'd certainly been to New York City before. I grew up in nearby Connecticut, but as a child, New York City was more an idea—even a fantasy—to me than a real place. My mother would tell stories about taking my oldest four siblings there on day trips. Her description of the shops, the lights, the food, the smells fueled my imagined vision of a magical city.

When the family grew to eight children, those regular trips became too daunting. But at about ten years old, I got an early Christmas present. My mom and I took a bus trip to Radio City Music Hall. There we saw the Rockettes perform and, later, stood in awe in front of the decorated Christmas windows at Macy's. But other than that one trip, I developed my impressions of New York's streetscapes from watching the annual Macy's Thanksgiving Day Parade on TV. On Thanksgiving mornings, my brother RJ and I would sit cross-legged on the floor in our pajamas. On the rug in front of us was a picnic of grapes, tangerines, and nuts. Cracking the nuts was as fun as eating them. We'd yell out the names of our favorite balloon characters as they floated down the streets. "Snoopy!" "Spider-Man!"

Laughter. Excitement. Awe. Each of these colored in my perceived outline of New York's skyline.

And fear.

Another vivid New York memory was boarding a train with my sister Lauren. She was a teenager then, eight years older than me. The train was supposed to take us from Washington, DC, where we'd been visiting relatives, to Bridgeport, Connecticut. Inadvertently, we were put on the wrong train and ended up in Penn Station. I was scared and so was Lauren, though she assumed a veneer of calm for my sake. While my father waited for us in a station in Connecticut, we were stranded in New York in the middle of the night.

Facing my fear, I think. *That's what I am doing by going to Ground Zero.*

My nightly dreams began to reveal the fear that gripped me as the New York trip came closer.

Images of the Rockettes kicking in unison morphed into a mass of people swelling and receding on the sidewalks around Ground Zero.

Then they ran, terrified, past me.

What if someone recognizes me? *I thought to myself, panic rising.* What if they blame me? *I hid near a storefront. It was closed. The metal shutter covering the door was cold and rough against my cheek as I pressed myself to it as closely as possible. A corner of a piece of loose-leaf paper scratched my arm. I inched my head back to see what it was. Wait. There were dozens of them. Faces. Handwriting. Names. "Missing" printed in block letters.*

Missing.

I must have groaned in my sleep because David shook me gently on the shoulder. "Hon, are you okay?" I struggled to open my eyes, and I woke enough to whisper, "Yes." But the reels of the dream continued to turn as I fell back to sleep.

I was at Ground Zero. How did I get beyond the construction fence? I didn't remember. I was breathing hard from the climb. I was at the top of the tallest crane. "I shouldn't be here!" My heart pounded in fear.

I looked down. Into the pit. "I don't belong here!"

"Join us. Join us."

Voices called to me from the darkness below. "You belong here," they said. "Join us."

I took a gun out of my jacket. I placed the cold metal next to my temple. "I do belong here."

I was falling.

My leg kicked against the quilt covering the bottom of the bed, a physical manifestation of trying to break my dream fall. I sat straight up, panting. "David, David," I whispered urgently, shaking his shoulder. I couldn't catch my breath. "David, if I don't come home from New York, it's not because I don't want to. Please come find me. Please."

"I will," he said, "it's okay, *shhhhh*," accepting without question my fevered plea and running his hand over my forehead like I was a small child until my breathing came easier and eventually I fell back asleep.

The next evening

We were leaving for New York City at dawn. Ann and I wanted to miss the morning commuter traffic. I put my suitcase in the trunk so I wouldn't wake everyone by dragging it down the stairs in the morning. When I came back in the house, David said, "Jack's still awake, and he wants you to come up."

"Hey, sweetie," I said as I settled into the rocking chair and stroked his hair. "Want me to sing to you?"

"Don't go New York, Mama," Jack said, reaching for me to take him into my lap. "Don't go New York. What if can't find way back home?"

His speech was childlike but there was no mistaking his meaning. Had he overheard me telling my fears to David? Or was there some deeper instinct beyond his or my understanding that prompted him to try to keep his mother safe? I didn't know the answer.

I didn't go.

CHAPTER THIRTEEN

"A COMPLETE COMEBACK"

January 1, 2003—Marblehead

I shivered no matter how close I stood to the kitchen fireplace. I lifted the mug of steaming hot coffee to my lips and surveyed the room. Towels were still draped over shoulders. Fleece caps pulled over wet hair. Damp stains dotted sweatpants where they covered wet bathing suits. Ten of us hovered near the warm flames. I had lit the fire the second I came back in the door. Even so, I couldn't get warm. Every nerve ending tingled. My feet were completely numb and covered in sand.

Jumping in the freezing Atlantic Ocean to start the New Year wasn't an original idea. But I was happy to claim it as a new tradition, as I toasted a fellow "polar bear" with my coffee mug.

In a couple of weeks, I'd start a new job, too.

Maddy was nine months old, and not going back to work wasn't an option financially, nor did staying home for good really occur to me. Even with the personal and career-shattering ending at Massport, succeeding professionally was how I defined myself. Could I do so again?

How would I even start? I knew Boston was in many ways a small town so I sought out the advice of a few business leaders and two people I knew at the *Boston Globe.*

Before politics, even more than politics, I had always wanted to be a writer. *Maybe that is how I start over,* I hoped.

***

"Congratulations on your new job, but I'm sorry about the letter." Gina, who had begun taking care of Maddy while I started job hunting, handed her to me and set Maddy's diaper bag down on the counter. I was soon to start as deputy editorial page editor at the *Boston Herald.*

"What letter?" I asked, kissing Maddy's soft cheek.

"You didn't see the story? It was in the *Globe*," Gina answered.

I hadn't had time to read the papers that morning. I picked the *Boston Globe* up off the counter, and Gina pointed out the small news item. I was conscious of her watching me read it. I tried to keep my expression neutral when I saw what it was about. I swallowed hard. Stunned, I read the item again.

The news item referenced a "letter" that, it turned out, was actually more like a petition. Forty of my soon-to-be-colleagues at the *Boston Herald* had signed it in protest of my hiring. The *Globe* item only excerpted a sentence or two, but I later read the entire text of the letter, which was sent to my soon-to-be-editor Rachelle Cohen, when it was leaked to the media critic Jim Romenesko:

> Dear Shelly:
>
> As you know, the newsroom staff deeply respects the "church/state" division between the news pages and the editorial/opinion pages. But the undersigned are compelled to register our grave dismay at the naming of Virginia Buckingham as chief editorial writer for the Herald.
>
> We acknowledge that the appointment is fully the province of you and the publisher. We are addressing this letter privately to you, and given that the decision

is made we will accept it as professionals and move on. But we conclude that Buckingham's appointment will be an embarrassment to the entire Herald staff for the following reasons:

1. She has no serious journalism experience.
2. She is familiar to most as a GOP political operative, with all the baggage that entails.
3. Her role as head of Massport during the 9/11 calamity undermines her credibility on issues of Homeland Security, airport safety, and the scourge of patronage appointments in state government. (Please see attached clippings from the Herald.)

Their third point hit me like a blow to the stomach. I stopped reading. *Why?* I wanted to demand. *Who better to write about safety issues?*

Because three thousand people were killed on your watch. I silently answered my own question. A familiar sense of despair settled on me.

The letter ended with this: "Buckingham's presence will be confusing and troubling to readers who have followed our aggressive and critical-minded coverage of her political career and of Massachusetts state government. Her appointment reflects poorly on all of us who labor as professional news people."

I didn't look at who signed it. I didn't want to know. I was supposed to show up in the *Herald* newsroom in just a few days. I wondered why Shelly, my new editor, hadn't told me about the letter. I didn't know her well enough yet to understand that the second she'd gotten it she'd crumbled it into a ball and thrown it into the trash.

The job offer from Shelly was unexpected. I was grocery shopping, literally picking up a bag of frozen peas, when my cell phone rang. "Ginny, it's Shelly Cohen. I have a job opening and I wondered if you might be interested?"

Interested? I nearly dropped the peas and yelped "Yes!" out loud.

"Sure, I'd love to talk to you about that," I answered, trying to keep my voice calm.

"Then let's have lunch. Sooner rather than later. How about Tuesday?"

I had last seen Shelly a few months before at the State House when the official portraits of Weld and Cellucci were unveiled at an event I was unexpectedly, and also ironically, asked to emcee when Jane Swift was unable to attend at the last minute.

"Tom Finneran?" I'd suggested when I was asked who should fill in for her, referring to the House speaker. "Bob Cordy?"—a justice on the state's highest court. "They want you," my friend Rob told me after running my ideas by Weld and Cellucci. There was an audible gasp in the Great Hall when I entered followed by the two governors—I hadn't been back in the building at all since the day I'd testified before the transportation committee after 9/11.

At the reception following the event, I asked Shelly if I could seek her advice about pursuing a writing career, as I had with other newspeople in town, a question she must have remembered when the position on her staff came open.

From Politics to Paper, Controversy Pursues Her
—Boston Globe, January 14, 2003

January 14, 2003—One Herald Square, Boston

I found an empty space in the already full parking lot behind the sprawling brick building housing the *Boston Herald*. The yellow box trucks with the blue lettering lined the row nearest the fence, already back from their early-morning deliveries.

I took a last sip of coffee, inhaled a deep, calming breath, and glanced one more time at the headline in the morning's *Boston Globe*: "Controversy Pursues Her."

"Her."

Me.

The story, printed the day after I started, was about the anger inside the paper spurred by my hiring.

"Hey, good morning," a shop-floor manager called out as I walked down the hallway past the enormous printing presses, long quiet from last night's run. His greeting reassured me somewhat that the "controversy" hadn't fazed everyone at my new paper. Upstairs, I passed the "dead room," having just learned that was what the space was called where old copies of the paper were stored—the most recent in piles on the floor, the oldest cataloged by topic and date and bound in enormous books. *I'd like to look sometime for some of the coverage of when I was in the State House,* I thought. I didn't need to look up the coverage of me and 9/11. I knew it by heart.

So why had I explored working for the *Globe*, and rejoiced at the job at the *Herald* if I thought their coverage of me and Massport was unfair? My first answer was that to be a professional writer was a life-long dream. I used to tell colleagues, even when I was a young assistant press secretary, that "someday I'd like to be another Beverly Beckham," a columnist who wrote on the *Herald*'s opinion pages. But I also real-ized in retrospect that both dissociation and denial played a big part. This was underscored when US District Court Judge Mark Wolf, a friend of mine and David's, invited me for lunch in his chambers to discuss my job search. When I told him about the *Herald*'s offer, he sat back in his chair, clearly surprised, and exclaimed, "Wow, that's a com-plete comeback." I smiled broadly. I wanted a "complete comeback," the promise inherent in his words, that I could regain who I once was, wrapping around me like a protective cocoon.

Mostly, though, it was the numbness, the dissociation accompa-nying PTSD, that had allowed me to continue to function normally, and also allowed me to keep a Berlin-scale wall between the words the *Herald* and *Globe* had published and my own feelings—anger, hurt, sadness, fear—about them. I knew the coverage existed, but it was "way down there" in that distant part of myself where I kept all the horror of 9/11.

After being at the paper for a couple of months, the furtive glances from other members of the staff as they walked by my open office door, like I was an exotic animal at the zoo, ceased. I learned the secrets of the tabloid's anachronistic word-processing system that was almost as old as me. I shared internet access at the office's one PC with three other people, along with a printer someone had brought in from home. My battered desk stood hard against cheap wood paneling and dented metal filing cabinets. Behind me, a large, dirty window with a bro-ken vinyl blind looked out on the crawling traffic of the Southeast

Expressway—a far cry from the skyline views and plush decor of my former offices in the State House and at Logan.

Each morning, after Shelly and I picked the next day's editorial topics, I worked the phones to get more information and perspectives from the same elected leaders I'd tangled with over politics and policy over the years. The afternoons were spent with my fingers poised on the keyboard, writing and erasing the green-glowing lettering that would represent the newspaper's view of pressing issues. When I nailed a headline, I laughed out loud as I sent it on electronically to copy editor Neil Cote.

"Amusing yourself, are you?" Shelly called out from her adjoining office.

"Yup!" I answered happily, reveling in the singular joy of finding the perfect word or turn of phrase.

I love it here, I thought one evening, as I tucked the proofs of tomorrow's editorial and op-ed pages in my purse. Besides the writing, the sense of being a player again at the center of city and state politics, shaping public policy, albeit on the other side of the pen, was exhilarating.

I began to believe Judge Wolf's assessment. A complete comeback was possible.

March 2003—Marblehead

"I'll be back in a bit," I called to David as I slipped my feet into brown Merrell loafers and pulled my winter jacket on.

It had been eighteen months since 9/11 and I was finally drawn to the sea again—to its beauty and comforting immutability. I no longer yearned for the waves to wash over me and make me disappear.

It was cold, but not the kind of cold that made me wince. More the kind that made me want to breathe deeply, to fill my lungs with fresh sea air.

The wind whipped my hair into my face. I hesitated at the end of my street, thinking I should go back and get a hat, but the sound of crashing surf, even from here, dissuaded me from turning around. The street that led to the beach was deserted, my neighbors likely huddling in their warm houses, crackling fires and warm tea warding off the chilly mist blowing off the water. As I moved closer to the beach, I could see the waves crashing through the covered promenade where, in calmer weather, I'd sit watching Jack devour an ice-cream cone among bathers seeking shelter from the summer sun.

The beach parking lot was completely flooded, and a police car with flashing blue lights was blocking access to the causeway that ran between the harbor and open ocean, connecting that spit of land called Marblehead Neck to the mainland. It was only then that I noticed the truck with the several telltale antennas—a TV-broadcasting truck— parked on the side of the road. Then I saw who was sitting behind the wheel.

"Hey, how ya doin'?" Stanley Forman asked, with a smile, his elbow crooked out the window. "How's the *Herald* treating ya?"

Before moving to Boston's ABC affiliate as a videographer, Stanley had been a Pulitzer Prize–winning photographer at the *Herald*. He also happened to be David's cousin, but I had known Stanley even before I met David since he had appeared, shouldering his camera, almost daily at the State House when I was the governor's press secretary.

As we both watched the water wash across the road in front of us, Stanley asked how I was liking the *Herald*. I told him that I was settling in, loving the work, and that I liked the people in the newsroom.

He said he had heard from his contacts at the paper about the turmoil my hiring had initially caused, but he advised, "Don't worry about it. It will pass. A newspaper staff is notoriously cranky. They'll get over it."

Stanley told me he'd checked in with some people he still knew in the *Herald*'s photo department and added, "It's not that big a deal, except there's this one guy, a photographer, whose father was killed in the World Trade Center. So that's tough."

"What?" I couldn't hide how stunned I was. I had no idea. The pho- tographers' office was right across the hall from mine.

Had I walked by him every day? I thought, my mind rapidly sorting through faces I'd come to see regularly in the hallway. *Did he think I was oblivious to his pain?*

I forgot that I was in the middle of a conversation with Stanley as my inner conversation raged and my sense of guilt, buried in the shallowest of graves, surfaced again. *Oh my God, did seeing me bring him more pain?*

And then this, the question that haunted me most of all: *Does he blame me?*

I'd feared running into a victim's family—in town, on the street, in a store, or even at my front door. I dreaded confronting their anger, their sorrow. Sometimes, when I'd get home late at night and I'd see a strange car parked on the street, my heart would begin to pound. I'd run to the front door as fast as I could. There was nothing rational about my fear. David would typically be right inside. If there were some stranger lurking, he'd hear me scream. But I wasn't only afraid of a stranger. I was afraid of meeting someone whose eyes carried the haunted look of pain that I saw constantly in my dreams. I was afraid to face their belief that I had a part in putting it there.

"Hey, you okay?" Forman called after me as I mumbled "goodbye" and walked away quickly, head down, back toward my house. A chill ran down my neck. I involuntarily shivered and clutched my coat tight as the damp wind swirled. I tried to ignore the contrast of the cold touching my skin with the warm throbbing in my wrists.

***

"Matt West." I determined that was the *Herald* photographer's name by asking discreetly around the newsroom. But I still didn't know what he looked like. I didn't have the courage to walk into the photographers' office and ask for him. My anxiety grew. I found myself constantly glancing up as photographers came and went from assignments. "Is that him?" "Or him?"

Some weeks later, in the early afternoon, I stood by the row of steel-gray bookshelves that lined the entrance to the city newsroom. I checked out the day's offering of "giveaways," typically books that had been sent in unsolicited by publishers hoping for a review. Sometimes there were promotional items like lotions or even candy or bottles of local wine, too, though those were scooped up quickly by *Herald* veterans who'd developed the same instincts as people who show up to yard sales before the posted hours.

I didn't see anything special that day and stood flipping through a galley proof of a novel. I noticed one of the *Herald* photographers standing next to me doing the same. I smiled at him, but got no response. *He's probably just focused on finding the right book,* I thought, though I could feel the tension building in my neck. Larry Katz, the *Herald's* movie reviewer, walked over.

"Hi, Matt," he said.

Was I imagining it, or did Larry glance my way and then look back at Matt? I panicked and fled to my office, ashamed I didn't have the courage to introduce myself.

I finally confessed to Shelly how I'd been agonizing over whether to approach Matt West. She and Wayne Woodlief, a veteran political reporter, suggested I ask Joe Fitzgerald, a longtime *Herald* columnist, for advice. Joe had been friendly to me in the past, and Wayne said he was close to Matt.

I learned Joe had written two columns after September 11 about Matt and his father. Peter West was only fifty-four when he died. He worked as a trader for Cantor Fitzgerald, the company that had lost more than six hundred employees when American Flight 11 hit the North Tower. Peter was a free spirit, Joe wrote, a daredevil of sorts, who rode a motorcycle, parachuted out of airplanes, raced vintage cars, and sucked every bit of adventure he could out of life. "The irony," Matt told Joe, "is that he took so many risks, but he was killed just by going into work."

The picture accompanying Joe's column showed a silhouette of Matt riding his father's motorcycle. I couldn't make out his features clearly, but it was obvious this Matt was not the one I had seen at the giveaway counter. I didn't know much more about what he looked like, but knew with heartbreaking clarity what he'd lost.

I asked Joe to pass a message on to Matt that I'd be willing to meet with him if he wanted to but that I also didn't want to intrude if he didn't.

Months passed. I don't remember Joe giving me a definitive answer about seeking out Matt. And I never gathered the courage to just walk into his office and look his grief in the eye.

CHAPTER FOURTEEN

A DUTY TO WARN

September 4, 2003—Boston Herald

I eyed the pile of newspapers I still had to read, five in all on a typical morning. I saved the *Wall Street Journal* and the *New York Post* for last, my two favorites. *I still can't believe I get paid to read newspapers every day,* I thought, smiling as I turned to the *Post*'s editorial page.

I picked up the phone on the first ring.

"Ginny, it's Joe."

I sat up straighter. Joe Savage, a former assistant US attorney, now had a downtown law practice. Since it was expected that Massport would be named along with the other airports, airlines, and security companies in litigation brought by some 9/11 families, I had been cautioned that I might be called to give a deposition. Before I'd left Massport, I'd hired Joe to represent me.

I hadn't heard from him in months. I leaned forward over my desk, one hand cradling my forehead, the other cradling the phone, an instinctive feeling of dread crawling up my spine.

"You've been sued," he said. "You've been named in a wrongful death lawsuit."

"What?"

I'd been sued? Not just the airport, but me personally?

My thoughts raced as I tried to focus on his words.

Joe related something about the plaintiff's legal strategy and the looming deadline of the statute of limitations. I couldn't take in what he was saying. Not a word of it.

Oh my God.

My worst fear had come true.

A family . . .

I could barely articulate the thought, even silently.

blames . . .

Oh my God.

. . . me.

I tried to conceal from Joe that I was crying. Shakily, I asked him the name of the family. "Abelman. Daren Abelman," Joe said. "He was on Flight 11."

Joe asked me to come to his office for a meeting in the next few days. I agreed and hung up the phone.

For a few minutes, I didn't move.

I couldn't move.

None of the angry letters or emails I'd received in the past two years were from people who indicated they had lost someone that day. So the "they" who blamed me after 9/11 had no real shape or identity as individuals. "They" were not left a widow or a young child without a father or mother because two airliners were hijacked from Logan Airport on my watch.

I moved slowly over to the computer, forcing one foot to take a step and then the other. I entered Daren Abelman's name into a search field.

As I started to read, I felt enveloped in silence, as if I were inside a sealed tunnel. No air, no light, no sound. Just him.

He was seated in 9B on Flight 11, I read. A flight attendant was being attacked by a hijacker farther up the aisle. The former Israeli military officer leaped up to defend her. Another hijacker was seated behind him. In row 10.

"A passenger had his throat slashed."

I could hear Ed Freni reporting this horrific fact on the morning of 9/11 in my office. A passenger. It was Daren Abelman. A father. A husband.

His wife is alone, I thought.

Wrongful death.

His two sons have no father.

Ed's voice: "A passenger had his throat slashed."

I read further that Abelman had been a very successful business-man. He and his wife seemed to have built a wonderful life. But now that life had been shattered. And his widow was asking a court of law to hold me responsible for it.

Am I? Could I have stopped them? The insistent inner voice of doubt gnawed at me. I felt a sudden, urgent, almost desperate, need to talk to Eva Abelman.

I'm not a monster, I would implore her, in my mind trying to meet her eyes. *I didn't know terrorists were going to attack us. I just didn't know. I am a mother, too. Please forg . . .*

My impassioned silent monologue stopped as suddenly as it had started. There could be no forgiveness for what happened to Daren Abelman.

And what if I am found responsible for his death?

His wrongful, horrifying death. His, and therefore the deaths of thousands of others?

I turned away from the computer screen. It was cold in the office, something I hadn't noticed before. I reached for my coat and left, not sure where I was heading.

Outside, I hailed a cab and called Jose Juves, the Massport media director. "Jose?" I said as calmly as I could.

"Yeah, what's up?" he answered.

I explained what had happened, my voice monotone.

"Well, you sound pretty calm, like you have it in perspective," Jose said.

"Yes, I do."

I didn't. I was in complete shock.

In a conference room at the law offices of Testa, Hurwitz & Thibeault, Boston

Sitting in Joe Savage's conference room sometime later, I had the sensation of observing the meeting as if I were at a great distance, like the room itself was shrouded in a thick fog. Dissociation was serving its purpose of self-preservation. Still, a phrase from the lawyers' conversation broke through. One lawyer was describing a recent meeting with the family's lawyer, a prominent Boston attorney, about the lawsuit. "We said to Joan, 'Are you going to try to take her house?'" he recounted.

My house! I thought, as my heart began to pound.

Literally and figuratively, since 9/11, my house had been both a refuge and the North Star I hoped to follow back to myself. When I started at the *Herald*, one published report noted that I'd been in "seclusion" in my North Shore home for much of the time since leaving Logan. While that was not strictly true, it was the one place where I felt shielded, and like some semblance of the person I used to be: a mom, a loved wife. There, I hoped I could find the rest of me someday.

I did not yet understand that was not possible, that the four walls of a home, of a self, could look the same on the outside while the inside was completely gutted.

The lawyers indicated that Massport's policy of indemnification, which assumed the legal liability of its employees, would protect my personal assets. Yet, I could tell they were truly surprised that I had been named individually as a defendant. Most of the lawyers' back-and-forth was trying to divine the legal strategy behind the move. "Not even the CEOs of the airlines or the security companies have been named," someone noted. Someone else offered a theory that naming individuals at Massport allowed some greater leverage down the road to secure a settlement.

"They're suggesting she had a 'duty to warn,'" Joe Savage said, as if "she"—me—wasn't sitting right there. "That she failed to warn the public about security weaknesses at Logan," he continued.

"Duty to warn."

Those three words were an immediate and powerful fertilizer for the seeds of doubt I carried in my conscience. One of my strongest skills had been my ability to draw media attention to an issue, to leverage that attention with policymakers, and to bring change. It's what I had done with great success as two governors' chief of staff. It's what I had done to advance the new runway project at Logan.

Yet, on the issue of problems with airport security checkpoints, I hadn't done this. There were reasons why I didn't. Legitimate reasons. The checkpoints were the responsibility of the airlines. They were regulated by the FAA. Security responsibility before 9/11 was clearly divided, and airport operators were not responsible for checkpoints. The airlines' trade group had balked at my simply trying to improve customer service; they would never have stood for overstepping on the checkpoints. But in the aftermath of the hijackings—in the aftermath of being sued—this sounded like a justification even to me, like an excuse for something that was inexcusable. I had a duty, they said. Did I?

CHAPTER FIFTEEN

THE RISING

September 6, 2003—Fenway Park, Boston

David and I approached the gate to Boston's Fenway Park. Our solemn demeanor was in stark contrast with that of the excited concertgoers around us. "Are you okay?" David asked, squeezing my hand.

I squeezed back but didn't say what I was thinking: Even in this throng of people—even with David holding my hand—I felt so alone.

"Here, from Pat," Shelly had said, smiling, a week or so before, referring to the paper's publisher, Pat Purcell. She thrust two tickets for the *Herald*'s private box into my hands. I had a feeling she understood my strong desire to attend a concert at Fenway Park had nothing to do with it being the first-ever concert held in the famed home of the Red Sox. What drew me was who was featured in it and the theme of his album: Bruce Springsteen on tour for his 9/11 album, *The Rising*.

I'd kept a poster of Springsteen on my bedroom wall in high school and in my dorm room in college, but, for the most part, I was a casual fan, not one who attended concerts and knew every song by heart. That changed after I read somewhere how *The Rising* had come about. I read that one day after the 9/11 attacks, Springsteen was seen in his native New Jersey. A motorist pulled up and rolled down his window. He said, "Bruce, we need you, man."

I immediately went out and bought the CD. I listened to it over and over again. "Empty Sky." "Mary's Place." "The Rising." Each word, each melody offering an assurance that the loss wrought by 9/11 was both universally felt and understood implicitly. I even had pressed a copy of the CD into Anne MacFarlane's hands when I met her for another lunch. "Listen to this," I told her. "He understands."

"Bruce, we need you, man."

I needed him. Somehow, in some way, I hoped his songs would speak to me, that hearing the lyrics firsthand would assuage the loneliness, my sense of isolation from most people's experience of 9/11.

"You've been sued for wrongful death."

I needed him.

As David and I entered the *Herald*'s skybox, a handful of people were already there. I noticed a young, muscular man with curly brown hair standing near the window. He seemed to be studying the ball field below.

"I'm Matt West," he said, reaching out his hand, first to me and then to David. It was only then that I noticed the camera equipment placed next to him on a chair.

I tried to hide my surprise. For months, I had wanted to—and feared—meeting him. But seeing him here was completely unexpected.

David moved away to give us a few minutes alone. I said quietly, "I'm sorry about your dad."

"Thanks," he answered, and turned to gaze out at the field below.

"This must be a hard week for you."

"It's no different than any other. There's just more attention on it." His pain didn't follow any calendar or anniversary. It was with him always.

Mine, too, I wanted to say, but I didn't want him to think I equated my grief with his, so I said nothing.

David rejoined us and we made small talk about how he'd snuck the camera with a telephoto lens into the box, a coup for the *Herald*'s coverage of the event. The concert was about to begin so we moved to the seats outside. Matt settled on the stairs, his camera aimed at the stage below.

The haunting picking of the guitar strings. The minor key. Of all the songs Springsteen could have started with, it was this one that brought me immediately back to Logan that 9/11 morning: "Empty Sky."

As he sang about the "empty impression" in the bed, wanting a kiss from his lost lover's lips, wanting an eye for an eye, and waking up to an empty sky, I found I, too, could hardly breathe.

"Two planes are off the radar."

"A passenger had his throat slashed."

"Can you give the official okay to open the family assistance center?"

I heard Springsteen sing of blood on the streets and in the ground. But I was no longer at Fenway Park.

The second plane.

The ball of fire.

Black smoke.

Bodies falling.

"They are suggesting she had a duty to warn."

"Abelman. His name was Daren Abelman."

I laid my head on David's shoulder. Tears freely flowed down my face. Nearby, Matt aimed his camera, trying to capture an empty sky.

CHAPTER SIXTEEN

A PROMISE

September 7, 2003—Marblehead

David and I had decided not to tell anyone about the pending legal action. It hadn't been picked up by the media and we didn't want it to be. We particularly didn't want our parents to know, sparing them the worry over what it might mean. While it didn't appear that a successful suit could have tangible financial ramifications for me, given the airport's legal indemnification policy for employees, its emotional consequences would be devastating. So when my friend Ann suggested she and I go out one evening, for what had become our tradition of ending the summer season with a drink on the porch of her waterfront club, I agreed. A night of not talking about the lawsuit seemed like a good idea.

As we entered the wide veranda, I saw the familiar tan wooden rocking chairs, gently worn by the sun and sea air, set along the edge of the porch. Ann and I claimed two, facing the changing colors of the sky. The swells in the harbor moved the boats, up and down, up and down. I unconsciously rocked back and forth in unison with them, sipping cold chardonnay, and talked to Ann about our kids and the school year ahead, her youngest son and Jack both entering their last year of preschool.

A good number of people had come onto the porch to enjoy the fading warmth. Ann stood to say hello to a friend talking with a group nearby. I followed her and introduced myself to an older gentleman also standing there, out of courtesy rather than any real desire to engage in conversation. He leaned toward me, the music making it hard to hear, and asked me to repeat my name.

"Ginny Buckingham," I said, more loudly this time.

"9/11," he responded.

It sounded like a declaration, as if we were playing a word association game and that was the first thing that had come to mind: "Ginny Buckingham—9/11."

I took a protective step backward. If the man noticed, he didn't give any sign.

"We owe you our thanks," he said. "You did a very good job."

He touched my arm as I answered, softly, "Thank you. That's very kind of you to say." I moved away toward Ann, who had sat back down in the rocking chair.

"Ginny Buckingham—9/11." Whether this linked identity was suggested in kindness as this gentleman meant it, or in anger or sorrow as the plaintiff who sought some recognition of her loss in court, it was an association I so desperately did not want that I almost felt a physical aversion to it, like my body was rejecting a new organ, my own cells attacking who I had become.

The sky was now a mix of vivid pink and slate blue. As I looked at it, I was struck by the jarring juxtaposition of my internal pain and such exquisite beauty. I forced my gaze away and nodded when Ann offered to get us another round.

I had spent years, since I came to Boston at the age of seventeen, building a "Ginny Buckingham" whose name would be associated with good things, with strong things. "Hard worker." "Smart." "Successful." "Competent." "Loving." "Good." Yes, "good" above all else. Through the black-and-white prism of my Catholic upbringing, I accepted a clear paradigm of good versus evil. I endeavored endlessly to fall on the right side. Yet would a "good" person have failed in her duty to warn? Would a "good" person have failed in her fundamental obligation to keep the people using the facilities under her purview safe?

David was already asleep when Ann dropped me at home. I restlessly tossed and turned in bed, the linked identity "Ginny Buckingham—9/11" transformed into an internal debate of "good or evil?"

Which was I? I had spent hundreds, possibly thousands, of hours wrestling with that question, but had come no closer to an answer.

I held my right hand up in front of my face. I couldn't see it clearly in the darkened bedroom, but I knew what I was looking for was there. It had always been there. In the exact middle of the back side of my right hand. A beauty mark. It was perfectly round, dark brown, set against a sea of white skin.

When I was about ten years old, I stood in front of my mother's light brown wooden bureau, distinguished from my father's by its large attached mirror. There, in the lacquered tray where odd things collected—pens, a safety pin, a memorial card—was a tube of her foundation makeup. Gently at first and then more vigorously, I rubbed it on my right hand. I was trying to completely cover the beauty mark. I wanted to see what my hand would look like without it. I wanted to be the girl without the hand that had a beauty mark. And even then, as I focused on rubbing the foundation even deeper, I knew there was more to it. I wanted to be someone else. Someone other than the seventh of eight children in a stress-filled, cash-strapped home. Someone recognized as "good" for more than simply not causing her parents any trouble.

I don't want to be a person who was sued for wrongful death. I don't want to be the person being held responsible for the death of two little boys' father. My silent pleas rang in my head.

I want to erase that person. I want to cover her up.

Ginny Buckingham—9/11. I want her to disappear.

September 9, 2003—Devereux Beach, Marblehead

I drove past my street and turned into the beach parking lot. David thought I was still at a meeting downtown. I glanced at the clock: 9:00 p.m. Maddy and Jack should both be asleep by now.

I noticed a handful of other cars as I parked at a slight angle, my headlights pointed toward the water. I had expected the beach to be empty at this time of night. I glanced around. In one car, the driver appeared to be alone. In the other, I saw a couple turned to each other talking, enjoying the romance of a deserted beach on a late-summer evening.

I was here with a different purpose. Could I do it? Did I really want to? There was a certain peace to it. To having the waters close around me. Yet, the water was cold. I involuntarily shuddered. Would it hurt?

I looked around. No one seemed to be paying any particular attention to me. No one was going to stop me.

Could I do it?

Jack. Maddy. I pictured their sweet faces. Imagined their eyes gently closed in sleep.

Would they be better off without me? Without my brokenness?

Springsteen's voice seduced me from the car's speakers. He seemed to be calling me, reminding me I couldn't breathe with an empty sky. *Ginny, put the car into drive. Press the accelerator.*

Make the pain go away.

I turned the key to start the car.

Could I have stopped 9/11? There was nothing I could have done, was there?

I looked toward the water. It was high tide. Maybe twenty yards of beach to the edge of the surf.

Even if I couldn't have stopped it, some people would always think I could. Ginny Buckingham—9/11.

Springsteen sang on, taunting me.

Jack. Maddy. They didn't do anything wrong. How could I do this to them?

"If I listen to those words again, I will," I said out loud, fiercely squeezing my hand around the gearshift. The moonlight on the water seemed to have drawn a path for me to follow. "Go," I ordered myself. "Go."

Drive over the sand straight into the waves until the car was enveloped, until the car was swallowed, until I could not breathe.

Go home. Go home. In my mind, I fought back. *Pull out of here and go home.*

Jack. Maddy.

Like pulling my body out of quicksand, it took all my strength to put the car in reverse, press the gas pedal.

I entered the house. It was dark except for the light in our bedroom and the light in the bathroom at the top of the stairs. I looked in at David. He still had his glasses on. A book was tumbled forward on top of the covers, evidence that he had fallen asleep while in the middle of reading a sentence. Maddy was in her crib, her daisy-shaped night-light glowing steadily in the corner. I could hear her breathing as I passed her door on the way to Jack's room. It struck me that her breathing was deep, in and out, even and effortless because that is what you do when you are alive, breathe in and out without thinking about it. I was conscious of my own breathing as I entered Jack's room.

He was sprawled in the middle of the bed, boyish arms and legs claiming every corner of the mattress, stuffed animals spilling out all around him, as if he had dropped down asleep in the middle of a game. I gently placed Special Doggie, the favored black-spotted Dalmatian, on the rocking chair and lay down next to him. The movement disturbed him for a minute, and he squirmed until he found a soft spot in the pillow, then settled back into a deep, peaceful sleep.

I brushed back the lock of blond hair that had fallen across his forehead and reached for his hand. Gently I stroked his palm with my thumb. "I love you, Jack," I whispered. I didn't want to wake him up.

But I also wanted him to know I was here, that I want to stay here.

I need something to hold me here, I thought. Like an anchor holding a boat as it is tossed in the waves.

I suddenly realized an anchor was right in front of me.

"Jack, I will never leave you," I whispered to him. "I promise I will never leave you."

Deep down I understood that it was a promise I could not keep, not really. We all leave one another sometime. But I wouldn't choose it. I couldn't choose it. No matter how desperate I was to escape my own torment. No matter that every time I took a step forward, it seemed I was pushed back two. No matter if the future held only pain. I would not choose to die.

"I promise."

September 11, 2003—Marblehead

On the second anniversary, the sky was a beautiful, cloudless blue, like in some cruel version of *Groundhog Day*. I lay in bed under the covers, wishing I could stay there. I wondered if the rest of my life would be like this. Simply surviving from one anniversary to the next. Until I didn't.

Stop. Jack. Maddy.

I finally got up and robotically went through the morning ritual. Showering. Drying my hair, picking the kids' clothes out, packing their lunches.

I had finally told David last night about my struggle at the beach. He tried to be supportive. But the idea of wanting to end life was so foreign to him, I wasn't sure he believed me.

"Don't you want to see the kids grow up?" he asked. "Don't you want to dance at their weddings and hold your grandchildren?"

I tried to explain that wasn't the reality of the choice. It wasn't between living a life of joy or accepting oblivion. It was living a life of unbearable pain or oblivion. David's blue eyes radiated concern and kindness, but they also betrayed a hint of frustration. We quickly fell into the pattern of our recurring argument.

"It wasn't your fault, Virginia," he said. "If you had made people wait in long lines and take off their shoes to get through security, they would have put you in a straitjacket and taken you away." He repeated the same points he had made many times before.

"I was blamed for it," I said, my voice rising. "I'm not making it up."

"That was just politics," he said.

We went on like that for a while, each clinging to our own certainties. Anger and stubbornness kept me from voicing this silent plea: *Please understand, David, how afraid I am that I am not strong enough to choose a life of pain.* But because I stayed silent, he did not understand. And because he didn't urge me to speak—didn't really want to know—a distance between us grew.

As I helped Jack into his jacket, I sensed I was clinging to the promise that I made to him like a life ring.

I will never leave you.

"C'mon, honey, time to go to day care." I picked Maddy up, carrying her on my hip as I took Jack's hand and led him to the car.

The allure of putting an end to the pain was like a powerful magnet. It drew me toward it even as I desperately tried to pull myself away. I wondered if this was how suicide happened. Was it something you thought about and carefully planned? Or was it a powerful impulse you couldn't overcome?

The other magnet that was drawing me on this anniversary was Logan Airport. A couple of weeks earlier, Jose, who was still Massport's media director, had suggested I come to the memorial service in the airport chapel. "People want to see you," he said.

The invitation appealed to me. After the lawsuit notification, I'd started to feel being there might be an answer to my loneliness. Maybe at Logan, among the people who had been through 9/11, too, I would find some secret to how they did it. How they got out of bed in the morning and went to work and raised their children.

How they "moved on."

As I neared the Logan chapel in Terminal C, a TV news crew waiting by the entrance stirred to life. "Hey, isn't that . . ." I heard one of the crew say, but I didn't slow down long enough for anyone to shoulder a camera.

I quickly found a seat near some of my former colleagues, whispering a quiet hello, as the service began. Representatives of United and American Airlines stood at the front of the darkened chapel and read a poem written in memory of their airline colleagues, called "American, United."

As they spoke about the shock of that September morning, I reached back to the pew behind me and grasped the hand of Betty Desrosiers, who had headed the Massport Care Team tending to families after 9/11.

Betty and I tightened our hold on each other, openly weeping, as the poem described the surreal turn our collective love of aviation took, in just minutes, at the hands of hate.

As the poem ended, the airport chaplain, Father Richard, said he would conclude the service by playing "God Bless the USA" by Lee Greenwood.

Oh no, I thought. *I can't do this.* As comforting as it was to be with Betty and my other former colleagues, I suddenly wanted to flee, conscious I was just yards from the gates where passengers and crew had boarded United 175 and American 11.

When I had first heard the Greenwood song at the airport memorial service in the Delta hangar, its words felt like permission to finally cry, to grieve like other Americans, away from the TV cameras and the questions about whether I would resign and what grave mistakes Logan had made that allowed the hijackings. But now it was simply a reminder that that moment, standing arm in arm with airport and airline colleagues, may have been the last time I didn't feel alone.

As soon as the first notes of the song played from the chapel sound system, the music abruptly stopped. Father Richard played with the dials on the equipment for a minute before concluding he couldn't get it to work. I closed my eyes briefly in grateful acknowledgment of the reprieve.

When the service ended, the attendees exchanged muted goodbyes.

As I turned to walk down the aisle toward the door, a voice piped up from a back pew. It was a voice I was starting to know well.

"I want to say something," the diminutive woman said loudly, instantly commanding the attention of everyone still standing around in the chapel.

Anne MacFarlane stepped forward down the aisle.

I had told Anne I was coming to the service and asked her to come, too, but I never expected she would. She had gone on extended medical leave from her own job at Logan after Marianne's death.

"Listen," she said firmly, as if she were gently scolding her own children, "I want all of you to go home, take off those dark clothes, and have a party." Then looking right at me, she added, "That's what Marianne would have wanted."

Her words themselves seemed to gently illuminate the chapel, as people moved toward Anne and hugged her. I shook my head in wonder. In trademark Anne fashion, she was reaching out and comforting us instead of accepting the comfort that was hers.

I walked down the aisle and stopped to give Anne a warm hug. "Thank you so much for coming," I said. I then turned to say hello to Father Richard, who was standing nearby. For a moment he didn't recognize me, which I attributed to some recent weight loss.

"Oh Ginny," he said, "you look terrific. How do you feel?"

"Scared," I answered, looking him straight in the eye. He was clearly surprised by what must have seemed like an odd response.

"Scared? Scared of what?"

"Of getting through 9/11," I answered.

"We already have," he said.

I hadn't. I would keep trying.

I promised.

PART III

CHAPTER SEVENTEEN

"THEY FOUND MARIANNE"

November 5, 2003—Downtown Boston

WBZ-TV reported live that I was testifying before the 9/11 Commission investigators. I didn't find out until later that someone had tipped them off. I didn't see any media in the lobby of my attorney's firm on Oliver Street in downtown Boston. I pressed the button for the elevator. *You can do this, Virginia,* I silently encouraged myself.

When I had learned weeks earlier that I would be questioned, I was as grateful as I was anxious. The panel had been authorized by Congress to investigate how the attacks had been planned and executed. I wanted to help them in their work. I wanted to answer their questions if I could. I wanted to tell them what security issues I felt were not being addressed, even now. Yet, I also knew, whatever their findings, theirs would be the definitive word on whether lapses in airport security had allowed the attacks.

Their judgment would be my judgment day. They would determine whether Logan Airport, and therefore I, as its leader, was to blame.

As I rode up in the elevator, I mentally reviewed the questions the lawyers said I might be asked. In meeting after meeting they had grilled me, carefully, without suggesting the correct answer, on time frames for the events at Logan before and after 9/11 and on the context within which I'd made certain decisions. I nodded, taking in what they said, but knowing all the while I had a different objective for the outcome of the interview.

I wanted to be exonerated.

"You shouldn't look at this as a chance to be exonerated," one of the lawyers cautioned me during a prep session, as if reading my mind. "Just answer the questions they ask you."

The elevator doors opened and I stepped onto a marble-floored hallway. A secretary pointed me toward a nondescript conference room, and Joe Savage, my lawyer, greeted me and gestured to the seat at the head of the table. I glanced out the window at the rooftop of a neighboring building as the Commission's staff assistant—"Lisa Sullivan" it said on the business card she handed to me—set up the audiotape equipment. Joe and Chris Moore, the attorney from a large Boston firm that Massport had retained, sat on one side of the table, directly across from the two 9/11 Commission investigators. Sullivan gave me a slight smile as she turned on the recorder. The small kindness calmed me, as if she were saying, *I have a name. I know you do, too. You are not just a subject of our inquiry, simply a voice to be recorded, but a person.* Her acknowledgment, whether real or imagined, strengthened my resolve, and I looked now directly at the investigators.

The two, John Raidt and Bill Johnstone, were part of Team Seven, the 9/11 Commission's aviation and transportation security subteam, they explained. Raidt noted they had the security clearances necessary to discuss classified information. My attorney nodded and agreed that if I had any classified information to share, I would indicate it to them.

As the lawyers and investigators conferred, I looked around the conference room. The walls, the tables, even the other people seemed to have faded to an even more nondescript shade of gray. Except for the investigators and me. We stood out in vivid color. As if we were superimposed on the bleak background. As if we were the only ones in the room.

I shifted in my seat, keeping my hands in my lap.

The interview would be conducted in three parts, Raidt explained. First, it would focus on security prior to 9/11. Then their questions would turn to the day of the attacks itself, he said.

The second plane.

The ball of fire.

The black smoke.

Stay here, Ginny, I admonished myself, recognizing the familiar feeling of leaving my own body in response to stress. Unlike descriptions I'd read of people in near-death experiences hovering over themselves in an operating room, the "leaving" caused by the dissociative aspect of PTSD was more like having your essential humanness—your personality, your humor, your love, your sadness, most of all your sadness—removed from your body so that all that was left was a shell, looking to the casual observer like a regular person, but unconnected to anyone, including itself. Did my dissociation project some sort of mask, I wondered later, making me, in the investigators' eyes, seem uncaring? When the reality was that I didn't know if I could stop from breaking down if the mask slipped?

Stay here.

Raidt was saying they also wanted my thoughts on how to improve security going forward.

"We realize that many of our questions will be asked with the benefit of hindsight," Raidt added.

I nodded and took a deep breath. I absorbed the word he'd used—"hindsight"—without yet absorbing how its application to Logan's, and therefore my, responsibility for the 9/11 attacks was a foundational ingredient for the blame heaped on me.

I cleared my throat.

"I know setting the record straight as to Logan's role in this pales in comparison to the enormous pain and suffering of so many families." I could feel the investigators' and lawyers' eyes on me. I didn't dare look over at Massport's or my attorney as I began to speak again. "But I do hope that this process can resolve the fact that there was unfair blame brought to bear on me and on the hundreds of hardworking Logan employees.

"Your job is to get to the truth and be objective," I added quietly. "I am hopeful that your work will lift the burden off those of us who were at Massport."

The two investigators had no visible response to my statement. I had no way of knowing if they even understood what I was asking: *"Please answer the question I've been asking myself for more than two years—Am I to blame?"*

The investigators asked if I was ready to move on to their questions. I nodded.

First, Raidt asked me to outline my background and the mission and responsibilities of the agency.

I detailed my past career in state government. I noted that because Massport operated infrastructure that was critical to the state's economy, there were community challenges over growth, pointing to the thirty-year runway battle as an example. "My job was to set the agenda. To drive the leadership team," I said.

As the interview continued, I felt my cheeks redden. Their questions, one after another, seemed drawn directly from the pages of the *Boston Globe* and *Boston Herald.*

"Did you know . . . ? Why didn't you do . . . ? What about this . . . ? When were you going to . . . ?"

"We were where we should have been on security and were pushing the envelope by going beyond FAA requirements," I said, referring to Logan's instituting of a requirement, from as early as 1998, that all airport personnel submit to fingerprinting for background checks. "Security responsibility at the time was trifurcated," I continued, trying to be firm without being defensive. "The FAA was in charge of the airspace, Massport was in charge of the airfield and public spaces, and the airlines were responsible for their operations areas and security screening." I pointed out that I felt this division of responsibility was the major problem with pre-9/11 security and the reason I had pushed to federalize aviation security after the attacks.

"Everyone at Massport recognized that security and safety were the core of our mission. Before 9/11, our major concerns were runway safety, perimeter security, and bombs, especially a bomb-carrying car at the entrance to a terminal.

"When I was called to testify before Congress it was about air traffic delays and customer satisfaction issues. That was what was driving public-policy debate that summer."

Even as I said this, I felt the familiar despair in the pit of my stomach. What I said was true—no one was focused on the threat of terrorism before the attacks. Not Congress. Not aviation leaders. Not me. But this rationale was no match for the acute stab of regret I felt in response to their continuing questions: "Did you know . . . ? Why didn't you do . . . ? What about this . . . ? When were you going to . . . ?"

Emotion tightened my throat. "If we had realized the degree of vulnerability, God dammit, we would have told Congress to turn security over to the federal government."

The interview turned to my recommendations for the future.

"Focus security on stopping bad people, not weapons," I said, seeing as I spoke the knife disguised as a pen that Detective Robichaud had shown me in the operations center in the days after the attacks.

"Treat airport security as a national security issue with a true federal system of information sharing. Now all it looks like is putting a different logo on the jacket of the screener, so it's basically the same system with different people operating it. If three thousand people dying didn't shake up the establishment, the responsibility for security needs to be put in the hands of people that understand the threat."

The interview wrapped up shortly after.

"I thought that went well," one of the attorneys said as we made our way down the hall when it was over.

"Well?" I exclaimed incredulously. "Every question came straight out of the newspapers!"

Any hope I'd had that the Commission would bring some national perspective to the conclusions they'd draw about Logan's—about my—culpability sank with the elevator I took back down to the ground floor.

An hour or so later, completely depleted, I sat at my desk, staring at, without reading, the word processor in front of me. *I should have gone home*, I thought.

The phone rang. I looked at it, trying to summon the will to lift the receiver. "Hello," I finally said, my exhaustion evident.

"They found Marianne."

It was Anne MacFarlane.

"What do you mean?" I asked quickly, sitting up straight, my full concentration now on her voice.

Anne said her son George had gotten the news from a buddy in the local police department. Some of Marianne's remains had been identified in the massive forensic recovery effort still ongoing in New York.

"I don't even know what they have—it could just be a fingernail," Anne said, the shock evident in her flat, emotionless tone.

I tried to take in what she had said, and I searched for an appropriate response.

"Do you feel relieved at all?" I finally asked. "Does it help?"

"Well," Anne paused, "all along, I think part of me just thought she had amnesia. I figured one day she would walk through the door and say, 'How ya doing?'"

I didn't say anything. I didn't know what to say.

"I'm going to need to lean on you for a while," Anne said, filling the silence.

"I'm here," I answered.

Although we continued to see each other only intermittently, our relationship was another life ring we hung on to in the years following the hijackings. We didn't always talk about 9/11 on these visits, but we usually did. And with Marianne's picture still prominently displayed right above her heart in the pendant, it sometimes felt like she was there also.

I hung up the phone, the worry about the 9/11 investigation's outcome now interwoven with Anne's unexpected news.

***

That evening, the small TV was on in the kitchen as I was preparing dinner. I was just about to change the channel from a sports network to the news when a song being played at the start of a NASCAR race stopped me, remote poised in midair.

It was Lee Greenwood. As he evoked losing everything, starting over, and his gratitude for America, I squeezed my eyes shut, and again, I was back in the Delta hangar at Logan, just a few days after 9/11. The lyrics to "God Bless the USA" echoed across my kitchen.

I was vaguely aware of Maddy tugging at my hand. "Mama, uppie." Maddy was insistent now, reaching her arms up to me. "Uppie, Mama."

I picked her up and held her on my hip, wiping my cheeks so my tears wouldn't upset her. Maddy loved music and she was delighted to have a better vantage point to see where the melody was coming from.

"Clap, Mama, clap," she said, giggling and clapping her dimpled eighteen-month-old hands in time with the music. I couldn't help smiling and then clapping along as she had commanded.

"Yay, Mama!" Maddy cheered.

***

"Mommy?" Jack interrupted my brooding thoughts the next day as we drove by King's Beach in nearby Swampscott on the way to do an errand.

"Mommy!" He yelled louder because I was not answering.

"*Shh*, my little love, you'll wake Maddy." I could see in the rearview mirror that she had fallen asleep, the sucking of her pacifier the only movement she made.

"Mommy, I have to tell you something."

"What, honey?"

"I love you deeper than any ocean."

I looked up, startled by his earnestness.

He was not done. "More than there are shells on the beach. More than anything on earth."

I smiled, as he pronounced our planet as "earf," not able to make the "th" sound yet.

"Mommy," he said, as if he feared that somehow I didn't believe him. "Everything I'm telling you is true."

It was possible, I realized then, to physically feel, not just sense, a shift in how you hold a painful memory. It was possible for one memory to move over rather than disappear to make room for another.

"That's how healing happens," Andrea said, when I told her the two stories.

A song that evoked a grief-filled airport hangar would also bring me the moment of holding my baby girl on my hip and dancing with her in the kitchen. The sight of the ocean, once a pleasure, but now a reminder of painful questions to which I had found no answer, also a reminder of a son's love, so deep, it was deeper than the ocean.

"I'm here," I said silently to Jack and Maddy as I looked in the rear-view mirror and blew him a kiss. "I'm here."

It was what I had told Anne, all I could offer to her, just as I had promised it to Jack that night I came home from sitting in my car at the beach.

"That's how healing happens."

I would try to hold on to that promise, too.

CHAPTER EIGHTEEN

MAYBE GOD CRIED, TOO

November 2003—Sharon, Massachusetts

I was here.

In a synagogue. I'd hardly set foot in any house of worship since 9/11, never mind a temple. And I had never been to a bar mitzvah. Yet, unexpectedly, the surroundings felt comfortable. Familiar.

The cantor began to sing. I closed my eyes and let the music wash over me, wondering if it would mean anything, not only because the language was foreign, but because music, just like prayer, had ceased being a way to God for me.

My mother had been the soloist in our parish church, her rich soprano a central part of the congregation's worship. While it had embarrassed my teenage sensibilities to see her standing behind the lectern each Sunday morning, it also taught me to pray through music.

"Turn to Me."

"Here I Am, Lord."

"Be Not Afraid."

Sometimes, through these favorite hymns, I felt God was speaking directly to me. Telling me He would be there if I needed Him.

As the unfamiliar music and Hebrew chanting filled the sanctuary, I thought back to a recent session with Andrea. She had, uncharacteristically, asked me about my relationship with God.

"I wouldn't typically talk about religion," she said, "but I have a gut feeling that the way you'll get back to yourself is through God." I was surprised by the comment, although I had once described to her the many times I would sit in the chapel at Boston College as a young student and think I felt God's presence.

"Go home tonight and write God a letter," she urged. "Just see what might come of it."

Our friends' son Jordan took his place next to the rabbi as the Torah was placed in front of him.

On the ride home from the appointment with Andrea, I thought about her suggestion. There was a chill in the damp air. A light rain had begun falling. I realized I was shaking, not with cold but with anger. The feeling made me uneasy. Who was I to be angry at God?

David squeezed my hand and said he was getting up to help his father, Marvin, who suffered from Parkinson's disease, join the rabbi and do an honorary prayer, called an *aliyah*. I nodded, still lost in thought.

Where was God on 9/11? I asked myself, maneuvering through the traffic as I neared home. *Did He just stand by and watch as the hijackers boarded the planes?*

It started to rain harder. I turned the windshield wipers to the next setting. My fury seemed to rise in concert with their increased tempo. *Did He choose to do nothing while the pilots' throats were slashed? While people jumped from the towers rather than burn to death?*

With a bitter shake of my head, I knew exactly what I would write in my letter. Four words. My response to the falsehood, "turn to me and be saved." My answer to the lies, "be not afraid" and that He'd carry me "on eagle's wings."

No. He. Will. Not. I wanted to scream it out loud.

"Dear God," I would write. *"Fuck You."*

***

David sat back down next to me and drew my attention back to the front of the temple. "Jordan looks great," he whispered as our friends' son began to read his Torah portion from the—altar?—I knew that wasn't right but I didn't know what to call it.

When Jordan finished, the rabbi stepped down from the bimah—that's what David said the raised platform was called, in a whispered answer to my question—and began telling the congregation the story of God destroying Sodom and Gomorrah. "Abraham challenged God," he said. "He urged God to stop." The rabbi moved toward the group of Jordan's Hebrew-school classmates. "What do you think Abraham is doing?"

A student ventured an answer. Then the rabbi provided his:

"Perhaps," he said, "Abraham was trying to teach God. Perhaps, we not only learn from God but also God learns from us."

The rabbi suggested, "God is evolving. Abraham is trying to teach God that if He is looking for perfection, for justice, he will never find it in flawed human beings. He will never find it on earth."

I looked up at the pitched roof above me, the wooden crossbeams providing an illusion of support, and then glanced at the stained glass window behind the bimah, so reminiscent of a church. David could sense my disquiet, and he leaned over. "Are you all right?" he asked.

"I might be," I answered and finished the thought silently. *I might be if this turns out to be true: on 9/11, maybe God cried, too.*

CHAPTER NINETEEN

A WARNING

March 2004—Singer Island, Florida

The sun and the sand wrapped themselves around us. Carrying pails and shovels, chairs and blankets, juice boxes and snacks down to the beach each day was a gift, a needed respite.

It was far too windy for an umbrella. I securely tied a sun hat underneath Maddy's chin and settled Jack's baseball cap more tightly on his head. We sat as close to the water's edge as the tide allowed. David got to work helping them dig a big hole to fill with buckets of water.

There was a yellow flag flying at the public beach a little to the right. I tried to remember what each color meant from a sign I'd seen that morning posted by the Juno Beach Park fishing pier. Purple for marine life in the water. Red for no swimming. Yellow for? Caution. "That's what the yellow flag means," I told David. This beach was prone to riptides and each time Jack or Maddy moved to the water's edge to fill their buckets, David followed them. He wouldn't let them venture beyond their ankles in the roiling surf.

I was struck by David's seriousness as he stood guard over them. Jack built walls of sand and Maddy promptly smacked them down with her shovel. I noticed David's hands loose by his sides, his knees bent. He was at the ready should a wave sweep up and threaten them. Caution, the yellow flag meant. We had been warned.

＊＊

I liked vacationing with my parents, except for the TV. It was on constantly. If my mother wasn't insisting on watching "Wheel," as she called the game show *Wheel of Fortune*, then it was *Jeopardy* with Alex Trebek. Occasionally, I'd try to join her, yelling out the answers, doing best in categories having to do with current events or literature, almost always forgetting to phrase my answer in the form of a question. Most evenings, though, David and I sat on the balcony with the sliding glass door closed after putting the kids to bed, trying to block out the noise and read our books.

Once the game shows were over, it was Dad's turn and he immediately switched the channel to Fox and *The O'Reilly Factor*. The host's voice carried through the glass door.

Giving up any hope for peace and quiet, I went inside to sit with my father. I immediately regretted it. The show was about 9/11 and the presidential campaign. *No matter where I was, there is no escape*, I thought, with a flash of anger, which quickly dissipated into disquiet as the show continued. Someone was saying that US Senator John Kerry, the presumptive Democratic nominee, must have known weapons were able to get through the checkpoints at Logan because an undercover Fox News investigation before the hijackings had spotlighted it.

That's ridiculous, I thought angrily, standing to leave the room.

"Did you know?"

I thought I must have misheard the question.

"What?" I asked, turning back to my father from the threshold of the bedroom.

"Did you know?" he asked again. His voice wasn't accusatory, just curious. But it stung me like an arrow dipped in poison. I didn't bother rushing to my own defense. I didn't bother explaining that the checkpoints were not even under Massport's control, that under federal law, they were the responsibility of the FAA and the airlines. That the small knives brought on board weren't even necessarily illegal.

"Yes," I simply said, "everyone knew."

But no one knew what counted. That a man in a cave thousands of miles away would send nineteen hijackers to America not just to sneak knives aboard but to use the planes themselves as weapons. There was no yellow warning flag for that.

***

We were scheduled to fly home the next day. The airport was just twenty minutes away. On the short ride there, the Florida sun, which the day before had warmed and soothed me, seemed too bright. It exposed the ugly concrete highway and blight of strip malls, one after the other. I felt exposed, too, the doubts I had sought to quiet about 9/11 back in force, fertilized by my father's question.

We had to return the rented minivan. "It will be easier to pull up to the curb and check all our bags," David suggested, before returning the rental car.

"Okay," I agreed. David dragged the bags one at a time to the sky-cap, while I waited behind the wheel in the car with Jack and Maddy. Then we switched, so I could check us in. I showed the skycap my license and he carefully examined it, questioning why my name was listed as "Buckingham-Lowy" but my airplane ticket only said Lowy. Then he asked whether all the bags were mine.

"No, one is my husband's," I answered.

"Well, then, I need to see his identification, too." I explained that David was in the car with the kids and couldn't leave them alone to bring over his license.

"Where?" he asked.

"Right over there." I pointed out the car and was surprised when the skycap stepped out from behind his desk and walked over to the driver's-side window.

"May I see your ID, sir?" he asked.

"Thank you," I said, touching his arm. "Thank you for being so careful."

"Yes ma'am," was all he said, smiling. He was doing his job. He had been warned.

***

Flying down to Florida, I had barely noticed being in the terminal, having been consumed with keeping track of the kids, balancing my purse and carry-on luggage on the back of Maddy's stroller, making sure Jack went to the bathroom one last time, checking that I had drinks and snacks for them on the plane.

But now my emotions careened between rage and despair. *Will I ever be free of these questions?*

Why didn't I do something? If my own father could wonder, how can I expect others not to?

The crowd of travelers swelled and receded around me. I felt trapped in one of those funhouses at a traveling carnival. Everywhere I looked there was a mirror image of me that was grossly distorted.

As we got close to our gate, I finally noticed the TVs suspended from the ceiling. They were tuned to CNN and the 9/11 Commission hearings. David saw that I was openly crying and took the handles of the carriage. "I'll wait here, honey," he said. In the ladies' room, I saw that my eyes were red and swollen, and a lady standing at the next sink offered me some Visine drops. I shook my head no and mumbled that I had contacts in, but I was calmed by her kindness.

When I emerged, David said, "They called our flight."

"Go ahead," I said. "We'll catch up." I handed him two boarding passes. Jack pulled on David's arm.

"C'mon, Daddy. C'mon, let's go."

I was several people behind them on the jet bridge and had to stop near the aircraft door to fold up Maddy's stroller. There was a bit of a backup of people entering the plane, and I shifted Maddy on my hip, wondering what the problem was.

As I got closer, I saw David standing by the cockpit. I was momentarily confused. What was he doing? "Oh my God," I whispered, as I followed David's gaze, my eyes filling with tears again. After 9/11, security protocol had virtually ended the once-common practice of showing children the controls in the cockpit, yet there Jack was, wearing the captain's hat of the Delta pilot, staring in awe as the captain pointed to the dials and numbers.

"You should take a picture," a nearby flight attendant said to me. "This doesn't happen much anymore."

As I fastened the children's seat belts and listened to the flight attendant's instructions about securing their oxygen masks in case of emergency, I asked another passing attendant if she'd get me the pilot's name. "Captain Eddie Briggs," the attendant wrote on a scrap of paper that I tucked in my purse. I leaned my head back against the back of the seat. Captain Briggs knew how vulnerable he was every day, and surely his life had changed irrevocably, too, the day thirty-six of his aviation colleagues were murdered. Yet he chose to do what he'd always done. He chose joy in the simple act of exposing a child to aviation's wonders.

A choice.

That's what I was making every time I let people's questions drive me to despair. I was choosing to accept a paradigm that fit neatly into the evening news, a cable TV talk show, and our political culture. Someone had to be held responsible for 9/11. Someone had to have missed something, an expired visa, flight school irregularity, a gathering in a foreign land, a weakness in security checkpoints. We couldn't simply be vulnerable. Life this fragile. Terrorists that evil. It had to be someone's fault. But why? Andrea once pointed out that human beings are the only creatures aware of their own mortality. "We are mortal, and we are conscious of it," she said. Did blaming me allow people to feel safer? Did they sleep better at night with the belief that if one person was responsible and that if that one mistake could be remedied nothing like this could happen again?

As we pushed back from the gate and began taxiing to the runway, my view out the window widened.

Like Captain Briggs, I could choose differently. I reached for Jack's hand and wrapped my arm around Maddy.

The engines roared to life and we gathered speed, lifting off the ground, headed home.

CHAPTER TWENTY

"APOLOGIZE"

March 24, 2004—Washington, DC

Former Clinton/Bush Administration chief counterterrorism adviser Richard Clarke testified before the 9/11 Commission and expressed his regret: "Your government failed you, those entrusted with protecting you failed you, and I failed you."

Spring 2004—Boston Herald

Back from vacation, a few mornings after Clarke's apology, my day started out like any other. I read the papers. Checked the wire. Jotted down potential topics for the day's editorials. I took a sip of coffee and grimaced. It was cold. I started to get up to walk down the hall to the publisher's office suite to grab a refill. The phone rang.

"Hello," I said.

The man on the line claimed to be from Lynn, a city northeast of Boston. "Is this Virginia?" he asked.

"Yes, can I help you?" I answered, already impatient, wanting to get on with the morning, wanting another cup of coffee.

"Did you get my letter?" he asked. "It had a lot of vulgarity in it. Sorry about that."

"If it had vulgar language in it, I would have thrown it away," I responded curtly, moving to hang up the phone. It wasn't unusual for me or my editor, the two female names on the paper's masthead, to receive letters, some crude, some even from state or county prisoners.

"So, when are you going to apologize for 9/11?" I put the receiver fully back on my ear.

"What?"

"When are you going to apologize so this city can move on?"

Silence.

He didn't say anything else. He was waiting for an answer.

I couldn't speak.

I could hear him breathing.

I tried. "I . . ."

I stopped.

He said nothing. Waiting.

I tried again. "I don't . . ." My voice cracked. "I have . . ." I breathed in. "Nothing . . ." *Breathe, Ginny.* "To . . . apologize . . . for." I was barely speaking above a whisper.

Still silence.

Except for his breathing.

I hurriedly hung up the phone.

That man never called back, but at least once a week, there was a voice mail message waiting for me when I got into the office. I knew who the message was from even before I dialed the code to retrieve it. "Virginia," it typically began, "this is Anne from South Boston." That was how she identified herself. Simply by her first name and the Boston neighborhood she lived in. She always called after she'd read the morning paper, but never when I had already arrived at work. Not once had she agreed with the editorial opinion of the paper, but it seemed my occasional bylined columns particularly goaded her. "I don't understand how you could have written what you did," she'd say, a pleasant Irish lilt belying the coming ugly turn she always took in the message.

"But then again, I don't know how you live with yourself, given what you've done."

Sometimes, I'd have a nightmare that took place, not in the sky, but under the water. I'd be underneath the surface. It was dark at first, then lighter, the sun penetrating the water as I swam closer. Drawing me toward it. Just as I was about to break through and fill my lungs with a deep breath of air, I was pushed back under.

"Apologize," he demanded. "I don't know how you can live with yourself," she said.

I was pushed back under.

***

Over the next several weeks, the 9/11 Commission hearings received around-the-clock media coverage. During this time, Shelly asked me to watch President George W. Bush's live press conference in case he made news we should editorialize about for the next day. I knew he would be asked about the Commission's progress. I sat alone in the conference room, waiting for the inevitable.

Reporter: "Mr. President, to move to the 9/11 commission, you yourself have acknowledged that Osama bin Laden was not a central focus of the administration in the months before September 11th. 'I was not on point,' you told the journalist Bob Woodward. 'I didn't feel that sense of urgency.' Two and a half years later, do you feel any sense of personal responsibility for September 11th?"

I couldn't believe he was being asked that. The three TVs lined up on the dusty metal stands in front of me all had the same shot, the camera tight on the president's face. His expression betrayed no hint the question surprised or bothered him. Back when he and Governor Weld served together, sometimes they would join late-night poker games in the hotel where national governors' conferences were held. Maybe this was his so-called poker face. Or maybe, unlike me, he harbored no doubts. *"Apologize."* I could still hear the breathing on the phone line. My hand tightened on the pen as I waited for the president's answer.

"Let me put that quote to Woodward in context, because he had asked me if I was—something about killing bin Laden. That's what the question was. And I said, you know, compared to how I felt at the time, after the attack, I didn't have that—and I also went on to say, my blood wasn't boiling, I think is what the quote said. I didn't see—I mean, I didn't have that great sense of outrage that I felt on September the 11th. I was—on that day, I was angry and sad. Angry that al-Qaeda—I thought at the time al-Qaeda, found out shortly thereafter it was al-Qaeda—had unleashed this attack. Sad for those who lost their life. Your question, do I feel—yes?"

The reporter repeated, "Personal responsibility for September 11th?"

"I feel incredibly grieved when I meet with family members, and I do quite frequently. I grieve for, you know, the incredible loss of life that they feel, the emptiness they feel. There are some things I wish we'd have done, when I look back. I mean, hindsight's easy. It's easy for a president to stand up and say, now that I know what happened, it would have been nice if there were certain things in place."

"Hindsight." That word again. As painful as being the target of blame in the immediate aftermath of the terrorist attacks was, I got no satisfaction from national figures being held up to similar scrutiny. Seeing the same faulty expectation of perfect hindsight applied again simply punctuated my despair that perspectives hadn't changed much in three years: someone still had to be blamed.

Nor was the sense of isolation I had felt when I was singled out assuaged now that others were being scrutinized. It was intensified. The media spotlight had moved on. There were no news trucks driving up and down my street, no microphones being stuck in my face. I was not part of the 9/11 narrative, yet I still felt utterly broken, like a rusted-out car on a front lawn that neighbors grew so used to, they no longer saw it when they drove by.

Around the same time as the president's press conference, National Security Advisor Condoleezza Rice testified before the 9/11 Commission. Her testimony was being aired live on the radio as I pulled into the *Herald* parking lot. I sat with the engine running, riveted by her recounting, stunned when she added, "I've asked myself a thousand times what more we could have done."

Oh my God, so have I, I thought, *thousands and thousands of times.*

But how could she sound so certain that the answer was that she could not have done anything? Would I ever stop seeking certainty about my role? Could I live with anything less?

***

I don't know if this next call was exactly in this time frame, but in my mind I connect it, another life ring thrown to me.

I was at my desk and received a call from Joe Landolfi, a friend I'd worked with in the State House.

"Hey, Joe, how's it going?" I said.

"Listen," he began, "this is going to sound a little strange, but a woman who lives in my town tracked me down because she knows I know you. She wants to talk to you. Her name's Lauren Rosenzweig. Her husband died on one of the planes on 9/11."

I felt my back stiffen. I tightened the grip of my hand on the phone. "What does she want?" I asked.

"I don't know," Joe answered. "And I didn't want to give her your number without asking you first. I see her around town and she's still very emotional."

I found myself shaking my head, even though Joe couldn't see me. I couldn't tell him, without sounding a little crazy, how afraid his call had made me.

"Can you try to find out what she wants, Joe?" He agreed to try.

Several days passed.

When he finally called back, the sound of his voice caused my heart to pound.

"I talked to her. She asked me to pass along a message."

I swallowed and responded, "Yes?" urging him to continue while at the same time wishing I could hang up so I didn't have to hear what she had to say.

"She said it's been on her list of things to do since 9/11." Joe's quiet voice was edged with kindness. "She said to tell you that she knows you did all you could." I silently began to cry.

I marveled at Lauren Rosenzweig's ability to reach beyond her own pain to comfort someone else, especially someone whom she could have easily seen in a harsher light. I struggled for days to express my feelings in a note to her and finally kept my message simple, too: "Thank you."

Her simple message cradled me like a gentle wave that then lifted me on its crest so I could see the horizon more clearly.

Thank you.

CHAPTER TWENTY-ONE

GANESH

In everyone's life, at some time, our inner fire goes out. It is then burst into flame by an encounter with another human being. We should all be thankful for those people who rekindle the human spirit.

—Albert Schweitzer

April 2004—**Boston Herald**

Why did I meet her then, just when I needed her most?

I had noticed Raakhee Mirchandani in the *Herald* newsroom many times. She was hard to miss. A diamond stud piercing her nose. Long, curly hair framing funky, dark-rimmed glasses. The Yankees T-shirt the young Indian American features writer from New Jersey sometimes wore to taunt the die-hard Red Sox fans on the copy desk.

Still, I didn't actually meet Raakhee until she burst into my office one afternoon.

"Shelly here?" the young woman asked, rushing through the door, looking for my boss.

"No. She's out for a few days," I answered.

Raakhee wasn't gone five minutes before she was back. "I'm so upset, I just have to talk to you," she said, pulling up a chair near my desk without being asked to sit down. "Look at this," she pointed to the headlines of the papers on my desk. Splashed on the front page of both the *Herald* and the *New York Post* in similar large print was this headline: "Savages." Below the headline was a picture of four American civilian contractors who had been killed in Iraq, their bodies dragged through the streets, mutilated, and burned beyond recognition.

"Who are we to call them savages?" Raakhee exclaimed. "We've never had our land invaded, our homes taken. We have no idea what they've been through."

Raakhee, whose family, I learned, emigrated from India, went on to say she felt "Americans have no idea what it's like to have foreigners occupying their land." She described how her grandmother had lost her home in 1947 when her homeland was partitioned into Pakistan and India.

"I swear I was not even this upset when my cousin died in the World Trade Center," Raakhee said, caught up in the heat of the moment.

I inhaled sharply. "I'm sorry about your cousin. I didn't know," I said.

"Yes, it was terrible. My aunt and uncle are devastated. He was their only child." Raakhee said they had taken his ashes back to India, to place in the Ganges, a holy river.

We both fell silent, but somehow it was a comfortable rather than awkward silence.

"How do you feel about me working here?" I finally asked, summoning the courage I hadn't found yet to ask the same question of Matt West.

"I was happy for you," Raakhee answered. "You're only one person. You deserve good things to happen."

An intense, close friendship grew out of that first conversation. Some fifteen years in age separated us, but our relationship was completely equal. We both gave and received advice and, often, just laughed at the quirks of working in a big-city newsroom. I cherished each walk we took in the South End neighborhood outside the *Herald*, me counseling her on whether she should move back to New York, her assuring me that one day my despair over my role on 9/11 would lift. During an evening spent at my house watching a political debate and eating the Indian food she'd introduced me to from a nearby restaurant, Jack found a hug and a warm lap in his new friend, "Rocky."

"Hey, Ginny," Raakhee called to me one day as I walked through the newsroom on the way to the copy machine. "I have something for you."

I crouched down next to her desk as she rummaged through her bag.

"Here." In her hand was a small glass object. It was blue and seemed to glow from within. She handed it to me.

The glass was slightly warm from her touch. I stood up and turned it over in my hands.

"What is it?" I asked.

"It's Ganesh," Raakhee said.

I looked more closely at what I could now tell was the frontal outline of an elephant figure, carved as if it were sitting on its haunches. About the size of the palm of my hand, the back and bottom of the glass figure were flat. I set it down on the edge of her desk. It still seemed to glow from within, the light transforming its blue color from aqua to deep navy.

I looked at Raakhee questioningly. "My grandmother gave it to me," she said. "Ganesh is the Hindu god for overcoming obstacles. I don't need it anymore."

Raakhee smiled gently and placed Ganesh back in my hands. "I want you to have it."

She didn't need it anymore, but she knew I did. When I got home that evening, I placed Ganesh on my bedside table, cherishing its glow and, more so, the warmth of being deeply understood.

June 2004—Marblehead

It was a beautiful early-summer day. A birthday party at my friend Kate's for her son was in full swing. Jack had his shirt off and was running through the sprinkler. The pleasant chaos of five-year-old squeals mingled with the chatter of parents sitting on blankets and lawn chairs. I leaned back on the rope hammock, Maddy sitting on my lap, and gently rocked her back and forth while watching Jack play. I thought about a conversation I had with him earlier that day.

Jack, at times a serious little boy, had become curious about death. As I helped him get dressed, he asked me: "Is everyone afraid of dying, Mommy? Is it true you turn to dust?"

"Well, your bones do," I answered, "but your soul goes to heaven to live with God, where you get to eat ice cream for breakfast, lunch, and dinner." Despite my own questions of faith, I instinctively tried to assuage Jack's fears with the same promise of heaven I had been brought up with, albeit with the added twist of a sweet-treat-filled menu.

"You know what I'm going to wish for?" Jack said, apparently unsatisfied with this rosy description. His blue eyes reflected his widening smile.

"What, my darling?" I asked, pulling on his white socks.

"To start life all over again."

"Wow. That's a great wish!" I said, giving him a squeeze and kiss on the forehead. *Just like your dad,* I thought to myself, marveling as I said my first prayer of thanks in many years that David's enthusiasm rather than my deepest moments of despair seemed to be defining our little boy.

I looked over from the hammock as the gate to the backyard swung open. I instantly recognized the man walking through it. Josh Reznick, his unusually styled thick white hair unmistakable, was the editor of a string of local newspapers, including in East Boston, which covered Logan operations most closely.

"What began at Logan on Buckingham's watch is a disaster whose outcome will follow her the rest of her life. . . ."

His harsh editorial had felt like a wave knocking me off my feet shortly before I resigned.

What is he doing here? I abruptly stood up, holding Maddy protectively, as if to shield her. I looked left. Right.

Even in the vast backyard, there was nowhere to hide.

Hide. That's what I wanted to do. From him, from his words.

"She is being swept away . . . like the salmon which swim upstream . . ."

Swept away. Like a bottle tossed in the sea. Tumbled apart over time by the fury of the waves.

I handed Maddy to David and fled through the kitchen. Other mothers were there, helping to bring out more juice boxes and plates for the birthday cake. I avoided their glances and climbed the stairs to the master bedroom on the second floor and shut the door. I sat down in the rocking chair in the corner, tucking my legs protectively underneath me. My arms hugged my chest as I rocked the chair back and forth, staring blindly out the window.

I had had no idea that Reznick's daughter was in the same preschool class as Jack. I had never seen him at pick up or drop off and so never made the connection. His unexpected arrival at a place where I felt safe, a close friend's home, made me feel exposed and vulnerable. No matter where I went, no matter how much time had passed, 9/11 seemed to follow me.

I have to go back outside, I thought, disgusted at myself for crumbling so easily.

Hold your ground.

My bravado faded as soon as I reached the backyard and noticed Reznick chatting with some of the other parents. I fled again, taking Maddy into the blow-up moon bounce where kids were jumping and tumbling, emitting squeals of laughter. She sat on my lap, the movement of the other children gently bouncing us up and down. Maddy giggled at the motion. Through the mesh netting, I could observe the party but not be observed, and I thought that I would spend the rest of the afternoon with this protective vantage point. But Maddy had other ideas and wanted to get out.

"Okay, honey, let's go," I said.

As we climbed out of the narrow opening, Maddy reached her arms out to David, who was standing nearby. I looked up and saw Reznick coming around the side of the structure. I didn't know whether he was purposely seeking me out, but he didn't seem surprised to see me. He reached his hand out and said, "I'm Josh Reznick."

"I know who you are," I answered as firmly as I could manage. I kept my eyes locked on his. My fear was suddenly replaced by a low boiling anger.

"You owe me an apology," I said, the words surprising me, as if they came from someone else. Someone tougher. Braver. Someone like who I used to be.

Reznick looked uneasy as his unmet hand dropped back to his side.

"What you wrote was far crueler than anything the *Globe* or *Herald* or anyone else did," I said. "I'm a writer now. Words matter."

Reznick objected. "C'mon, what I wrote wasn't that bad."

"Go back and read it," I challenged him. "I think you'll agree that you owe me an apology. If you don't think so, fine, but I think you will."

The next week, I attended a ribbon cutting for a massive renovation project to make a state-of-the-art YMCA in East Boston out of an old railhead shed in the shadow of Logan Airport. The event had brought out many of the well-known anti-airport activists to celebrate the community milestone. I greeted some of the people I'd gotten to know from community forums on Logan operations. One longtime activist seemed surprised to see me. "In the paper this week, it said you would never be seen in East Boston again. I guess they were wrong."

I was puzzled by the reference. *Why would the local newspaper say that?* I wondered. Then I put two and two together. I had heard Reznick wrote an anonymous column in the paper with gossipy, sometimes snarky items, and one of the items that week recounted our meeting at the birthday party. Instead of apologizing, he must have decided he was in the right.

Years later I ran into Reznick again at a local coffee shop. We said polite hellos and exchanged pleasantries and inquiries about each other's children. "You know," he said, "I'm not really into covering those politics anymore," referring to Logan and East Boston. It wasn't an apology. But I no longer demanded one. I had come to see Reznick was partially right. His words hurt because they rang true. The events of 9/11 did sweep me away as he predicted, though the aftermath didn't so much "follow me" as become part of me. The question for me was finally becoming this: What could I do with that reality other than simply carry it?

CHAPTER TWENTY-TWO

FOOTNOTE #1

July 13, 2004, 7:00 a.m.—Boston Public Garden

Boston's famed public park was nearly deserted. I saw only the occasional student or commuter making their way along its winding paths. Some paused momentarily, as I usually did, to appreciate the mallard ducks congregating on the side of the lagoon. The swan boats were still tethered to the dock. I walked slowly toward the garden's southwest corner.

The Garden of Remembrance, the official memorial to the victims of 9/11 from Massachusetts, had been dedicated in a private ceremony the day before. The governor and the mayor had spoken. Tom Kinton, my colleague at Logan, had stood discreetly in the back of the crowd.

I approached the stone bench flanking the side of a granite crescent. As if she were still standing there, I could clearly see the face of a little girl with long dark hair, pictured in the morning paper, holding a perfect white rose. Her dad, the account said, had been on one of the planes. Somewhere, carved in the granite, was his name along with the 201 others with connections to Massachusetts.

I began reading each of the names, which were listed in alphabetical order. Slowly, left to right. I tried to hold each name in my mind, to pay each victim honor. *Were you that little girl's father?* I asked silently as I read one name. *Who were you?* I silently asked another.

I took a step closer to the crescent as I reached the *M*'s.

Marianne MacFarlane, I read silently. Anne had told me she wasn't up to coming to the dedication, so I knew she hadn't been here the day before. I bent down. With my forefinger, I traced each letter of Marianne's name. When I finished, I kissed two fingers and gently pressed them on the carved letters. "From your mom," I said quietly. I continued to read each name, pausing again to press my palm against the name "Daniel Trant." I had never met him but knew he was the brother of a former deputy director of Massport, Matt Trant, who had served before my tenure. *I'm sorry for your loss, Matt,* I said silently.

My eyes swept back across the names. "I'm so sorry," I mouthed silently. I repeated those words over and over again. My dark glasses hid my eyes, but the heaving of my shoulders couldn't hide the sobs that were now wracking my body. "I'm sorry." I spoke to the 202 names etched in the granite, to the little girl clutching the white rose, to every family member who had stood in this same place just the day before. "I am so, so sorry."

What did I mean? Was I apologizing, as the caller to the *Herald* had demanded, for something I felt responsible for? Or was I expressing my despair that I knew there was nothing I could have done to stop their deaths but desperately wished I could have? Try as I might to discern my own meaning then, I couldn't. I only knew those words came from a place inside as elemental as the instinct to draw breath into my lungs, my sorrow swirling like mist into the shape of the face of a little girl holding a white rose.

July 22, 2004—Boston Herald

The TV was on in Shelly's office. Coverage of the live press conference to release the findings of the 9/11 Commission was about to begin. I sat, frozen in my chair, which I'd moved into her doorway so I could see the TV.

This is it, I thought. *Now I'll know the answer.* Andrea had tried to warn me in a recent session not to place so much emphasis on the Commission's findings.

"They could come out either way," she had said. Her caution did no good. The report's possible conclusions hung over me like a dagger, as their official word about the methods and strategy of the 9/11 hijackers would publicly define my guilt or innocence, whatever the reality. I had nodded as if I agreed with her, although I didn't.

In a few minutes I will know whether I'm to blame, I thought as the two Commission chairmen took their places behind the press lectern.

"Will you run over to Barnes and Noble and get us a couple copies of the actual report when this is over?" Shelly asked, as casually as if she were asking me to pick up a copy of the latest State House report on transportation funding. Thousands of copies of the report had been shipped to bookstores across the country with strict orders to keep them sealed in boxes until the official release this morning.

"Sure," I answered, endeavoring to mimic her professional demeanor.

As the press conference concluded, there was still no mention of Logan Airport's role. *I still don't know,* I thought, fearful and frustrated as I hurried to the bookstore and back to the *Herald* clutching two copies of the softcover book.

I handed Shelly her copy and sat at my desk, opening mine to chapter 1, entitled "We Have Some Planes." While factual, the report had been purposely written like a chilling nonfiction account of a horrible crime to make it more readable. I swallowed the same feeling of nausea I'd had hearing some of those same details in my Logan office three years before. Still, as I read through to the end of the chapter and the details of the hijackings, I saw no mention of security flaws at Logan.

I suddenly remembered one of the Commission's chairmen commenting on the thoroughness of the Commission's investigation during the press conference. "There are more than seventeen hundred footnotes," he'd said.

I quickly flipped through the report. The footnotes were organized by chapter.

"Oh my God," I said under my breath, my heart pounding.

I couldn't believe what I was reading: "Notes to Chapter One. Though Logan was selected for two of the hijackings (as were both American and United Airlines) we found no evidence that the terrorists targeted particular airports or airlines. Nothing stands out about any of them with respect to the only security layer that was relevant to the actual hijackings: checkpoint screening."

Oh my God, they did it. Tears ran down my cheeks.

The 9/11 Commission didn't have to make a special point about its conclusion on Logan security to detail the movements of the terrorists, but it did. I thought back to my interview. "Your job is to get to the truth and be objective," I'd said. "I am hopeful that your work will lift the burden off those of us who were at Massport." That they did so in the very first one of seventeen hundred footnotes was likely simply the result of following the chapter-by-chapter format, but its placement seemed like an exclamation point on the initial flood of relief that coursed through me.

I read and reread the conclusion of the footnote: "They simply booked heavily fueled east to west transcontinental flights of the large Boeing aircraft they trained to fly that were scheduled to take off at nearly the same time."

"So, you've finally been exonerated, eh?" assistant *Herald* city editor Jose Martinez quipped as I made my way to the copy machine at the front of the newsroom.

"Exonerated." The word, the act I'd longed for and never thought I'd hear had finally been uttered. I had a preplanned lunch that afternoon scheduled with former governor Paul Cellucci, and I could see the relief on his face when I told him the news. I knew he worried about me, and I wanted to answer his relief with my own. But I couldn't. I didn't feel anything. I was numb. The exoneration offered in the footnote triggered an immediate dissociative response. I didn't understand why until later that evening when I called David on the way home. He, too, had been relieved, almost elated, when I called him earlier in the day and read the footnote. Now, he repeated how happy he was, and it was like he pulled a pin out of the grenade of my explosive rage.

"Why?" I screamed into the phone. "Why did I have to go through this? Why did I have to get blamed?

"It's not fair," I screamed louder, sobbing. "It's not fair." I don't remember what David said in response; I think he just let me scream and cry until I was depleted. Empty. And yes, relieved the Commission came out the way it did. Relieved, yet broken, utterly, still.

August 6, 2004—**Boston Herald,** *the publisher's dining room*

I slowly pushed open the door. The editorial-board meeting wasn't set to start for another fifteen minutes, but I knew the two people we would interview were already there.

"Ken, I don't have to attend the meeting, I understand," I'd said a few days earlier to the *Herald*'s editor, Ken Chandler, when I'd learned two members of the 9/11 Commission were scheduled to brief reporters and editors on their findings.

"Why wouldn't you attend?" he asked, his British accent conveying a mix of the skepticism, humor, and thoughtfulness that I'd come to know during his tenure at the helm of the paper.

"It might not be appropriate, given my role at Logan," I answered.

"Well, you probably know more about it than anyone else, so I think you should be there."

Fred Fielding and Jamie Gorelick were seated at the table and looked expectantly at me, perhaps assuming I was there to simply welcome them or offer water or coffee.

"Hi, I'm Ginny Buckingham." I could tell my name didn't trigger any recognition. "I wanted to come in and introduce myself before the meeting," I began.

Now they looked a little puzzled.

"I used to run Logan Airport," I said. "I just want to thank you for your painstaking investigation. It means a lot to me and to the people I worked with at the airport." I didn't reference the first footnote, but I thought from her softening expression that Gorelick understood.

As the interview was set to begin, several reporters, the publisher Pat Purcell, Ken, Shelly, and other senior editors took their places around the table. A photographer clicked away as one reporter posed this question: "So why was Logan chosen?" I looked quickly from the reporter to the two commissioners, and then down at my notebook. It was the right question to ask, no matter my presence in the room.

"We found no evidence that Logan was chosen for anything but logistical convenience."

I kept my head bowed so no one saw the tears pricking the corners of my eyes.

Someone else asked about early reports that additional planes had been targeted.

"Part of our job was to dispel myths," Fielding said. Gorelick caught my eye and smiled.

Myths. Surely, I had held on, as tightly as my most vocal critics, to the myth that had I been smarter, older, more experienced, somehow I could have prevented the hijackings. Would I be able to let the myth go now? Was this official recognition going to be enough to help me move on at last?

CHAPTER TWENTY-THREE

"THE LITTLE CHAPEL THAT STOOD"

August 2004—Lower Manhattan

Seated in the back of the cab, I pressed the button to lower the window for some fresh air. With my right hand, I felt around in my purse. I was reassured when my hand closed around the statue of Ganesh, the glass cool to the touch, my finger stroking the outline of the elephant-god.

The cab pulled to a stop.

"Is this where you want to get out?" the driver asked.

"Yes," I answered, handing him the fare.

A massive metal fence at least ten feet high surrounded the site on the opposite side of the street.

I waved off a hawker trying to sell World Trade Center memorabilia. I crossed the street and moved toward the fence but had to pause while a group of tourists posed for a picture in front of bouquets of flowers that had been laid on the sidewalk and stuffed into the holes of the fence's metal grid.

What are they doing? This isn't some tourist attraction, I thought, with a flash of anger. But I quickly reconsidered. *People should come here. Take pictures. Remember.*

I finally stepped forward. I approached the fence, which was covered in most places with some kind of matting, impeding a clear view. I found an opening and pressed my face against the cold metal.

A void the size of a small canyon spread out beneath me. It was crawling with construction machinery. Far across the void, I could see a battered staircase, the "survivor's staircase" that had been used by some who had escaped the towers to reach the street level from the World Trade Center plaza.

The void was mirrored in my body. In my head. I pictured the terrified people streaming down the stairs. I saw the clouds of dust, the darkness, the fire. My eyes widened. The void. A mirror image of what I had become.

It was so noisy from the work of the backhoes and cranes that I put my hands over my ears. There had been no resolution among New York leaders and the owners of the site about what would go here, so the activity still involved just cleaning, clearing.

After a while, I walked to the left, along the fence. I wanted to find Ten House, the first station that responded on 9/11. Six of its men had been killed. *That must be it,* I thought as I neared the end of the fence line, passing what appeared to be a spontaneous memorial to the first responders, police and fire badges from all over the country posted on a wall.

By a small side door was a brass rendering of the six who died that day. I considered knocking but couldn't bring myself to lift my hand. Seeing the faces of the men who died and reading their names jarred me out of the shock of finally seeing Ground Zero. Weeping openly, I walked around the corner. There was a large glass window facing the street. I could see a couple of firefighters standing there.

"Thank you," I mouthed when they noticed me. "Thank you."

One of them gestured toward the side door. When he opened it, I opened my mouth to speak but nothing came out. He seemed to understand.

"Is this the first time you've been here?" he asked.

I nodded.

"Where are you from?"

"Boston," I choked out in answer, nearly sobbing now.

"Well, thank you for coming," he said, reaching for my hand.

"Thank you, thank you so much for what you did," I said and squeezed his hand as he turned to go.

I paused by the outdoor chessboards that dotted a nearby park. Old and young, men and women, and a handful of children were at the tables, intent on their games, seemingly paying no mind to the enormity of what happened across the street. Similarly, a steady crowd of shoppers streamed in and out of the busy clothing store nearby, their arms laden with bags.

I was puzzled by the nonchalance of the people going about their daily routines around Ground Zero. *What is their secret?* I wanted to know. *How can they live their lives beside such horror and not have it consume them?*

I walked another block to Fulton Street. I saw the wrought iron fence before I saw the building I sought—"The Little Chapel That Stood." I knew St. Paul's was a historic church, once attended by George Washington, but I was there to try to feel another part of the 9/11 story.

I was there to try to feel.

Despite its proximity to the Twin Towers, the chapel had survived completely intact, even while gray ash blanketed its graveyard that day like a freakish fall snow.

The black wrought iron fence was empty now. But I walked alongside it and tried to envision it as it was right after the attacks. Covered with pictures, paper, homemade posters of the missing. And on the spikes, the shoes and boots of the firefighters who had rushed to the scene, hurriedly exchanging their footwear for protective gear, thinking they'd claim their civilian shoes later.

A man was selling cold waters at the edge of the stone steps that led to the door. I took one gratefully and drank nearly all of it down at once.

St. Paul's had become a refuge in the days and weeks after the attacks for rescue workers and volunteers, who gathered there for hot food or coffee. At one point, the historic pews held podiatrists instead of penitents to treat the aching feet of first responders.

I paused inside the door. The chapel was slightly darkened and hushed like I would expect a church to be. Immediately to my left was a folding table holding the first of a series of displays from the disaster's aftermath. Among the memorial cards and snapshots, I spied a piece of lined loose-leaf paper like I had used in grade school. The image on it looked familiar. I leaned forward for a closer look.

It's Marianne, I thought, and breathed in, stunned. Someone had written on the paper "United 175. Always Remember." It was underlined in thick black marker.

Like seeing a friend in a room full of strangers, the picture of Anne's daughter at first surprised me but then put me at ease. I looked over at the center of the chapel. Large banners hung from the upper balconies. They had been sent from all over the country in a show of support, made by a church, a Boy Scout troop, one, seemingly, from a whole town. "Our prayers are with you" was written on one. "Thank you" on another.

I slowly walked from one display to the next. They ringed the entire chapel, each bearing the small remembrances left by the loved ones of the lost. It was unbearably sad, but I couldn't stop feeling a strange but persistent feeling of companionship.

I reached the last display. Next to it was a small gift area. I purchased a video made about the volunteer effort and, impulsively, reached for an illustrated children's book about the chapel's role in the 9/11 response.

Maybe I'll read it to Jack and Maddy someday, I thought.

"Did you see the place to leave a note?" the volunteer manning the register asked. I followed her pointing finger and walked to a small room at the back of the chapel. There, set on an easel, was a thick pad of paper, like that used in a corporate meeting room to record participants' ideas. It reminded me of the blank white wall of paper set up on the Boston College library plaza on the first anniversary of 9/11. Like I did that day, I pressed the marker against the white paper. I wrote the same thing I did then. "Make meaning. Find Joy. For Jack, Maddy, and Marianne."

I hesitated for a few seconds.

Do I deserve it?

At first tentatively, and then more firmly, I pressed the marker to the paper.

Make meaning. Find joy. For Jack, Maddy, and Marianne.

"And me," I added.

And me.

I pushed open the heavy door to the outside and breathed in the sharp New York air. *I was wrong, all this time,* I thought. *I was never alone at all.*

Later that same evening—Upper East Side, Manhattan

The party on the rooftop deck with a view of the East River was well underway when I came to the top of the spiral staircase. I surveyed the scene, knowing almost every person I saw from past campaigns. It was a beautiful evening, and I accepted a glass of chardonnay.

The official reason I was in New York was to cover the Republican National Convention for the *Herald*. My old boss, former governor Bill Weld, had moved to Manhattan and was throwing this party, ostensibly in my honor, but really just as a good excuse to gather his former staff and operatives together.

I moved from group to group, chatting about the convention, and the latest political news of the day.

I didn't tell anyone where I'd been that day. The alcohol was doing its job of clothing the sharp emotions in a gauzy haze. It was making me the Ginny Buckingham they had always known. Smart. Politically insightful. Successful. And this: the Ginny Buckingham who had moved on from 9/11.

The next day—A Manhattan video production studio

"Hey darlin', how ya doin'?"

Stuart Stevens greeted me with a warm hug and a kiss on the cheek. A Mississippi native, Stuart had produced the ads for all the Massachusetts campaigns I'd worked on and now was on President George W. Bush's reelection team. At the party the night before he'd invited me to come to the studio where they were editing the convention video that would introduce Bush before he addressed the delegates.

I settled on a stool behind Stuart and other members of the video team.

"Recognize that voice?" Stuart asked.

I listened closely.

"It's Fred Thompson," Stuart said, relating how easy it was to work with the actor turned US senator who was narrating the video.

"Watch this. Have you heard Ashley's story?"

I shook my head no as a picture of a young girl, maybe twelve years old, appeared on the screen. Her face was burrowed into the crook of President Bush's arm, his chin resting on her hair. Compassion and concern were etched in the lines of his face as he held her tight.

Ashley Faulkner's mother, Wendy, was killed on 9/11. The president was making a campaign stop in 2004 in Ohio where the Faulkners lived. Ashley went to see him, as she and her mom had done four years before. As Bush greeted the gathered crowd, a friend of the Faulkners told him, "This young lady lost her mother in the World Trade Center." The president turned to Ashley. "I know that's hard. Are you all right?" And he took her in his arms.

"He's the most powerful man in the world and all he wants to do is make sure I'm safe, that I'm okay," Ashley later said.

Stuart was busy telling the technician where to cut the video and mix in sound. He didn't notice how quiet I'd become.

It reached me. That's the only way I could describe what happened when I saw the picture of President Bush holding Ashley Faulkner. It reached the self who was pushed behind the wall of dissociation the moment I heard the words "Two planes are off the radar." It reached the person shattered by being sued for wrongful death, the person who hadn't "moved on" from 9/11 and never would. It reached the person desperately seeking exoneration, forgiveness, and someone to "keep me safe" from the trauma of being blamed. It reached me and left me aching at the realization I might never find those things. It would be many more years after I first watched that video before I understood its ultimate lesson was finding this: the closing scenes show the president on the pitcher's mound at Yankee Stadium, readying to throw the first pitch in a World Series game, but more, delivering a message of strength to the wounded city. Fred Thompson's melodic voice intoned, "No matter what, you keep pitching. No matter what, you go to the game. You go to the mound. You find the plate. And you throw. And you become who you are."

PART IV

CHAPTER TWENTY-FOUR

TWENTY SECONDS AND THE THIRTY-MINUTE RULE

You have to be your own hero.

—Andrea Bredbeck

January 2005—En route by air to Washington, DC

"Ladies and Gentlemen, we are now thirty minutes outside of Washington, DC. Federal rules require that you stay in your seats for the duration of the flight." The FAA had settled on the so-called thirty-minute rule after finally reopening Reagan National Airport some weeks after 9/11.

I stared at the frayed cloth above the latched tray table on the seat back in front of me and tried to ignore the anger mixed with despair that the announcement of the rule gave rise to—*as if that will stop terrorists*, I thought. *Focus on what you will say to him*, I chastised myself.

When I told Jack I was going to meet with President Bush for an editorial-board meeting after his reelection, my five-year-old said confidently, "He'll remember me." His certainty was adorable—and understandable. Each morning he'd seen the picture on my bureau with me holding him at seven weeks old, flanked on one side by Texas governor George W. Bush and on the other by Weld and Cellucci.

I felt the plane begin to descend. I knew I would get, at most, twenty seconds or so to speak privately to the president before or after the interview.

"Please make sure your seat backs are upright, tray tables secured, and seat belts securely tightened," the flight attendant intoned through the intercom.

What did I want to say to him?

Minutes from touchdown, I tried to dismiss the familiar feeling of longing that inevitably arose when I thought about how things might have been different if President Bush had known about the intensity of the blame aimed at me and Logan Airport and said something, anything, to condemn it at the time. Andrea had tried to probe my feelings about that, but I dismissed her questions out of hand. "He was protecting the country," I told her. The Logan controversy wasn't on his radar screen nor should it have been, I felt, but still, over the years I'd watched enviously as the president vigorously defended members of his administration from assertions they'd missed signs of the impending attacks.

Why didn't you defend me? I pushed the thought from my head, embarrassed to even think it. *He was a bit busy, you loser,* I chastised myself. If he even knew.

Did he know?

Stop it, Virginia.

I was ashamed to admit how much I wanted him to know, to acknowledge what happened to me, to express his sorrow, his understanding. To figuratively hold me in the crook of his arm like he had held Ashley Faulkner, to keep me safe. The implicit exoneration of *The 9/11 Commission Report* hadn't lessened my ache for something more, something I hadn't learned yet wasn't possible, to not just move on but to return to who I was.

Twenty seconds. That's all I had.

The White House

The *Herald* team stood around quietly, a little awkwardly, awed by simply being in the waiting area of the West Wing. A military guard stood near the door, and a young aide offered to take our coats and briefcases.

Pat Purcell and I stood near a glass-front wooden bookcase. It contained bound volumes of the collected speeches of recent presidents. We shared a laugh that Bill Clinton, renowned for his long oratory, had twice as many volumes as Ronald Reagan.

Framed artwork of what looked like historic battle scenes graced the dark-red walls. Combined with the low ceilings, a church-like aura caused us to keep our voices low.

Another aide told us we'd be meeting with the president in the Roosevelt Room. I hid my disappointment. We had hoped to see the Oval Office. Karl Rove, the president's chief adviser, who had helped me arrange the interview, walked through the waiting area. He and another campaign aide paused to say hello. "You guys were great during the campaign," he said. The other aide commented that one of her favorite media moments had been the *Herald*'s depiction of Senator John Kerry touring a NASA site while clothed in what looked like a surgical gown and a cap. In the picture, he was emerging from a structure resembling a space capsule. "Bubble Boy!" the *Herald* dubbed him in a front-page splash.

Another young press aide said, "It's time to go." She asked if I'd like her to hold my purse and reporter's notebook.

"Why?" I asked.

"You'll want your hands free to shake hands with him," she answered.

The aide led us down a warren of small dark hallways. She paused at a large heavy-looking door.

"Are you ready?" she asked me since I was right behind her.

I answered, "Yes, sure."

She pushed open the door. Instead of the Roosevelt Room, beyond the open door was the Oval Office.

My mental image, like most people's, of the Oval Office came from photo opportunities on the evening news. The two chairs in front of the fireplace. The president sitting behind a stately wooden desk flanked by flags. But when you enter it from the darkened narrow hallways of the West Wing, the contrast with the soaring ceilings and bright light streaming through enormous windows makes what's been dubbed the "world's greatest home-court advantage" even more extraordinary. I tried to take in the impressiveness of the room, when I saw, straight ahead, standing in front of his desk, President Bush and White House chief of staff Andy Card. The president walked briskly toward us.

"Hello," he said, shaking my hand.

"Hello, Mr. President, Ginny Buckingham," I said, reintroducing myself. "It's really nice to see you again."

The president paused, and seemed to remember. "You look good," he said warmly. As he moved on to greet the rest of the *Herald* team, Andy Card and I exchanged a quick hug.

"Thank you for doing this," I said.

The president gestured us toward the two cream-and-rose-striped couches facing each other in front of the fireplace and took his seat on one of the chairs.

I was seated closest to him on the couch to his right. An official photo we later published in the paper showed everyone leaning forward on the edge of their seats, except me. All you could see was the tip of my boot on my crossed leg because I was comfortably leaning back. *Why was I so comfortable?* I've wondered since, despite the importance of the moment to me. I still don't know for sure, but it may have been this simple: I liked President Bush immensely and had always felt comfortable with him. Despite the august setting, with his manner so reminiscent of Paul Cellucci's warmth, I felt like I was about to have a conversation with an old friend.

Herald editor Ken Chandler sat next to me and Greg Rush, head of the company's string of smaller community papers, was next to him. Across from me on the other couch were Purcell, then Shelly next to *Herald* Washington, DC, bureau chief Andrew Miga.

A few hours before, the *Herald* team had met for lunch at the National Press Club. There we planned out the questions we would ask the president. We assumed that only two of us, at most, would get to pose a question, so we wanted to be sure the questions we asked had the greatest chance to "make news." Miga would ask about the hunt for Osama bin Laden, we'd decided. Shelly wanted to get a sense of his thinking on Supreme Court appointments.

To our surprise, the president solicited a question from each and every one of us, starting with Purcell. Shelly asked, as planned, about the courts, Miga about Bin Laden.

Chandler and Rush had their own relevant, current-events-oriented questions.

I was last. I sensed we were running over time as some of the aides standing nearby had started to shuffle nervously on their feet. I saw one looking at his watch as if wondering whether to interrupt. But the president seemed to be having fun sparring with a friendly media audience and indicated he was in no hurry.

"Mr. President," I said, finally leaning forward. "I told my son Jack, who's five now, that I was going to see you. I asked him what he would want me to ask you." I looked over at the opposite couch and I saw Miga looking nervously at Purcell. *What is she doing?* his facial expression seemed to be asking.

The president looked amused. "He knows that you used to own the Texas Rangers," I continued. "He wants to know how you could have traded A-Rod to the Yankees."

The president chuckled. "Well," he answered, "we were trying to give you a little help."

I smiled in return and the rest of the group laughed, relaxing a bit. Without waiting to see whether I'd be given an opportunity, I immediately turned to a more serious question.

"You said earlier that for people to follow, a leader needs to know where he wants to go. Do you think people get it? Do they keep 9/11 present like you obviously do and many others do?"

My words came out in an earnest rush. By "many others," I was referring to myself, too. Watching his features soften, I thought it was possible the president understood the answer was as much for me personally as it was for the benefit of the *Herald*.

"You know, after 9/11," he answered, "I made some statements that I knew there would be a natural tendency for people to kind of settle in and forget the moment, and that's natural. Who wants to relive the . . ." His voice trailed off. "No one wants to relive that horrific day on a regular basis. And that it would be my duty to remind people of the nature of this war we're in and that it's a different kind of war, the enemy is different, they are not nation-states that we're dealing with.

"I think most Americans, however, do understand and get glimpses into the real world, based upon certain things that take place," the president continued.

Andy Card came back into the room. "Mr. President, you have another appointment."

There was so much more I wanted to ask him. *Do you ever doubt yourself? Do you lie awake in the dead of night, like I do, wondering what more you could have done? Has your faith in God changed at all?*

We all stood up as the president did, and Purcell and Shelly shook his hand and thanked him for his time. He turned toward me and wrapped me in a warm embrace.

Twenty seconds. I couldn't control what he would or wouldn't say to me, what he did or didn't know about Logan four years earlier. I could only control what I would say to him.

"I just want to thank you for all you've done since 9/11," I whispered so only he could hear. "It's given me a lot of strength."

I stepped back. President Bush looked me directly in the eye.

"You're a good person," he said. "You're a good person."

A "good person." His words were kind, though not what I had longed to hear for all these years. He didn't say, "It's not your fault." Or "You did nothing wrong."

But, I appreciated it because I had been defined so harshly as the opposite of a good person. It would have to be enough, even as I knew, achingly, in the deepest part of myself that it wasn't, and I didn't yet know what would be.

***

A more normal rhythm moved me through the rest of 2005. I continued to see Andrea but not as regularly. Shelly gave me the opportunity to write a twice-weekly bylined column. I tried to include references to true accountability versus blame whenever I could and also threw myself into covering the budget tussles and other debates at the State House and in Washington, DC.

Despite my Republican roots, I was a frequent critic of then governor Mitt Romney, who seemed to choose policy positions based on his national ambitions, not Massachusetts's best interest. When Pat Purcell told me that Romney personally complained to him about my coverage, I grinned with pride. I relished the role I was playing again shaping the public-policy debate in Boston.

Jack entered kindergarten in September, and his young life's passage seemed a moment of passage for me, too. A line from Springsteen's "Waitin' on a Sunny Day" popped into my head as I watched him follow the line of new classmates into school, proudly shouldering his Thomas the Tank Engine backpack. Yes, everything would be okay; just like those lyrics promised, we'd survive the devastation of 9/11.

I marked the fourth 9/11 anniversary by attending the small ceremony held by our town's firefighters and police in a local park. I stood alone, grieving just like all of those around me, as taps was played by a local firefighter and the American flag was lowered.

I began to believe what Andrea had once told me. "Think of your life as a tapestry," she'd said. "One day, 9/11 will be a thread in that tapestry, brighter perhaps than all the rest, but one thread."

CHAPTER TWENTY-FIVE

A SWIM ON NEW YEAR'S DAY

December 28, 2005—Marblehead

"Neil," I said, leaving a message on the copy editor's voice mail. "I just sent my column in. Let me know if you didn't get it."

I took one last look to double-check that the email to him was in my sent folder before shutting down the computer. *I hope Shelly doesn't mind,* I thought as I started rummaging through the refrigerator to figure out a dinner plan. In that quiet week between Christmas and New Year's, I'd decided to take a break from writing about politics. Instead, I penned a column about my fourth annual polar bear swim that upcoming New Year's Day.

There was no exact count that I knew of, but each year hundreds of New Englanders from Maine to Rhode Island start the New Year with a swim in the frosty Atlantic Ocean.

The most famous of these in the Boston area were the L Street Brownies, so named for the well-known bathhouse on Carson Beach, at the end of L Street in South Boston. The tradition of this hardy group started in 1904. Now, each year hundreds of honorary Brownies joined them for the jump into Boston Harbor. Screaming and preening, the Brownies' swim was faithfully captured by local TV stations for the evening news and featured in front-page photos in the city's two dailies. Seeing the spectacle, Bostonians shake their heads in wry bemusement at a tradition that was as much a part of Boston's celebration of the New Year as the ball dropping in Times Square was New York's.

A few friends and I had decided to copy the tradition in January 2003. We each gathered a couple of other people, and that first year we met at Devereux Beach in Marblehead. Instinctively, we agreed our impromptu group didn't want to garner any publicity like other polar bear clubs in nearby towns. Kate, her husband, Alex, and the others surely had their own reasons for participating. For me, the appeal was ingrained in my Catholic upbringing: water and renewal.

The column ran on Thursday, December 29:

Cold Comfort on New Year's Morn

On New Year's Day, otherwise sane humans along the frigid coastline of New England will take a swim. I will be one of them. I'm still trying to figure out why.

This will be our fourth consecutive year of voluntarily freezing our tokhes off. We have few rules. We do the deed in the morning, the better not to dread it all day. We have to wear a bathing suit (a wet suit being so beside the point). We run into the water together. We must dunk our heads. Oh yes, video and still photographs are freely taken—I wish I had thought at the beginning to impose a waist-up rule—the better to use for blackmail later on.

The night before my first dip, I asked a cardiologist-neighbor if it was dangerous. "It won't kill you," he said, "but I wouldn't recommend it."

This column, actually, isn't meant to recommend it either. I have no profound message, or

discovery of deeper meaning, to impart. Interest-
ingly, our group hasn't even discussed amongst
ourselves why we do it. We all agree, usually with
some measure of wonderment, that, post-dip, we
feel extraordinarily good. For some, I suppose,
the decision to dip started much like Sir Edmund
Hillary's timeless explanation for summiting Everest—"because it's there."

I bought a refrigerator magnet recently which
summed up, as only refrigerator magnets can, the
philosophy of life as I aspire to (not as I do) live it.
"Dance as though no one is watching you, love as
though you have never been hurt before, sing as
though no one can hear you, live as though heav-
en is on earth."

To this, I would add "jump in the ocean on
New Year's Day" if you want to. Happy New Year.

I usually received a few emails from readers in response to my columns, sometimes agreeing with an opinion on one political issue or
other, but often not. I liked best the responses from readers who dis-
agreed, as part of the fun of the column was provoking a passionate
reaction. Given the nonpolitical nature of that column, though, I didn't
expect much of one that time.

It was evening before I had a chance to sit at my computer in the
kitchen and open my *Herald* email. I had seven new messages, but
from their subject lines, only three or four looked like they might be
from readers.

I clicked on one. It was from Michael Welsch, a friend I'd once
worked with. Welsch, an amputee, was a regular competitor in mara-
thons and triathlons. He was amazing.

"I know you will do fine," he wrote. "Just think, you can do anything for a minute. Go for it!"

I clicked on the next message. This reader corrected me on my commonly misattributed Sir Edmund Hillary quote. It was actually British
climber George Mallory, the email pointed out, who said "because it's
there" when asked "Why climb Everest?"

I opened the next email from "Evelyn." She wrote, "Today's article about jumping into the ocean on New Year's Day was delightful. . . . What I liked more than anything was no politics!" I made a mental note to pass that one on to Shelly, who preferred hard-hitting political columns. I smiled as I clicked on the next email, expecting more of the same from "J. Paul."

"Ms. Buckingham: Contrast the cold Atlantic Jan. 1 with the intense heat people at the upper floors of the WTC were feeling 9/11; hot enough to jump 100 stories if that's hot enough for you. . . . Thanks for giving the world and civilization half of 9/11."

I stared at the words, at first not comprehending them. I breathed in, conscious of drawing the air in through my mouth, but I couldn't expand my lungs. The words of J. Paul pressed like a weight on my chest.

David came into the kitchen after checking on the kids, who were asleep upstairs. I turned away from the computer screen and looked toward him, not meeting his eyes.

"What's wrong?" he asked.

Wordlessly, I turned back to the computer and pointed to the email. He read it, standing behind me, one hand gently resting on my shoulder. "This is ridiculous," he said. "Will this ever end?" Then he added quietly, "I'm sorry, hon."

"I know," I said, as I shrank from his touch.

"Do you want to talk?"

"No," I answered, too sharply, pushing him away with my tone. I moved to the refrigerator and filled my glass to the brim with cold white wine.

I set it on the marble table next to the couch in our sitting room and lay back against the pillow.

"Are you going to sleep down here?" David asked, his face creased with worry.

"I guess so," I mumbled.

The sound of David climbing the stairs faded. All I could hear was the soft hum of the refrigerator. The quiet was oppressive, J. Paul's words all I could see.

"Ms. Buckingham: Contrast the cold Atlantic Jan. 1 with the intense heat people at the upper floors of the WTC were feeling 9/11; hot enough to jump 100 stories if that's hot enough for you."

I had heard about a recent documentary being released containing never-before-seen footage of the World Trade Center that day. You couldn't see the bodies falling, but you could hear them hitting the ground. The idea was too horrible to even think about. I knew I could never see the documentary, but at that moment I could hear them, the bodies hitting the pavement.

"Thanks for giving the world and civilization half of 9/11."

I sat up abruptly, jostling the wineglass. I drank it empty and then set it down on the side of the sink. I switched off the kitchen light. Reaching the top of the stairs, I turned into Maddy's room. The light from the hallway gently fell over the jumble of covers and books and stuffed animals strewn across the big-girl bed she'd started sleeping in when she turned three. I pulled the pink-and-yellow blanket she had kicked off up and over her shoulders. She squirmed under it and turned on her side before settling back into a deep sleep. I kissed my fingers and placed them on the top of her curly brown hair. "I love you, angel," I whispered and turned to Jack's room.

Jack was still awake, waiting for the rest of his bedtime ritual. I had sung "Edelweiss," from *The Sound of Music*, to him almost nightly for the past seven years, starting when I was pregnant with him. Instead of the actual ending—"bless my homeland forever"—I always substituted "Bless my baby Jack forever."

It was a tradition we both loved. Usually after I was done and had rubbed his back for a few minutes, Jack tried to extend our time together—or more accurately, forestall sleep. "Mom, what galaxy is Earth in?" was a typical stumper that kept me in the rocking chair for a minute or two. But tonight I didn't have anything left to give him.

"Mom, what's a practical joke?" Jack asked, as I got up to straighten his covers and leave. I sat back down.

"Well, it's when you make someone laugh by doing something to them rather than making a joke with words," I tried to explain.

"I don't understand. Mom, have you ever done a practical joke?"

"Yes, back in college. There was a group of guys who lived near our dorm, and we were always playing practical jokes on each other."

"Like what?"

"Well, silly things like they'd steal our underwear and hang it in a tree."

Jack giggled.

"But the best," I told him, warming to the subject, "was when we were sophomores and we borrowed a bunch of chickens from a farm. We snuck into the boys' dorm and left the chickens. When they opened their door, you could hear clear across upper campus, 'There are chickens in our room!'"

Jack collapsed on his pillow in laughter, and I started to laugh, too, caught up in the joy of pulling off a doozy of a practical joke. "I have some pictures of the chickens that I'll show you sometime," I promised. "Now go to sleep." I kissed him gently and turned out his light.

J. Paul's email receded into the darkness now gently illuminated by Jack's smile.

January 1, 2006—Marblehead

They are terrified. I can see the faces of the people inside, pressed up against the window. I can't hear them but I understand what they are saying. "Let us out. Please help us." Their mouths are moving, their fists pounding on the glass. Dozens of people. Looking right at me. Waitstaff in uniform. Businessmen in suits. A woman about my age. Their eyes pleading for me to do something. I am just on the other side of the glass. Suspended somehow outside the Windows on the World restaurant in the World Trade Center. I am motionless as they mouth, "Help us. Help us."

There is nothing I can do.

I woke with a start. Sat straight up in bed. Panting. *Just a dream, it was just a dream.* I looked over at David and extended my hand to shake his shoulder. I stopped myself. I didn't want to tell him that the nightmares were back. I lay back down but didn't close my eyes. If I did, I was afraid I would see them.

Just as they had in the days and months after 9/11, the nightmare cast in sharp relief the subconscious burden of guilt and shame I still carried, guilt that I may have contributed to the events of 9/11, shame that I could not help the people affected. I also started to be more aware of being ashamed that I wasn't "over it." One ugly email still had the power to send me right back to where I had started. I didn't yet understand the role of triggers in PTSD. J. Paul's email was clearly a trigger. And I didn't have the mental tools and perspective to be able to figuratively shrug, not in nonchalance but in self-awareness, an understanding that, of course, the email was a trigger, of course the nightmare was a result. I didn't have the power to depower the trigger with that simple act of self-kindness.

Later that morning—Devereux Beach

It was 10:03 a.m. when David, the kids, and I pulled into the beach parking lot. The waiting group gestured for me to hurry. The twenty-two-degree air temperature made every extra minute feel like ten. "C'mon, Ginny!"

My friends and I stripped down to our bathing suits on the ice- and snow-covered sand. A blast of cold air hit my exposed skin. All week, I'd considered canceling, haunted by the fresh accusation in response to my column.

We posed for our traditional picture, shivering, arms around one another.

I need this, I thought. Giving up this new tradition would be more than letting go of a quirky annual bit of fun and camaraderie. It would be akin to giving up hope.

"One! Two! Three!" I counted down, loudly yelling to the others, "Let's go!"

With shrieks and screams and laughter, we ran to the water's edge.
Keep going.

I was about in the middle of the group. Two or three people were already in as deep as their waists. I saw Kate gracefully dive beneath a wave.

I realized then: *This hurts.* The icy cold of the water cut through the familiar emotional numbness.

I wasn't a great swimmer and was about to drop to my knees underneath a breaking wave when suddenly I was picked up off my feet.

Hold your ground.

The freezing water filled my ears and I felt rocks and sand scratch my right thigh as the wave dumped me onto the ocean floor. I scrambled to find my footing, my hands pushing me up. The wave passed and I got to my feet, sucking in air and rubbing water out of my eyes. The air hitting my skin felt like a thousand fingers pinching me all at once. I turned back to the beach and stumbled out of the water. David was waiting with a towel. He wrapped it around me.

"Are you okay, hon? How was it?" he asked.

"It was great," I answered, looking back at the water.

I could feel.

CHAPTER TWENTY-SIX

SUBPOENA

February 2006—Marblehead

"Mommy, why did you leave your old job? I liked it when you were at the airport."

I put down the plate of half-eaten chicken fingers I was about to clear from the table and sat back down next to Jack. I looked over at David, who was researching ski conditions at the computer for an upcoming trip to Vermont.

"Well, honey, I'm going to give you the kid version of my answer," I finally said. "And when you're a grown-up I promise I'll answer any questions that you have."

So far, so good. David nodded, looking impressed, unaware that I had no idea what to say next.

"Some people got mad at the airport, and now I have another job that I love at the *Herald*," I said.

Jack looked off to the side, like he did when he was pondering one of his life's more typical questions, like which episode of *Star Wars* was his favorite. I looked imploringly at David, who intervened. "C'mere, buddy, let's look at a trail map."

My reprieve was brief. About a week later, Jack and I pulled into the Starbucks parking lot, a favorite after-school treat—cookies for him, coffee for me. As I shut off the engine and started to unbuckle, Jack said from the backseat, "Mom, I don't understand, why were people mad at the airport?"

I turned to look at my forty-three-pound inquisitor.

Okay, you can do this.

"Well," I said gently, "there were some bad guys at the airport and they stole some airplanes."

"They did?" he asked, wide eyed. "What did they do with them?"

"They crashed them."

"How many?" he asked.

"Four."

"Where?"

"Two in New York and one each in Washington and Pennsylvania."

"What happened?"

"Well, they hurt," I paused. He deserved the truth, as much of it as I could tell him. "No," I started again, "they killed a lot of people."

"Why?" Jack asked. "Why would they do that?"

Why.

"Well, you know how you love me, and Mommy and Daddy love you so much and Maddy, too?" I ventured.

Jack nodded, uncertainly.

"Well, these bad guys didn't love anyone. They just wanted to hurt people."

I opened my car door, hoping my simple explanation was enough.

"Mom?"

Not so fast.

"What, honey?"

"Were you at the airport when the bad guys were there?"

"No, sweetie. I was on my way there but not there yet."

"I'm glad," Jack said, his concern making my eyes prick with tears.

"But Mom?"

"Yes?"

"I still don't understand. Why were people mad at the airport?"

How did I explain to a child what I wasn't even sure I fully understood?

"Well," I started slowly, choosing my words carefully. "Sometimes when people are scared, they get mad. And instead of thinking about what makes them scared, they blame someone for making them feel that way."

A few days later

What a great day, I thought to myself as I pulled in the driveway. I had taken the day off and driven about forty-five minutes north to a small ski area. I had skied only a few times before but figured I should try to improve since David was a strong skier and Jack had been skiing since he turned three. I spent three hours at nearby Bradford, taking the rope tow to the top of the learner's slope and slowly making my way down. *Tiring, but fun,* I thought. I opened the front door to the foyer. A letter-sized envelope was on top of the stack of mail. It looked official, like a tax document or something. I took a closer look and saw the return address: "United States District Court."

I dropped the rest of the mail and tore open the envelope. "Subpoena in a federal case," it read in the right-hand corner. Typed in what appeared to be some kind of form letter was "Re September 11 litigation."

There was no postage on the envelope so I must have been served in person.

"You are commanded to appear at the place, date, and time specified below at the taking of a deposition in the above case."

An office in downtown Boston was specified. The date just one month away.

I stood frozen in place. No one at Massport had warned me the subpoena was coming. My wrists ached dully as I dialed my lawyer's number. He explained the subpoena was for a deposition in the remaining wrongful death cases, for the families who had not either reached a settlement or taken part in the federal fund set up to compensate victims.

Unable to sleep, at about two o'clock I sat cross-legged on the dining room floor and began going through a box I hadn't looked in since I'd left Logan.

I lifted out a file and pulled out a sheaf of legal documents.

One of the few disagreements I'd had with members of my senior staff at Massport right after 9/11 was over a decision to retain outside attorneys in the eventuality that the authority would be sued. Massport's chief legal counsel made the case to me within days of the hijackings to hire experienced lawyers on behalf of the agency's potential defense. I rejected his advice. I felt we should be focused on the airport's safe operations, not future legal wrangling. At the direction of the Massport board chairman, however, he had hired a law firm anyway. When I found out, I was furious. Yet, soon after the disagreement, notices of intent to sue began arriving in my in-box. I obviously knew about the one wrongful death case I had been notified about in 2003 that had named me personally. But it looked like several other families had also considered a lawsuit against me.

I don't remember getting these.

Each of the legal notices, a half dozen or so, were stamped in the right-hand corner "Received. Massport Authority Executive Director." I knew this was the procedure for any incoming mail to my office at the time. Each of them was addressed personally to me. Yet, I had no memory of having seen them.

Maybe Julie sent them right to the legal office without showing me? I wondered, thinking my assistant may have tried to protect me. Or maybe I had completely repressed the memory because it was so painful.

October 10, 2001

Dear Executive Director Buckingham: The following constitutes notice for a formal demand for damages arising out of the wrongful deaths of Sarah Siffitz and her viable unborn child who died on American Airlines Flight 11. . . . Ms. Siffitz was seven months pregnant at the time of her death and eagerly awaited the birth of her first born.

Oh God. I pursed my lips tightly to try to keep from crying out loud. I would have been nine or ten weeks pregnant with Maddy when I received the letter.

> The Siffitzes believe that the circumstances surrounding the ease with which the hijackers were able to smuggle weapons on board the aircraft compel a conclusion that the Massachusetts Port Authority was negligent in its failure to provide adequate security and breached its duties to Ms. Siffitz and her viable unborn child and that this breach of duty was the proximate cause of their deaths. In addition to the Massachusetts Port Authority, suit will be commenced against Ms. Virginia Buckingham.

I put the notice back in the folder. I rocked back and forth, my face buried in my hands.

At the 9/11 memorial at Ground Zero, the name of every victim is carved into the reflecting pool walls marking the base of each tower. Next to some women's names is "and her unborn child." I didn't know how many unborn children were killed that day, how many people like the Siffitzes lost not only their loved ones but someone they would never have the chance to love.

I also remembered that sometime after 9/11 *People* magazine had published a story about the babies born to widows of 9/11 victims. On the cover was a picture of some of those babies, gathered for a photo shoot. The picture and story were meant to be hopeful. To give the sense that life miraculously followed the death and destruction of the terrorist attacks. Impulsively, I bought a copy I saw in the checkout line at the grocery store. I put it on the seat next to me as I drove home, casting sidelong glances at the picture. Instead of the hopefulness intended by the publishers, all I could think about were their fathers. For months, I kept the magazine in my car under the passenger-side seat. A reminder. Knowing it was there, a kind of penance.

February 2006—South Londonderry, Vermont

"God dammit, Jack, then next time I will just stay home!" I said and stormed out of the ski house bedroom, as Jack began to sob. I'd been trying to get Jack and Maddy to sleep for an hour. Neither wanted to stay in the bunk room down the hall from the master bedroom. Jack kept insisting on sleeping in the bed with David, like he had done when the two of them had come up for a ski trip earlier in the winter. My frustration grew as I came back into the room for the fourth time after turning out the lights, and I finally snapped at him in anger.

"Go upstairs," David said quietly. Firmly. "Go sit by the fire and read your book. I'll take care of this."

Losing control and yelling at my kids. It was what I swore I'd never do. Throw a coffee cup across the room. Impatiently dismiss the little girl wanting to help her mother in the kitchen. These memories of my mother, understandably stressed, are certainly not the only ones I carried, but these burned most brightly. However far-fetched, I didn't want Jack and Maddy to have any childhood memory stand out unless it was a particularly joyful one. But, like the signs that a volcano was preparing to erupt, the yelling had been happening more and more in the last few weeks. I'd yell at small things. Childish antics that wouldn't have bothered me at all before. Screaming at Jack and Maddy to stop bickering. To pick up their toys. To go to bed without any pushback.

I sat by the fire, my eyes burning with exhaustion. I hadn't slept much since receiving the subpoena. The house we were staying in for the weekend respite was the same one we had come to with Jack just after 9/11. I glanced out the floor-to-ceiling windows. The view from the edge of a meadow, ringed by woods and mountains, was reassuring in its peaceful immutability but also contrasted with my fear that I would never feel that kind of peace inside. No matter how I tried to make peace with all that had happened, another shoe dropped and sent me reeling. And now it was affecting my parenting.

I could hear Jack's whimpering and David's soft voice trying to comfort him. I went back downstairs. "I'm so sorry, buddy. I shouldn't have yelled like that." Jack clung to my neck, moistening it with his tears. "Want me to sing to you?" I asked. He nodded and I tucked him under his blanket and softly sang "Edelweiss." As I finished, Jack's eyes grew heavy, and before I left the room, he was sound asleep.

Shortly after, David came upstairs. "They're both asleep now," he said.

"Thanks." I was too embarrassed by my outburst to look at him. "I'm sorry. It's the deposition."

"I know," he answered. He sat next to me on the couch, and reached for my hand. We sat, saying nothing, and looked at the fire, as if some answer burned there. I took a deep sip from my glass of red wine, and felt it travel down my throat and into me. I grew warm from the fire and the wine. I reached for David and kissed him deeply, urgently. I lifted my shirt off over my head, and he reached behind me to undo my bra. I lay on the couch as he pulled off my pants and quickly undressed. He took my wine from the table and poured a little onto my belly and then inside me. With his tongue, he tasted the wine and me together. I closed my eyes and tried to feel him there. When he pulled up and kissed me, I tasted the wine and my wetness in his mouth. He put himself inside me and as he went deeper, I opened my eyes. There was a skylight directly above us. It was dark out now, so I could see our reflection in the sloped glass. David was moving on top of me. I stared at the reflection. I was not there.

CHAPTER TWENTY-SEVEN

"WE SHARE A PAIN"

September 2006—Marblehead

"Why Is This Maine Man Haunted by 9/11?"

I stared at the headline on the front cover of *Yankee* magazine. Haunted. Like me.

My mother, a longtime subscriber to the New England–based magazine, had called that morning after reading about Michael Tuohey, the gate agent at Portland International Jetport. "I turned to your father," she'd said, "and told him, 'This is how Ginny feels.'"

When we'd hung up, I grabbed my keys and rushed to the local newsstand to find a copy.

I sat cross-legged on the floor of my bedroom, the article about the man who checked Mohamed Atta and Abdulaziz al Omari in for their commuter flight to Boston opened in my lap.

"I thought I could put it behind me," Tuohey said to the interviewer. "I thought I could just grab it and confront it. I figured, the more I confront it, I won't let it bother me." He paused. "I was wrong. There's never a day without thinking about that day. It's just there. It's in your blood, your system. Your feelings. It's like the sky—always there. It's like you know your name. How do you try and not know your name?"

Me, too, I thought. *It's always there.*

I read on about Tuohey's experience on 9/11. He was about to take a break after checking in the flight to Boston, when he saw two men hurrying to the check-in counter. "I motioned them over," he said. "These guys showed up twenty minutes prior. Back then, I didn't think anything of it. Back then, it was all set up for convenience of passengers." I found myself nodding my head as I read.

Tuohey recounted that when he saw that Atta and al Omari had one-way first-class tickets to Boston connecting to American Airlines Flight 11 to Los Angeles, he decided to issue them only a boarding pass to Boston. "I never liked the system where you give a boarding pass to a follow-up flight. I worked for US Airways, not American," Tuohey told the interviewer. "So I just gave them a boarding pass from here to Boston."

The decision prompted a confrontation with Atta. "They told me 'one-step check-in,'" Tuohey said, relating Atta's insistence.

"Everyone knows the pictures of the guy now," Tuohey continued. "That cold, hard picture. Well that is a warm and cuddly look compared to what I saw. My stomach literally turned over when Atta looked at me . . . We locked eyes," he said. "We were this close. And I said, 'Mr. Atta, if you don't go now, you will miss your plane.'"

Goose bumps rose on my arms as I pictured the scene with Atta. I tried to put myself in Tuohey's place, staring into the terrorist's eyes.

The interviewer described tears welling in Tuohey's own eyes. "Why didn't I recognize the devil? I did recognize him. But I didn't stop him."

"You couldn't," I whispered out loud, as if somehow he could hear me. "You just couldn't."

It was after *The 9/11 Commission Report* was released in 2004, Tuohey related, that the full force of his experience hit him. "I just started crying," he said. "I'd say, 'Get over it. Get over it.'"

Get over it. Get over it. I thought, *Just what I'd told myself and what I'd been told by others.*

Tuohey said that he'd be at the mailbox and he'd see Mohamed Atta driving by in a car or at the mall and Atta would be walking ahead of him. "My heart would pound. My stomach felt like ice," Tuohey said. "I ran after him . . . I knew it wasn't him, but at that moment it was."

My dreams. Planes blowing apart. Crashing. Trying to get there. To save them. Never being able to.

As soon as I finished the article, I went to the computer and watched the episode of *Oprah* that the article said Tuohey had appeared on.

I needed to contact him. Right away. I typed in the address for the *The Oprah Winfrey Show*'s website. There was a place to register comments, and I quickly typed that I would like to get in touch with Michael Tuohey. I briefly explained my role at Logan and wrote something like, "I think I can help him."

I heard nothing back from the show's producers. I knew Tuohey lived somewhere in southern Maine near Portland, so after a few days of waiting, I took a chance and called information. His number was listed.

One ring, two. My heart was pounding. An answering machine clicked on. I left a message. "Mr. Tuohey, my name is Virginia Buckingham," I said. "I, I, just want to thank you. For telling your story. You helped my family understand what I have been unable to explain for the past five years."

Before hanging up, I added, "I want you to know you aren't to blame. You did the best you could."

Tuohey returned my call a short time after. "Ah, Virginia, I thought I recognized your name," he said, when I told him who I was.

I don't remember most details of the conversation, but we talked for a very long time with the instant familiarity of two people who didn't have to know each other to understand each other.

Tuohey had retired from US Airways, he told me, and it was then that he began fearing to leave his house, began to see Atta when he went out.

I told him a little about my own fears.

The second plane.

The ball of fire.

The black smoke.

The bodies falling.

The people mouthing "help me" in the Windows on the World restaurant.

We talked and talked. We interrupted each other with exclamations of "exactly" or "I felt that way, too." When we both were finally exhausted, we started to say our goodbyes.

"I don't know if we will," I said, "but I hope we talk again."

"Well, Virginia," Tuohey answered simply, "we share a pain."

***

We didn't talk again, though I thought of Michael Tuohey a lot. Sometimes I'd see him on TV around 9/11 anniversaries advocating for additional security changes. Mostly though, I saw his story in my mind. Atta driving by his house. Atta in the mall. I felt his pain like it was my own. "We share a pain," he had said. And oddly, however dubious, those words were a gift from him to me. I had been understood. I hoped he felt the same.

PART V

CHAPTER TWENTY-EIGHT

NEW YORK

May 2007—**Boston Herald**

Like too many in the journalism profession, when I was recruited for a position in the private sector, I reluctantly said yes for the financial security it offered. Yet, the position in government affairs for the bio-pharmaceutical company Pfizer posed an additional challenge for me. While I would be based in New England, its corporate headquarters were in midtown Manhattan. I knew I would have to spend time in a city I had once feared would reject me, or worse.

Was I ready?

On my last day at One Herald Square, I was presented with a mock-up of a front page, a traditional parting gift, and I smiled with a sense of belonging so different from when I had started four years earlier. I realized that working at the *Herald* had offered me more than a job when I needed it; it had helped me begin to rebuild the person I had lost. As I turned to leave, Shelly and I embraced by the dusty door-frame. "You saved me," I said quietly to her. "In more ways than one."

How much rebuilding I still had ahead of me was punctuated by an offhand comment by a new friend I soon made at Pfizer. My office was on Beacon Hill, just steps from the State House. I'd hung an assortment of pictures on the wall, including a favorite of me as a young press secretary standing over Governor Weld and Lieutenant Governor Cellucci, who were seated at a table. They were looking up at me expectantly as I briefed them on an issue and likely, given my role, told them what to say to the press. I didn't remember the moment, but I remembered the feeling: the confidence, that I knew exactly what I was doing and didn't hesitate for a moment to rely on my instincts. Looking at the picture—my posture, my face—my new friend Heidi, with insight and concern, noted, "I don't recognize that person."

Neither do I, I thought to myself. I wondered if I ever would again.

I flew to the company's New York headquarters about once a month. The flight from Logan took only about thirty-eight minutes. Once in a while, on the approach, the plane would follow the Hudson River and circle around Lower Manhattan. One early morning, a few months into the new job, I was seated in the window seat on the left side of the plane. As the city came into view, I pressed my face against the pane, and I felt my heart rate increase. Any minute I knew I would see them. The footprints of the Twin Towers, yawning, empty, as clear from the sky as the World Trade Center targets must have been that September morning. As they came into view, the familiar throbbing in my wrists returned. I craned my neck so I could see them for as long as possible through the small oval window. As the plane banked wide over the mouth of New York Harbor, I also could see the Statue of Liberty. Triumphant, beckoning, its promise of shelter unbowed. I wanted to feel awed, I wanted to fill up with pride that it and all it meant were still standing. Instead, the fog of dissociation began to form, wrapping me in its protective tendrils. I welcomed its embrace, even as I began to understand it was keeping me from myself.

In our sessions, Andrea tried to illustrate the impact of dissociation by holding both of her arms horizontally from her body. "This is the range of human feeling," she'd say. And then folding one arm at the elbow toward her body, she'd explain, "And if you cut off feeling one extreme, pain, you can't fully feel joy either." I understood by then I wasn't doing this purposely. Andrea had often said that a more accurate name for my condition would be "post-traumatic stress order." She re-explained that my mind was protecting me as I tried to make some sense of what had happened.

On the New York business trips, I needn't have feared that I'd be swept away by the ferocity of my emotions because this automatic response of dissociation never let me down. I learned my way around the corporate culture and did what I'd always done—worked hard. I was aware that many of my New York–based colleagues must have experienced the events of 9/11 firsthand, but I didn't know if any knew my own experience until one day when I stepped into the elevator. A longtime employee said hello, not unfriendly but not friendly either, and nodded toward me, saying to the person standing next to her, "She's googleable." My face burned red, as I wondered whether the neutral statement was more than that. Pushing down an instant defensiveness, I brushed off their questions about my past with a "wrong place, wrong time" type of answer, my blitheness a cover for renewed despair. Others I soon met, though, were genuinely curious and supportive.

Slowly, like muscles that grow stronger from the work of carrying heavy cases of goods, I realized that just being among these colleagues with their own 9/11 stories and being in New York itself brought their own measure of healing. Walking the few blocks from my office in Midtown to my hotel, moving past the Chrysler Building, its sloping spire rising above Forty-Second Street like a watchtower, being buffeted by the rush of the crowd emerging from Grand Central Terminal all made me feel less alone, despite my presence in the midst of thousands of strangers. *Yes,* I imagined them thinking, *we might be afraid sometimes. And it still hurts, but we'll be okay.*

By that time, Raakhee Mirchandani, my *Herald* colleague who had gifted me with Ganesh, had left Boston for a job writing at the *New York Post.* One evening, we walked the streets of the city continuing the same kind of conversations we'd had in Boston about the meaning and the inheritance of 9/11. Nearly six years had passed. Jack was eight years old and Maddy was five. Yet, I didn't offer to give back to Raakhee her statue of the Hindu god of overcoming obstacles. She didn't ask. She knew I still needed it.

CHAPTER TWENTY-NINE

"BLAMELESS"

September 2008—Logan Airport

Massachusetts governor Deval Patrick looked surprised to see me. I could tell from his puzzled expression that he was trying to figure out why I would be at the Logan Airport 9/11 Memorial dedication. By then, I'd interviewed him many times for the *Herald*. But evidently he also knew I'd left the paper for Pfizer.

"How's the new gig?" he asked.

I reached for his outstretched hand, looked him in the eye, and instead of answering his question, I said, "Thank you for being here."

His expression instantly softened, as it seemed the pieces fell into place. *Oh, that's right,* I imagined he was thinking. *You were here.*

I was here.

A front-page story on the memorial had been published in the Sunday *Globe* a day or two before. Referring to Logan Airport, the piece began with this simple summation: "It is the place where a nation's nightmare began."

As I read, I tucked my legs underneath me and squeezed as far into the corner of the couch as I could manage. *The nation's nightmare,* I thought. *And a nightmare for so many families.* I closed my eyes as the phantom throbbing ran through the veins of my wrists. *My nightmare. Mine, too.*

I read on: "The airport's connection to Sept. 11 is especially fraught because both of the planes that brought down the World Trade Center in New York departed from Boston. Though investigators found airport personnel blameless in the hijacking—no aviation security protocol was violated—the deaths of more than 2,700 people will never really clear the conscience of many who were working at Logan that day."

"Blameless."

I turned the word over in my mind, accepting its small solace. The writer had gotten it exactly right. No matter the official findings, the deaths of thousands of people would never be fully gone from my conscience. Somehow, by acknowledging this reality, it felt like the writer had helped me dial the combination of a lock, the tumblers opening to a sort of acceptance upon hitting the right series of words, opening a safe containing the greatest of treasures: an understanding of the difference between moving on and moving forward.

Now, on the slight rise in front of me was the glass cube, the centerpiece of the new Logan 9/11 memorial. The light was reflecting off the glass. I couldn't take my eyes off it.

As I settled in my chair in front of the makeshift stage festooned with American flags, I saw Carl Stevens, a reporter for the city's leading radio news station. He was plugging his recorder into the sound system. Carl had called me that morning, asking if I would do an interview. I demurred, saying I was just heading into the airport for the dedication.

It was Carl who had shocked me by stopping me in the grocery store a few years earlier and saying, "I owe you an apology." For what, I asked, confused. "For going along with the crowd," he'd said, "in my coverage after 9/11."

I listened to the series of speakers—the architects who designed the memorial, the head of the airport, the CEO who had replaced me,

Governor Patrick. Tom Kinton, Logan's longtime aviation director, welcomed past CEOs and board members.

John Quelch, chair of the Massport board of directors, came to the podium. The Harvard Business School professor had been appointed to Massport after I left. He was hailed in the media along with my successor as part of new leadership bringing needed changes to Logan. Quelch moved the microphone down slightly, clearing his throat. I tried not to let my face betray anything as he began to speak, stiffening as I expected a reference to be made about all the improvements he and others had implemented to make Logan safer after my departure.

"For the past seven years," he said, "there have already been in place two memorials at Logan Airport, dedicated to the 147 men, women, and children who perished the morning of September 11, 2001, on American Airlines Flight 11 and United Airlines Flight 175. One stands outside gate 32 in American Airline's Terminal B. The other stands outside gate 19 in United's Terminal C."

I gazed up at this man I did not know as he summoned the sense of pride and heartbreak that marked Logan personnel in those early days.

"Both memorials," he said, "appeared spontaneously, raised by airport and airline employees without fanfare or ceremony. These two memorials are one and the same. And there is no grander memorial. That memorial is the flag of the United States of America. The flags fly proudly to this day, and will likely fly forever. They symbolize the determination of this airport, this nation, and the community assembled here to recover from the grievous wound of 9/11. Today, we dedicate a third memorial as a remembrance of that day and its impact on all of us."

I gripped my arms tightly, trying to contain my emotion. Betty Desrosiers reached over and placed her hand gently on my arm.

"The weight of September 11 also bore heavily on the entire Logan airport community who were devastated to learn that two of *our* flights—*our* Flight 11, *our* Flight 175—were instruments in the tragedy that unfolded. We at Massport and the entire Logan family hope that you—and we—will find comfort in this place."

The light had shifted slightly and the memorial seemed to glow from within as Quelch continued to speak.

"Changing our own lives will be the greatest gift we can give to the departed. They surely expect more from us than to merely memorialize their names. They surely want us to do more, work harder, be better, to be inspired by remembering them. So, for the sacrifice of those we honor here today, may this memorial make us better fathers and mothers, sons and daughters. For their sacrifice, may we be better custodians of the public trust, ever vigilant for the public safety. For their sacrifice, may we be better citizens and neighbors. And in the morning, with the rising of the sun, and with the sounds of freedom in the sky, in this place we shall remember them."

As if on cue, a departing jet took off from a nearby runway, its roar like an exclamation point on Quelch's exhortation "to be better." For the first time in years I wanted to do as he said. I wanted to "be better." I wanted my life and my experience here to mean something.

Once upon a time, well before 9/11, I'd thought about the possibility that a new terminal or the new runway would be completed on my watch and there would be a dedication ceremony, a plaque placed there in perpetuity like those in the older terminals naming a long-past governor and Massport leader. It was not an unusual political vanity, but now it seemed like it was from someone else's life, someone who naively, even arrogantly, but mostly innocently, thought her path would be seamless, straight, empty of flags adorning two gates and a list of names etched in glass.

After the ceremony, the speakers filed off the stage and began to walk to the entry to the memorial grounds. Joined by Betty, I followed behind.

Carved at our feet by the entrance were the words "Remember This Day." And then "This memorial is intended as a place of reflection for all those who were forever changed by the events of September 11, 2001."

"Forever changed." I, of course, knew I wasn't the only one at Logan forever changed by 9/11, but sometimes it had felt like that, that I was alone on this journey. Betty quietly explained that there were two paths to choose from to approach the memorial. "They are supposed to represent the two flight paths of the planes," she said. "But to me they represent the different journeys taken to move forward from 9/11."

"I like your interpretation better," I responded.

As we approached the glass cube, I saw the entrance on the corner. I stopped abruptly, staring at the first glass panel facing the entrance. "7:59" were the numbers etched there. "The time," Betty said, in a whispered explanation. "The airline people on the memorial committee really cared about the time, because that is so important to their work at the airport." I knew before she said it that 7:59 was the time that American 11 had left Logan.

As I walked into the structure, I heard, rather than saw, the news photographers kneeling on the ground, circling the inside of the cube.

Click, flash, click, snap, click.

They surrounded me as I stood there, yet I was completely alone. On two glass panels that faced each other in the center were the names of each of the 147 innocent people who had died on the planes. The TV videographers jostled for position as I looked upward. Overhead were small square-shaped glass panels hanging at various heights representing "the fractured sky." One photographer knelt quickly at my feet as I approached the panel listing the passengers and crew on United 175. She aimed her camera up, as I searched for Marianne MacFarlane's name.

When I finally found it, I clutched my hands tightly at my waist. The memorial began to feel too small. I felt trapped. *I have to get out of here,* I thought.

I started to leave the glass enclosure but stopped again at the final glass panel. "8:14." The time United 175 had departed.

Losing the effort to maintain my composure, I began to quietly weep.

"Ah, Ginny," one former colleague said, reaching over to hug me. I could tell by the tone of his voice that he was taken aback by my intense emotion.

The governor hesitated and then moved toward me, reaching for and squeezing my hand. "Thanks," I said quietly to him and began to move down one of the paths.

"Excuse me," a voice called from my right. I stopped and turned to the young journalist with his pen and notebook. "Can I have your name?" he asked. "Virginia Buckingham," I answered, automatically spelling my last name before he asked. As I started to move away again, he called out one last question.

"And what's your connection to the event?"

He had no idea why I was there or that there were those who had once said it was my fault we needed a memorial at all.

My connection? My connection to 9/11?

How to answer? A second, maybe two, passed. I looked at the newly planted trees alongside the path. *I am as rooted to 9/11 as these trees will be to the soil,* I wanted to say.

His question hung there in the quiet air. He waited expectantly, pen poised to write "widow" or "friend" or "coworker," filling in the blank that might correspond to my overwhelming grief.

"I was the CEO of Massport on 9/11," I said quietly, and as he wrote it down, I continued to walk down the path.

September 11, 2008—Goldthwait Reservation, Marblehead

The morning of the seventh anniversary was bright and beautiful, just as every anniversary had been. David took the kids to school. I drove to the beach and sat on the edge of a picnic bench, my arms crossed protectively across my chest. As 7:59 a.m. and then 8:14 a.m. went by, my cries of anguish were swept up in the salty wind and captured in the roll of the crashing surf. I watched the distant planes landing and departing from Logan and then turned my gaze to the horizon.

"Be better," I said in a whisper, to the ocean, to myself.

"Changing our own lives will be the greatest gift we can give to the departed. They surely expect more from us than to merely memorialize their names," John Quelch had said.

Be better.

Be a better mother, a better wife, daughter, friend. I closed my eyes and tried to implant the words in my brain, in my soul, where the image of the burning towers lived.

I stood and turned away from the water. As I reached the top of the wooden walkway that led from the rocky bluff to the parking lot below, I turned to take one last look at the planes on the horizon. My eyes then automatically swept the ground for a telltale sparkle of sea glass. Seeing none, I walked slowly down the path.

Unbidden, the lyrics to the Springsteen song "Waitin' on a Sunny Day" played in my head, just like it had years earlier the day Jack started kindergarten with its promise that everything would be okay.

I put the car into reverse. Backed out of the parking lot. Headed toward home and, I hoped, the start of something, someone, better.

CHAPTER THIRTY

AN ELEVATOR AND A TRAMPOLINE

What has happened cannot be undone.
                                        —Bessel van der Kolk, MD

2008–2010

My job at Pfizer increasingly took me in and out of New York and Washington, DC. Each time I flew out of Logan, I sought a view of the 9/11 memorial. I'd keep my eyes on it as I moved along the walkway connecting the airport's central parking garage to the terminal until it was long out of sight. Was I doing a kind of personal penance? Yes, at first. But over time, seeing the glass structure also became a comfort, like an old friend who could acknowledge a shared painful experience, no explanation needed.

From my higher vantage point on the moving walkway, I looked down at the suspended glass panels at the top of the structure, much like looking down on cumulus clouds from the window of an airplane.

Each panel caught the light individually and, with this perspective on the symbolic fractured sky, I saw all that was lost on 9/11 but also the possibility of beauty.

Could beauty and loss coexist?

With this fresh perspective in mind and with the passage of time, I began to hope it was possible that the shift from the blame being assigned to me and Logan would be permanent.

It did not take long for that fledgling hope to be destroyed.

9/11 Kin Seek Release of Secret Documents

9/11 Kin to Judge: Hold Massport Accountable

3 Victims' Kin Demand 9/11 Justice

This Brings It All Home to Logan

In real time, the appearances of the headlines in the *Boston Herald* were intermittent; months could pass before new developments in the Logan wrongful death cases prompted another bout of scathing coverage. But to me it felt like a constant barrage. I also never knew when to expect the next story, and I felt assaulted by them anew every time. Massport lawyers didn't keep me informed of developments because I wasn't personally a party to the lawsuits. I understood, but the lack of communication deepened my isolation and heightened a sense of inner shame. Why had I been so shattered by what others clearly considered finished for me?

Each headline was also an instant trigger for a post-traumatic stress reaction—not unlike, I'd learn, Fourth of July fireworks or a backfiring car could be for military veterans.

Andrea had over the years tried to explain the science behind PTSD to me, but I resisted trying to fully understand it. I wanted it not to be true. I wanted to be okay, just like the lawyers and others assumed I was.

Ginny Buckingham—9/11. I still didn't want to be her.

As the years had passed, though, and veterans from the Iraq and Afghanistan wars came home, many suffering from PTSD, the media began covering the issue more and more. And I tentatively, hesitantly at first, started to learn more about it.

Later, in a wonderful book called *The Body Keeps the Score* by Bessel van der Kolk, MD, I finally read more than I ever had about PTSD's cause and impact.

The book echoed much of what Andrea had explained to me in years past: that your brain had an alarm system or "smoke detector" that helped you identify and respond to danger; how this led to the release of stress hormones, and the fight, flight, or freeze response; and how, if you were unable to flee or otherwise react or escape, the stress hormones kept being fired even after the danger had passed. How the very same reaction could be triggered by something as commonplace as a smell that brought you back to that traumatic moment. And how the stress reaction even years later was often the same as if no time had passed at all. Andrea spoke about a "steel-lined emotional elevator" and how when we are unable to process or experience feelings in the moment, we use our "dissociative skills" to push them away. She'd say that once feelings had been "sent down that elevator" they incubate, remain static, unchanged. And that when they are triggered or catapulted back to the surface by whatever stimuli set them off, they haven't matured at all. Thus, she said, "it's as if they come up just as they were when we originally sent them away."

This wasn't on purpose, not conscious, she assured me, probably seeing the shadow of shame flicker on my face. "It's an essential part of our species' ability to cope," she said. These were "adaptations," and she said it was my work to learn to see them as the absolute best I could do at the time, that learning to be grateful for whatever it was that enabled me to get through and continue to live, to parent, to do as much of my life as was possible, was essential. She told me again and again that learning to make decisions in my own life that were respectful to those adaptations was an essential and potentially wonderful part of the recovery process.

In *The Body Keeps the Score*, I also read about the discovery of so-called mirror neurons in the frontal lobes of the brain that were the basis for human empathy. Andrea had explained this in the past, too, and had pointed out that when someone is not "mirrored" or under-stood, or is treated as "other" after trauma, PTSD was far more likely to occur.

"Why?" I asked.

"A lot of it is how you are received after the trauma," she said, drawing a parallel between many Americans' rejection of Vietnam veterans and my being scapegoated. "This was one of the reasons Vietnam veterans suffered PTSD so profoundly," she said. The com-parison made me extremely uncomfortable because I certainly didn't fight in a war, but I came to understand what she was saying. I was traumatized, like many others, by the horror of 9/11 itself and then by being singled out and blamed, and finally by being dismissed with the oft-repeated "you weren't really blamed, it was just politics." Van der Kolk similarly explained, "Trauma almost invariably involves not being seen, not being mirrored and not being taken into account." In other words, being blamed left me feeling completely isolated and vul-nerable to even unexpected triggers of post-traumatic stress.

***

"Mom can't watch violence," I had overheard Maddy, then about seven or eight, say when arguing with Jack over what TV show we would watch that evening. The exchange made me sad, rather than grateful. I'd done my best, however misguided, to shield Jack and Maddy from the worst of the impact of PTSD on me, but they knew anyway.

"You don't *want* to," Andrea would explain, prodding me gently to understand that avoiding violence was a choice, not a "can't." Maybe someday, I thought, but at the time it felt like it was a definite "can't."

The worst was when violence in the media snuck up on me when I was least expecting it. "Cover your eyes, hon," David would say, quickly moving to change the channel when a violent scene appeared in an otherwise calm documentary we were watching. The evening news was off-limits. Reading the newspapers in the morning became akin to tiptoeing through a visual minefield—avoiding this headline, looking quickly away from that picture. Even my favorite pastime of reading fiction was fraught. I became absorbed in *Loving Frank*, the best-seller about Frank Lloyd Wright and his great love, Mamah Cheney.

I couldn't put it down, enjoying the relaxation and escape I'd almost always found in reading since I was a child. And then, without warning, at the end of the book, Mamah was vividly, violently murdered by a hatchet-wielding madman. The machete split her skull, and instantly I felt as if my own skull had been split. I couldn't get the image of the blood spewing out of my (her) head out from behind my eyes. That's what it felt like, that the image sat there for hours, coming back over the following days, as real as if I were experiencing it in person. And here was the thing: what I knew and tried to describe to Andrea was that I didn't just see violent images or upsetting scenes through my eyes; I actually felt them in my brain, sometimes like a vise gripping either side of the front of my scalp. But sometimes it felt like the violent act or image of destruction or pain also imprinted itself on me, like an impression made by pressing a hand down in wet clay to make a handprint. My brain tissue the clay, the impression the horror.

Besides violent images and news coverage of 9/11 anniversaries and the litigation, the other main PTSD triggers for me were obvious ones, like seeing a plane flying near a tall building, the orange "go bag" or emergency kit my colleagues based in New York headquarters were required to keep in their offices, or the sight of a building partially collapsed at the hands of a wrecking crew. But the triggers could be unexpected, too, like seeing a toddler inconsolably crying on the sidewalk or a puppy being harshly handled by its owner. Were these triggers for me because vulnerable creatures were being hurt, like the vulnerable people on the planes or in the Towers? I didn't know.

What I did know was that while the nightmares began again with each headline about the lawsuit, the numbness, the feeling of floating through space without emotional connection, surrounded me like an airbag, keeping me from harm. Van der Kolk explained that trauma "compromises the brain area that communicates the physical embodied feeling of being alive."

I understood instinctively what he meant, but when my adult niece Kaitlin asked me to describe what it felt like to be "shut down," I struggled to find the words. "It's like not being in your own body," I tried, "like you're not there at all."

Jack and Maddy were fast approaching middle school, and I was grateful the numbness didn't extend to my feelings for them. They continued to be the source of whatever determination I could muster to find my way to who I had been and who I wanted to become. During this two-year period, I was promoted at work and, to all appearances, seemed to thrive. This ability to function, often at a high level, should be called the PTSD paradox. Paradoxically, I could feel nothing during periods of dissociation, or feel everything excruciatingly during times of being triggered. And at the same time appear to be "doing a life" successfully, as Andrea called it.

But I knew much of the time something was missing; I was missing. When I read more on Van der Kolk's view of trauma's impact, "the fear of losing control; always being on alert for danger or rejection; the self-loathing; the nightmares and flashbacks . . . ; being unable to fully open your heart to another human being," I wanted to swear, laugh, and cry at the same time. The book was describing the me—*Ginny Buckingham—9/11*—I had become. Yet it was also suggesting I could be more.

The author recounted the story of family friends who had dropped their five-year-old son off for first grade at a school right near the World Trade Center. Noam, with his father, fled through the smoke and debris and made it home safely. Van der Kolk went to visit the family, who were able to process the trauma they had witnessed in part, he wrote, because they took an active role in escaping and saving their lives. Even young Noam, who had, horrifically, witnessed bodies falling, was able to find a way to process it. He showed the author a drawing he'd made of the burning towers, including rounded stick figures, the people jumping. But an unrecognizable circular image caught the author's eye at the base of the tower. "What's that?" he asked. "A trampoline," Noam explained, "so the next time when people have to jump, they will be safe." Noam was making sense in his own way of what had happened, finding his way forward from the horror he'd seen, by building a trampoline.

How could I construct my own trampoline, all these years later? How could I make myself feel "safe" enough from the pain of being blamed, and blaming myself, to finally let myself bear it, to lift the fog and let myself feel the crushing anxiety, the self-loathing, the fear, the anger, and then—possibly, hopefully—peace?

"Naming and claiming," Andrea had said, was a start.

"What do you mean?" I asked her.

As she explained it to me, a key path to healing was to put words to my experience, every painful piece of it, and make it my own, acknowledge it. For starters, simply accept the truth of it. Similarly, the author of *The Body Keeps the Score* suggests "integration," or "putting the traumatic event into its proper place in the overall arc of one's life." I remembered when Andrea had put it this way: "One day 9/11 will be part of the tapestry of your life, but just one thread."

Before that could even be a distant possibility, though, I had to find a way to break free of my mind's automatic resort to dissociation, the numbing. I couldn't "name and claim" my experience if I was so shut down emotionally that I couldn't feel it.

But how?

By now, some years after I'd first met her and challenged her with the quest I was on—"Was I guilty or innocent?"—Andrea had grown used to my need for concrete answers and strategies. She had one for this challenge, too. Simply, she said, "Notice." Notice first when I felt "not there" or dissociated. And then notice, on ever-deepening levels, what I was feeling and thinking, even smelling, or seeing. Putting words to my inner experience, she said, and asking myself "and what else am I able to feel?" held many possibilities. Not only the obvious one of coming to peace with the actuality of my feelings but also the possibility that, by witnessing myself without judgment, I could move toward the accountability required to accept me as me, with my "adaptations," living with them, not in spite of them.

"What can I be aware of?" she said was the question I should answer. And then, "What else can I be aware of?" and so on.

I tried it and felt silly at first.

I am aware I am sitting in my car.

I am aware I feel like an idiot trying to be aware.

Van der Kolk's approach also involved "mindfulness," even the simple act of noticing yourself sitting in a chair with your feet on the ground. *I am sitting in this chair,* I'd think to myself, feeling the wood or cushion underneath me, and as ridiculous as I felt, I would come back to my own body.

I forced myself to keep noticing. And sometimes I'd just notice small things, like the warm breeze on my face, and the smell of dry leaves. But other times I'd notice that every time I wanted to cry, I'd forcibly stop myself; that crinkles appeared around David's blue eyes when he smiled but also when he looked deeply in my eyes with concern, and that I often turned away when he looked at me that way. I noticed that sometimes I seemed to forget to breathe and would need to take a deep breath to remind myself that I was alive, and that, as I lay in bed at night, I listened carefully to the roar of an airplane overhead to see if it sounded normal, to see if I could detect anything wrong, my anxiety rising as I mentally wished it safely on the ground.

The small "noticing" moved to this painful "noticing" quickly, and the intensity of the pain was not a bit lessened by the passage of years, having been pushed down in that "steel-lined emotional elevator."

I finally needed to try to let my emotions come back up and, beyond being simply aware of them, express them, "name and claim them." I told Andrea about a Holocaust survivor whose obituary I had just read. Her son, as I remembered it, was quoted talking about how she'd lived a full, happy life when she came to America after being freed from a concentration camp. She got married, raised a family. She never spoke of what she had endured. Until she began to slip into dementia and in her nursing home bed would scream and cry out about the horrors she was seeing.

"What was wrong with that?" I probed Andrea: "Why isn't that a perfectly legitimate way to handle trauma?" I don't remember Andrea giving me a concrete answer. She knew I had to answer that one for myself.

"I am afraid if I start crying about 9/11, I will start screaming and never stop," I had said to Andrea just a year after the attacks.

"You know now that's not true, right?" she said, more than a decade later when I repeated the same fear.

Did I?

Beyond the effort to be aware, I found another way to ease the grip of the painful images in my head. As much as possible, I surrounded myself with beauty. Fresh flowers on the counter and the coffee table in the winter, containers overflowing with annual flowers on the deck in the summer. I'd park by the shore and watch a seabird land on a rock jutting in the harbor, the sweep of the sea washing over the rock but barely disturbing the bird. I listened carefully to the wind rustling the leaves, covered myself in a blanket and watched the sunset from my back deck long after summer's warmth had faded. My unscientific observation? Beauty, like trauma, did not just enter the eyes; it, too, imprinted itself on the brain, a gentler hand making an impression in wet clay.

I was making dinner one evening, and Jack was doing his homework at the counter. I had a fire going in the kitchen fireplace and turned on the small TV on the counter. It was tuned to the evening news. I don't remember the exact story, but there was a mention of 9/11, and Jack turned to me and said, "That must make you feel sad, Mom." I looked at him, surprised and, unexpectedly, comforted. I had been "seen," acknowledged, understood.

Jack, barely a teenager, was aware.

What else could I be aware of?

CHAPTER THIRTY-ONE

I AM OTHER

In early 2011, my lawyer, whom I hadn't heard from in months, contacted me. "As we expected, you are on the witness list for the remaining 9/11 wrongful death case," he said. "The trial date is expected to be set soon."

A trial. The focus of the first nightmare I'd had shortly after 9/11. I again pictured the courtroom in Manhattan. Walking down the center aisle. All eyes on me. Onlookers jeering.

Now, years later, I tried to picture the reality of being seated in the witness box, the judge above me, a jury seated nearby, the plaintiff's attorney, like he did at my deposition, accusing me of ignorance and worse. "Were you aware of al Qaeda?" "Did you know what a fatwa was?" "Why didn't you do anything about the checkpoints?"

I couldn't do it. That much I knew. I could not walk into that courtroom.

I could not take that stand.

I could not be accused.

I could not do it.

The case against me personally hadn't been pursued, but I knew that if Logan was found liable, I, as its leader, would be, too, where it counted most to me: in my heart, in my soul.

At my lawyer's request, I went to a meeting much like the ones I had to attend before the 9/11 Commission testimony and the deposition. Several lawyers were arrayed around a large table. They laid out the possible scenarios, the preparation I would have to undergo. They would make motions, they said, to remove Massport from the case, but if they were not successful, there would be a trial and I could have to take the stand. I answered their questions, an edge of emotion barely noticeable in my voice. I welcomed the numbing. We agreed to set up a schedule of meetings. Robotically, I nodded.

No. I could not do it.

That night, David tried to comfort me by saying he would come with me to the courthouse. By then he had been a trial judge for several years and was known as a stickler about decorum in the courtroom. So when he said not only that would he come with me, but that I could sit on his lap in the witness box while I was being questioned, I couldn't help but laugh at the absurd image. A bit of the terror of the moment eased. We had learned a lot in the past years about reaching toward each other in the hardest times. The deep wrinkles around his eyes crinkled in concern. I didn't look away.

Jack and Maddy were in their rooms doing homework, and I sat with my legs tucked under me in the corner of my favorite couch in my favorite room, the one where I kept fresh flowers and, often, lighted candles. Beauty and pain. In my mind's eye, I saw the sign Andrea kept in her office. "Sometimes courage is simply being able to say, I will try again tomorrow."

I would try again tomorrow.

***

In 2003, David and I had traveled to Canada to attend the wedding of Anne Cellucci, the daughter of the former governor who had been named US ambassador to Canada. One of the guests at the wedding was the Canadian minister of foreign affairs, equivalent to the American secretary of state. David and he got into an in-depth conversation about 9/11, and David told him about my experience. "It was absurd to blame her," the Canadian leader said, noting it was a geopolitical issue.

David rushed over to me and excitedly related the conversation. "He's the secretary of state of Canada, hon, and he thinks it's absurd that you were blamed."

Rather than giving the pleased response to the comments that David expected, I shrank into myself and felt tears prick my eyes. I didn't yet have the words to respond: "Just because he thinks it was absurd doesn't mean it didn't happen."

Why did it happen? Why was I blamed? The reality of the coming trial began to force me to look at questions I hadn't had the ability—or courage—to face right after the attacks.

Did it matter that I was blamed, beyond its impact on me and my family? "Everybody needs a scapegoat" had been said to me more than once with a shrug of acceptance. What purpose did scapegoating serve, and perhaps more important, was there a societal toll paid in addition to the obvious personal one?

The author and speaker Brené Brown has suggested that blame is "a way to discharge pain and discomfort." So, like a collective breath being exhaled by the body politic, maybe my forced resignation temporarily eased the palpable sense of anger and fear in Boston following the attacks. It didn't matter that Massport had no authority over the security checkpoints under federal law at the time, not that this had any bearing on the hijackers' simple plan of carrying small knives onboard and overpowering unsuspecting passengers and crew. It didn't matter that security at Logan Airport was no different than at any other, as the 9/11 Commission eventually pointed out.

But perhaps it did matter that by blaming me, leaders, the media, and the public were able to push away the debilitating fear that the attacks wrought and avoid addressing the deeply complicated issues we faced in aviation and national security after 9/11. Certainly blaming me didn't make us any safer. I understood this bumper sticker approach to governing. At times I had been a practitioner of it. What I'd finally come to understand, though, was that blaming was not leadership, and certainly not in a world where the issues we faced were anything but simple.

Why else was blaming destructive?

I had never been able to get out of my mind a dream Andrea had told me she had right after 9/11. She dreamed, she said, that all the citizens of the United States had come together in the days after the attacks and worn head scarves in solidarity with Muslims. At the time she told me about it, I thought it was the craziest thing I'd ever heard, and I even wondered if our politics were so different that she might not be able to help me after all.

It was years before I finally understood that what Andrea described as "othering" was at the core of our resort to blame. In the dictionary, othering was defined as to "view or treat a person or group of people as intrinsically different from and alien to oneself." What did that have to do with scapegoating? Everything. It was the heart of it. It was the reason horrors like the Holocaust or the Armenian Genocide happened. Blame could be placed on one person, as was the case with me; the media was able to define me as "intrinsically different"—I was inexperienced, incompetent, a political hack, someone who put ambition above people's safety. I was not a human being who could be related to, empathized with. I was other. So I could be blamed. But more societally damaging was when blame was placed on an entire people, with horrifying results.

Andrea had also talked over the years about how assigning blame was an antidote to a natural fear of dying. "We are the only species that is mortal and conscious of it," she'd said. I came to understand that I was blamed because the attacks of 9/11 shifted something fundamental in Americans' sense of safety, and our belief that complete safety for us and our loved ones is achievable. The blame leveled at me in the immediate aftermath was later leveled at federal officials, including the president and intelligence agencies, for missing or ignoring signs of the attack. I realized this was not much different than a propensity to blame the victims of violent crime. If "she wasn't wearing that," or "hadn't accepted that ride," or "hadn't been walking alone in that dark place at night," she wouldn't have been raped. Therefore, we're safe because we don't do those things.

If the president had paid attention to the presidential daily brief entitled "Bin Ladin [sic] Determined to Strike in US" delivered to him in August of 2001, or if I had acted when I received a memo on terrorism and aviation, similarly vague and unactionable, in April of 2001, and later reported as evidence of my guilt, the intimation was that 9/11 could have been stopped. I, for too many long, painful years, held on to this possibility as well. Could I have stopped it?

No.

Finally, I not only believed it, I knew it. I could hear my inner voice. It was no longer being drowned out by the noise of the crowd, of a culture, telling me that I had to have done something wrong or I should have done something more.

I could finally hold on to what I knew was true. It was not my fault. It never was.

We rely on blame—by others and of ourselves—to avoid the truth that our lives and those of our loved ones are fragile. What if, after we came together to address, to the extent humanly possible, our vulnerability to terrorism, we acknowledged our mortality, the fragility of our lives? Would we live differently? How would it change us and our choices, and our leaders' choices? Those were big questions that I didn't pretend to have the answers to. I only knew they were worth asking.

CHAPTER THIRTY-TWO

THE RESILIENCE OF SEA GLASS

Suit: 9/11 Logan Screeners 'Unaware'
—*Boston Herald*, June 21, 2011

Massport Seeks to Head Off 9/11 Suit
Victim's Family Says Airport Liable for
Security Lapses
—*Boston Globe*, July 7, 2011

July 27, 2011—La Jolla, California

"The ordeal is part over." I stared at the words in the email from my lawyer. Could they mean what I thought they did?

On July 27, 2011, federal judge Alvin Hellerstein dismissed Massport and Logan Airport from the last remaining wrongful death case stemming from the Logan hijackings. I received the news via an email from my lawyer while I sat in a windowless conference room at a business meeting in California. If my colleagues noticed the heightened color in my face and the slight tremor in my hands as I gave my presentation, they didn't give any sign.

As soon as I could, I rose and walked quickly to the hotel driveway outside. I could smell the rosemary growing alongside the pavement and briefly closed my eyes and turned my face up to the sun. I pressed the numbers for David's cell phone into my BlackBerry. "He did it," I said, referring to Judge Hellerstein, as soon as he picked up. "He did it."

David didn't need any further explanation. "Oh, honey," he said.

***

"The ordeal is part over." I puzzled over the phrase chosen by my lawyer. He likely was referring to the fact that other litigation involving the World Trade Center's owners and their insurance companies was ongoing. But I think it stood out to me because of the truth in it. The "ordeal" would never be "over" for me.

I thought back to when Judge Wolf had exclaimed that the job at the *Herald* meant I'd made a "complete comeback." How, for many years, David had insisted that while I'd been changed, I was changed for the better. How some in my family said much the same thing. I understood. It was what they wanted. It was what I wanted, too. The Kelly Clarkson hit "Stronger," voicing the familiar American adage that "what doesn't kill you makes you stronger" and popular at the time, underscored the dissonance with my own reality. I wasn't stronger. What was I?

A couple of years later, the call to be "Boston Strong" after the attacks at the finish line of the Boston Marathon similarly seemed to insist on a one-size-fits-all approach to resilience. But I also didn't feel "strong" after the Marathon attacks. Boston being attacked again by terrorists, the subsequent lockdown, and the civic unity, so different from what happened with me and Logan after 9/11, left me with a sense of alienation even deeper than before.

And I felt a deep shame that I wasn't stronger.

A hard word that. Shame. But I was ashamed that I wasn't healed or whole or even close to it nearly ten years after 9/11. I hadn't "moved on." I wasn't "better than before." I wasn't resilient.

Or was I?

What if resilience didn't mean being "unbroken" by trauma and loss, as the title of the best-selling book about Louis Zamperini, the Olympic athlete who was captured and tortured during World War II, promotes? I loved everything about that book but the title, and had even noted wryly in some talks I've given that the title of my story could be "Broken."

I was broken by being blamed for the 9/11 hijackings. Not instantly, not shattered like handblown glass, but over time. Like a bottle tossed into the sea, tumbled apart by the motion of the waves. The bottle as we knew it no longer existed. Yet that wasn't the end of that bottle's story, was it? I'd long collected pieces of sea glass at low tide. It took twenty, thirty, even fifty years for the waves, the salt, and sand to smooth the jagged edges of the glass. To make what was broken beautiful.

I began to think about the editorial written in the weeks after 9/11 that I had found so devastating: "What began at Logan on Buckingham's watch is a disaster whose outcome will follow her the rest of her life. . . . Call it bad luck, bad timing, call it a mixture of chance and fate, call it what you will, Buckingham cannot come back from this."

What if the cruelty of this statement was actually true? What if I couldn't "come back," that I would never be the same? What of that bottle tossed in the sea and the resulting smooth-edged sea glass scattered on the beach? Green, milky white. And if you were ever so lucky to find it, deep, deep blue. It was broken. Changed forever. Yet still capable of bringing joy to she who picked it up from the sand and cradled it in her hand. Might that not be a different way, a truer way, of defining resilience?

I hadn't moved on. I had moved forward. I wasn't stronger, I was wiser. I would carry 9/11 with me like I carried memories of the first time I held Jack and Maddy in my arms, and the image of the people jumping from the tower, the first time David took my hand, and the pendant bearing Marianne MacFarlane's picture. Beauty and loss, pain and hope, carried together. As resilient as sea glass.

***

Would that realization help me through the upcoming 9/11 anniversary? How did one mark the tenth anniversary of hell visiting earth? Each anniversary before that one had seemed much the same, something to get through, pain to be endured. But I feared this one. There would be heightened media attention to it certainly. Former president

George W. Bush and President Barack Obama both planned to attend the memorial services in New York.

I worried that the media would want to talk to me. And I worried that they wouldn't, the fear of reliving the intensity of being blamed, competing with the despair of my utter isolation.

My former editor Shelly offered me the entire op-ed space in the *Herald* for the Sunday paper on the anniversary itself, and the Boston TV station I did occasional political commentary on asked if I'd tape an anniversary show. What could I say or write to adequately fill the one-thousand-word space or fill the airtime; how could I be adequate to the moment at all?

Van der Kolk in *The Body Keeps the Score* wrote about the necessity to put words to your experience. "Finding words where words were absent before and, as a result, being able to share your deepest pain and deepest feelings with another human being," he wrote, is "fundamental to healing the isolation of trauma—especially if other people in our lives have ignored or silenced us. Communicating fully is the opposite of being traumatized."

Andrea had taught me to "hold on to what you know is true."

And this: Sometimes your truth is all you have to hold on to. And you need to hold on to it with all your strength.

So using words to tell the truth as I saw and felt it would be what I tried to do.

I was scheduled to pretape the TV interview on the Thursday before the anniversary. I hesitated when I was told I would be joined by a 9/11 family member. "Can we appear separately?" I asked, the fear of being blamed still omnipresent despite the judge's ruling.

In the lobby of the station, I recognized Christie Coombs, whose husband, Jeff, had been on American Flight 11. She had taken a leadership role as a voice for families, and I'd seen her on the news over the years. I introduced myself, doing my best to hide my nervousness. Our initial interaction was polite, if distant, but I detected no animosity and felt my shoulders relax a little. In the greenroom, the producer asked each of us to read a transcript of a recording, just publicly released, of Mohamed Atta's voice during the hijackings. The producer told us they would play it during the show and ask each of us for our reaction. Christie and I read in silence, our own 9/11 stories reflected in our eyes.

"If we could have done anything to stop it, we would have, anything," I said during the taped interview, responding to host Ed Harding's question. He noted he could tell by the look in my eyes that the pain was as fresh ten years later as it had been that day.

Christie watched my portion of the interview on the feed in the greenroom. When I saw her waiting as I left the studio, she hugged me warmly. "What are you doing for the anniversary?" she asked. "Come to the State House." I had never been invited to attend the official Boston remembrance. I demurred, saying I just wanted to be home with my kids, but inside I felt another gentle moment of healing—like sand and water smoothing jagged glass—spurred by her generous compassion.

In the *Herald* piece published on the anniversary, I wrote that many people had urged me to "move on" and that I'd learned that wasn't possible, but "moving forward" was. "The difference? The first suggests a false promise of closure, the other a way to rebuild a life of meaning, even joy, cognizant of the foundation of loss."

***

Fall turned to winter, and as January 2012 approached, I planned to jump into the freezing Atlantic on New Year's Day for the tenth year in a row.

"I want to do it with you," Maddy said. My confident and outspoken daughter would herself turn ten in April.

"She's tough as nails," David and I would often comment to each other, wondering if, somehow, being inside me during 9/11 and the aftermath had imbued her with a steely strength.

As our group of fifteen or so ran into the ocean, I looked over at Maddy as she dunked her head under the water. As she came up for air, she smiled broadly and gave me a thumbs-up.

Jack and David were waiting on the beach. As we ran toward them, I felt the sharp rocks dig into the soles of my feet and the wind on my exposed skin. David wrapped Maddy, who was now crying from the biting cold, in a towel.

I looked at my family and then back at the roiling gray water. "Let's go home," I said.

EPILOGUE

LETTER TO READERS

Dear Readers,

I have been told by many—not least by our culture—that I need to conclude my story with a happy ending. "I want to read about the woman who was broken and then triumphed" is a common refrain. The thing is, that isn't my story and I don't think that neat narrative is most of our stories. At least not in the way our culture seems to require.

I am still struggling, though the shadows and light of that struggle change as I move forward on a journey that is at times arduous and, at times, full of grace. Beauty and loss, pain and hope, carried together.

I once read a quote from Doctor William Petit, whose family was brutally murdered during a home invasion in Connecticut in 2007. He has since remarried and had a child, yet he said, "I don't think there's ever closure. I think whoever came up with that concept's an imbecile."

I wanted to stand and cheer. And cry.

I continue to try to parse the lessons of my story and offer them in the hope that they are of use to someone. To those who struggle, you are not alone. Your healing will come in its own time. At its own pace. But know, and hold on to the idea, that you are as resilient and as beautiful as sea glass. To leaders and citizens faced with a world still rocked by terrorism and many other complex challenges, I hope there is a growing recognition of the destructiveness of blame, an understanding that the easy act of blaming is in fact a formidable obstacle to finding real solutions. Ultimately, it keeps us from embracing our fragility and discovering the meaning and joy that might offer.

I also continue to care deeply about leadership in our world. I am not actively involved in politics anymore, but in July 2015 I graduated with the inaugural class of Presidential Leadership Scholars, a joint initiative of the presidential libraries of Presidents Bill Clinton, George W. Bush, George H. W. Bush, and Lyndon Johnson. The purpose is to use the leadership lessons of those presidencies to instill in participants a deeper understanding of core leadership characteristics like deliberation, intentionality, self-awareness, decisiveness, and resilience.

During the six-month program, I did get to spend time again with President George W. Bush and learned that he never had heard about the blame directed at me in Boston. I also accepted, in the deepest part of myself, where that elevator at times still rests, that "being my own hero" means just that. No one, not him, not anyone, was going to protect me from the pain of blame I still carried. It was up to me to "hold on to what I know is true" with all my strength and, if I could, use it to help others.

Our graduation was held at the George W. Bush Presidential Center in Dallas. As I crossed the stage to stand between former Presidents Bush and Clinton, a summary was read about my 9/11 story and the goal of this book: "On September 11, 2001, Virginia Buckingham was serving as the CEO of Logan Airport and has dealt with the aftermath of the attacks launched there. Virginia is developing a memoir to shed light on both the personal and broader implications of scapegoating in our culture and provide insights on building resilience."

David was in the audience and we both understood how profound it was to be "seen" in this way, in front of two former leaders of the world, joining my 9/11 story to a much larger one. As I left the stage, I sought out David, and as we made eye contact, I saw that he was weeping. He took his index finger and scratched his heart, a signal he'd long used to send his love silently to me and Jack and Maddy. Our signal of home.

My story continues now as all of ours do. Thanks for coming this far with me.

Ginny

ACKNOWLEDGMENTS

WITH GRATITUDE

While there were times when I felt alone on this journey, I realize I never really was. First, no one believed in me more than David. His voice of clarity and love, even when delivered in a way I could not hear, was a life raft. He was and is my *bashert*, my destiny. I am awed that I get to be the mom to Jack and Maddy, smart, kind, insightful young adults now, whose wisdom and love from the beginning were my anchors. I also felt your strong support, my Buckingham brothers and sisters, Tom, Shelley (Donahue), Michael, Lauren (Lundebjerg), Lisa (Gabrielle), Bill, RJ, and broader family, and that of all the Lowys, Fallmans, and beyond, especially Barbara and Marvin Lowy.

My mom and dad have passed and won't see this moment, but oh, how I know they would have driven as far as they needed to in order to buy and cherish their copies, like they used to so they could read my columns in the *Boston Herald*. A large measure of whatever intellect, strength, and drive I possess was their gift. Thank you, Thomas (Bucky) and Florence Buckingham.

The Best Writers Group Ever (BWGE) individually and collectively put my fingers on the keyboard and welcomed my words. Thank you, Sara Foster, Kate Kahn, Jazz Newhall, Cheryl Byrne, and Phyllis Karas.

And Presidential Leadership Scholars (PLS), this book is not just for you, it's from you. My participation in PLS and my project—which was finishing this book—not only returned me to myself but gave me the courage to put my story out in the world. Thank you especially to former Presidents George W. Bush and Bill Clinton, their presidential libraries, and the presidential libraries of George H. W. Bush and Lyndon Johnson. Cassie Farrelly, your immediate grasp of what I was trying to say was both affirming and wise. Thank you also for founding Cavan Bridge Press to support works like mine. And to the rest of my PLS family, Mike Hemphill, Michael O'Leary, Stephanie Streett, Holly Kuzmich, Margaret Spellings, Kathryn Carr, Lori Zukin, Kristin King, Katie Lyman, Neill Sciarrone, (the other) Neil Grunberg, AnnMaura Connolly, An-Me Chung, Davy Carter, Haley Holm, Clarissa Martinez De Castro, Sean Fellows, Shelley Cryan, Jim Mauldin, Daniel Anello, Gina Warner, Brian McPeek, Steve Ressler, and all of the Class of 2015, you are forever part of me.

Andrea Bredbeck, my guide, my counselor, my path home. Thank you.

To my Pfizer friends, who have encouraged me and, no matter what, made me laugh, especially Heidi Cosgrove, Amy Goodrich, Meredith Sharp, Rachel Hooper, Steve Janson, Robert Popovian, Robert Jones, Daren Sink, Frances Devlin, Jim Sherner, Lisa Bellucci, Karen Boykin-Towns, Paul Critchlow, and instigator of my midlife adventure in New York City, Sally Susman, who also brought me Jessica Soffer, writer-inspirer extraordinaire.

To my political and news posse, Rob Gray, Stephen O'Neill, Dominick Ianno, Andy Antrobus, Kristen Lepore, John Brockelman, Stuart Stevens, Neil Newhouse, Andy Card, Patrick Dorton, Brian Kaminski, Jan Cellucci, Tom Reilly, Martha Chayet, Andrew Goodrich, Julie Mehegan, Shelly Cohen, Neil Cote, Beth Teitell, Raakhee Mirchandani, Frank Phillips, Janet Wu, and Mary Anne Marsh—campaigns and news careers end, but not friendships.

Boston College became my home at age seventeen and welcomed me home again many years later when I needed it most. With love to my forever-BC friends.

Eddy Foley, it happened! Tell Rose, and thank you for your belief.

To my mentors, Governor Bill Weld and Governor Paul Cellucci, with love and deep respect.

To those who call or text me every single 9/11 anniversary, or leave a Jersey tomato on my desk, please know how much it means to me.

I loved leading Massport and the remarkable people there. Thank you, Joey Cuzzi, Jose Juves, Julie Wasson, Tom Kinton, Lowell Richards, Chris Gordon, Betty Desrosiers, Dave Mackey, Leslie Kirwan, Bob Donahue, Ed Freni, Joe Lawless, James Roy, Katie McDonald, Russ Aims, Mike Leone, Tommy Butler, John Duval, and the entire Logan Airport community.

To my Marblehead community for so many deep friendships and kindnesses, especially David and Marla Meyer, Ann Fitzgerald, Kate Brooks, Sue McNeil, and Tammy Waite.

Thank you, Girl Friday Productions, especially Christina Henry de Tessan, Dave Valencia, and Georgie Hockett, and Smith Publicity's Sarah Miniaci, for bringing this story on its final journey.

Finally, to Marianne MacFarlane—I promise to try every day to live a joyful, meaningful life in your name as your mom, my friend Anne MacFarlane, in her inimitable way, instructed.

ABOUT THE AUTHOR

Virginia Buckingham was born in Connecticut and has lived in Massachusetts for nearly forty years. She was the first woman to serve as chief of staff to two consecutive Massachusetts governors. Buckingham was subsequently the first woman appointed to head that state's Port Authority, owner and operator of Logan International Airport. She has also worked as a deputy editorial page editor and columnist for the *Boston Herald*. In 2015 she was selected for the inaugural class of Presidential Leadership Scholars, a joint initiative of the presidential libraries of Presidents George H. W. Bush, George W. Bush, William J. Clinton, and Lyndon Johnson. The completion of this manuscript was her Presidential Leadership Project, a key element of the program, which teaches scholars to apply leadership lessons from those presidencies, such as courage and resilience.

CPSIA information can be obtained
at www.ICGtesting.com
Printed in the USA
LVHW032249060420
652382LV00001B/45

9 780998 749327